Jails: An ACA Reader

Mission of the American Correctional Association

The American Correctional Association provides a professional organization for all individuals and groups, both public and private, that share a common goal of improving the justice system.

American Correctional Association Staff

Daron Hall, President
James A. Gondles, Jr., CAE, Executive Director
Gabriella M. Klatt, Director, Communications and Publications
Alice Heiserman, Manager of Publications and Research
Jeannelle Ferreira, Associate Editor
Xavaire Bolton, Graphics Associate
Cover design by Xavaire Bolton
Cover photo by Shoshana Frishberg, taken at the Alexandria Dentention Center in Aexandria, VA.

This publication may be ordered from:
American Correctional Association
206 N. Washington St., Suite 200
Alexandria, VA 22314
(800) 222-5646 ext. 0129

For more information on publications and videos available from ACA, contact our worldwide web home page at: www.aca.org/store/

Library of Congress Cataloging-in-Publication Data

Jail Reader.–2011 ed.
 p. cm.
ISBN 978-1-56991-324-6
1. Jails–United States. I. American Correctional Association.
HV8746.U6J34 2011
365'.34–dc22

Contents

continued on the next page

Contents *(continued)*

Foreword

The number of inmates in county and city jails was about 767,600 at the end of June 2009, according to the Bureau of Justice Statistics (BJS). While prisons are run by state government, most jails are operated by local authorities, generally a county sheriff or jail administrator. Most jails hold inmates for a year or less. In 2009, approximately 62 percent of jail inmates were being held pending arraignment, awaiting trial or conviction. The remaining 38 percent had been convicted and were awaiting sentencing; had been sentenced to serve time in jail; or were awaiting transfer to state or federal prisons, according to the BJS.

At midyear 2009, jail authorities were also responsible for supervising more than 70,000 offenders outside of their detention facilities, including 11,800 under electronic monitoring, 11,200 in weekend programs, 17,700 in community service programs, and 12,400 in other pretrial release programs, BJS noted. This supervision of offenders outside of jails is a growing trend as jails are seeking lower-cost ways to supervise offenders. It is also an example of the complexity of jail operations and the movement of their populations.

Some of the chapters in this reader provide innovative ways to lower costs and achieve less recidivism. For example, a student-centered tutoring program in the District of Columbia is a partnership with a department of pharmacy at a college where students work with inmates. Health care costs for inmates are escalating rapidly and are a major portion of jail budgets. Since so many inmates have neglected their health, they have more health care needs than those outside of jail. This includes dental care and mental health care as many of the chapters demonstrate. In fact, some contend that jails are running the largest mental health facilities in our nation.

ACA has long supported standards for jails and detention facilities and our *Core Jail Standards* released in 2010 offer jails a way to achieve certification. An article on certification is included in this reader and information on certification and accreditation may also be found on ACA's Website at www.aca.org/standards.

This reader also explores other critical issues facing jails today including leadership and training of staff, security, technology, environmental issues, and reentry. The unwritten subtext in all of these articles is how to do more with less. We hope that correctional administrators and staff, and students in colleges, will find this collection useful to advance the innovative ideas and programs occurring in our nation's jails.

As Sheriff of Arlington County, Va., from 1980-1990, my goal was to ensure public safety while building a reputation of humane professionalism for the organization. When I came to ACA, I proudly reaffirmed that commitment. I believe the works featured in the *Jails Reader* show the scope of our members' expertise, integrity, and zeal for the advancement of modern corrections.

Many of the articles were originally featured in *Corrections Today*, ACA's bimonthly members-only magazine, or in *Correctional Health Today*, the peer-reviewed journal of the association's Healthcare Professional Interest Section. Photos were graciously provided by the Alexandria (Va.) Detention Center. Details about ACA membership, programs and publications can be found on our Website at www.aca.org.

James A. Gondles, Jr., C.A.E.,
Executive Director

Section 1

Training and Management Issues for Jails

Critical Factors in Jail Staff Training

By Lt. Gary F. Cornelius (retired)

I am a jail correctional officer. There—I have said it. I am not a "turnkey," "screw," or "guard." To the public, those terms that they may use to describe the professional men and women who staff our nation's jails may be convenient. Yet, those using these terms are blatantly misinformed about the roles of today's jail correctional officer.

I spent twenty-seven years working in a local jail and have written extensively on the events, inmates, staff, and policies and procedures that go on behind the walls. In my travels and tours of many jails throughout the United States, I have found that there are good, decent people who patrol the cellblocks, work and booking areas of our local jails.

What makes a person become a jail officer? Is it the pay? Benefits? The "glamour"? In my case, it was three things. First, I enjoyed the intrigue of jail work. It was interesting maintaining custody of people who did not want to be there and are known to be nonconformists when it comes to obeying the rules and norms of society. Second, having come from other non-correctional law enforcement agencies, I thought, then and still do now, that jail officers and staff—civilian and sworn—provide a valuable, but often overlooked public service in keeping offenders safely confined until they are released or sent "down the road" to other jails or the department of corrections. Third, I was one of the first at my college to study criminal justice and found corrections fascinating.

Jail correctional officers are not what have been frequently portrayed in films and on television as county "bumpkin" deputy sheriffs or brutal, bigoted jail "guards," who treat inmates in a negative manner. The jail officers of today are professional, well-trained, intelligent, and highly motivated. After decades of being in the background, jail staffs are receiving up-to-date equipment, such as computerized jail information systems, state-of-the-art inmate identification systems, high-grade-security audio and visual hardware, and personal alarm systems to enhance officer and inmate safety. Training for jail officers has improved greatly over the past thirty years.

But how do we in the correctional system effectively train jail officers? While there are many opinions on what should be taught besides the required constitutional law, firearms, and searches, I am of the opinion that the best approach to jail training is for trainers to examine three areas concerning jail officers and provide training curriculum that complements each:

- Traits of a good correctional officer
- Formal duties of jail officers
- Informal duties of jail officers

Traits of a Good Correctional Officer

Jail training consists of a lot more than saying that security is the number one priority, never trust an inmate, and always be firm but fair. While those slogans may have sounded sufficient thirty years ago, they remain basic even though jails are much more complex to staff and operate. The traits of a good jail correctional officer are as follows:

- Shows concern for inmates and desires to help them
- Creates and maintains a positive environment
- Carries himself or herself around inmates without exhibiting fear, anxiety, or timidity; is assertive and professional; maintains safety, control, and order
- Has good insights into inmate behavior and culture
- Maintains good mental and physical health, positively manages stress
- Is accessible to inmates, answering questions and grievances, and addressing their concerns
- Develops a rapport with inmates and is credible
- Has the ability to resolve inmate conflicts and problems fairly and promptly
- Maintains effective and positive relations with colleagues and other law enforcement agencies

In looking at these traits, the jail training staff may notice several critical factors: concern for inmate safety and well being, self-assuredness, and confidence in carrying out duties, a positive outlook on the job, and an ability to keep stress under control. Also, inmates are regarded as people.

Training should include such subjects as managing stress, following ethical procedures, communicating positively, maintaining a positive jail climate, maintaining boundaries, and resolving inmate conflicts. Most jurisdictions require some type of legal rights review for jail staff; this subject should show the jail officer that properly handling inmate grievances, maintaining safety, and having a pro-active approach to inmates' problems and disputes can head off much, but unfortunately not all, inmate litigation. Federal and state correctional training standards and standards from professional correctional organizations, such as the American Correctional Association (ACA), protect the agencies from engaging in staff practices that are ineffective or hamper operations.

Besides classroom training, jail training should also instruct the officers and staff in how to look and act as a professional. Inmates usually respond well to staff who look and act professionally—both in appearance and manner. Ethics and professionalism training may sound boring to the staff, but training staff should use innovative methods to present these critical issues, such as getting inmates' views on the types of jail staff they respect.

Maintaining effective and positive relations with staff in other sections of the jail facility requires training in teamwork. I know from supervising a jail programs unit for eight years that many custody staff appreciated the efforts of counselors, mentors, teachers, chaplains' staff, and volunteers after efforts to familiarize them with their roles in the jail. Conversely, bringing custody officers into civilian training and orientation sessions gave civilians insights into the difficult job of jail officers and their concerns. However, this can be accomplished best if agency management ranging from sheriff, directors, department heads, and senior staff on down to sergeants and corporals get behind this approach.

Formal Duties of Jail Officers

Two foundations in jail work include the formal and informal duties of jail officers. Because of movies and television, jail and prison officers are frequently portrayed as people who try to do a good job, but often the inmate "heroes" slip right by them by dodging floor checks, headcounts, contraband searches, and the ever-popular spotlight. How I cringe when I watch a movie where the officers are "gotten over on" or shown as brutal, mindless custodians who could not find a hen in a henhouse.

Every training plan should focus on media, curriculum, and instructors, to provide both innovative and up-to-date information to enhance job performance in the following formal job tasks: [1]

- Performing regular checks and headcounts in all areas to which inmates have access
- Performing searches for contraband on inmates' persons, their property, and any areas to which inmates have access. These searches include the routine frisk, strip searches, and body-cavity searches (the last with supervisor's authorization and by qualified medical personnel)
- Processing inmates into the facility and maintaining order in the booking area,
- Observing inmate behavior and activities: including observation for rules violations, unusual behavior, depression, suicidal behavior, security breaches, criminal violations, signs of escape, and so forth
- Supervising inmates on work assignments
- Enforcing laws, institutional rules and regulations
- Investigating crimes and preparing cases for disciplinary hearings and possible criminal prosecution
- Inspecting the facility security system, equipment, and environment
- Escorting and transporting inmates
- Participating in administrative and disciplinary hearings
- Admitting authorized visitors

Traditionally, the training in these areas has been mandated by state or federal standards and standards from such organizations as the ACA. Officers are instructed in performing thorough searches, preventing escapes, enforcing discipline, conducting proper headcounts, to name a few. This training is required. The trainees must pass written exams and practical exercises to test their skill levels and proficiency. In some jurisdictions, jail training is combined with law-enforcement training so when a jail officer graduates from the academy, he or she is dually certified in law enforcement (police) and in corrections.[2] In addition, all of these tasks are covered in agency standard operating procedures and state/federal guidelines.

Training in the formal duties is generally cut, dry, and straightforward. Basic training and in-service refresher training conducted to maintain certification have clear learning objectives and specify what material is to be covered.

Informal Duties of Jail Officers

A challenge for jail trainers is to present training in a way that jail officers understand that they have a crucial role in keeping the jail secure, safe, and operating in a positive climate. Also, through informal roles, they keep the pressure of incarceration on inmates from boiling over. The informal roles of the jail correctional officer are the following:[3]

- *Psychologist:* This does not mean that jail officers diagnose mental illness and recommend treatment. However, mental health staff depend on the observations of line staff. Line staff report the symptoms, behavior, and management problems of inmates that they suspect are mentally ill. Jail officers have to know the basic symptoms of mental illness; their "gut" tells them that suspected mentally ill inmates are not dealing with reality.
- *Legal advisor:* Jail officers cannot give inmates legal advice and should be careful not to do that. They should know that prompt responses to inmates' questions about court dates, bonds, and so forth are important. The inmates' behavior should be gauged carefully; if an inmate is very anxious about an upcoming court appearance, staff should take the time to let the inmate vent and ascertain if there are any dangers or risk issues.
- *Parent:* Jail officers should be positive role models to inmates, many of whom never had any positive influences in their lives. Jail officers must realize that taking proactive steps in such matters as correcting behavior and hygiene issues can keep tensions in the inmate population at a low level.
- *Information agent:* Due to jail being a nerve-wracking stressful experience for inmates, jail officers must clearly communicate to inmates how things in the jail work—the daily routine, sick call, rules and regulations, and most importantly—how to contact staff, especially if personal safety is a concern. This includes inmate thoughts or actions involving self-harm.
- *Counselor:* Jail officers must give advice to inmates on how to properly conduct themselves, how to handle conflicts, and how to handle problems.

- *Diplomat:* There is conflict in the jail. Not only do inmates have conflicts with each other, but also with staff. Jail officers, especially in direct supervision units, intervene in and defuse disputes. By doing so, many arguments do not have to escalate into heated verbal and physical altercations.

Jail trainers must take an approach to training that emphasizes the human nature of jail work. In other words, jail officers are in a human service profession; their clients are people—not "subspecies" of the human race. While the formal nature of the job stresses security, enforcing rules and laws, and preventing escapes, the informal nature focuses on the fact that inmates are people who have concerns and fears, and that their behavior must be observed and managed in a positive way.

Trainers must focus on the diversity of the jail populations. This is not just the diversity of different racial and ethnic groups. There is also diversity of age (including special concerns of the elderly), gender, mental health, sexual orientation, and other categories. Each group deals with their incarceration differently. The informal roles of the jail officer can aid in inmate adjustment, providing concerned and calm communications, taking into account that not all inmates behave the same.

Out of all of the aspects of jail training, training in the formal duties is less challenging than training in the informal duties. Most jails have instructors' schools and certification courses where formal lesson plans and objectives are developed, taught, and tested. Formal training has a script to follow, whereas making the jail officer aware of his or her informal duties requires innovative research into the material and teaching methods to make the training interesting and valuable. For example, the "diplomat" aspect of jail officers' duties is important. Officers must defuse possible volatile and heated conflicts. Training must show the officers that using good people skills and speaking to inmates in a mature and calm manner are vital. If the officers are resistant and have the attitude "if I see inmates arguing, I grab em' and lock them down … I don't give a _____ about what they think," the trainer now has a challenge—how can he or she get through this narrow mindedness?

The much touted "war story" can be used in training as an illustration or example. The war story should be a training tool and not the only curriculum. War stories should back up the learning objectives, and the trainer must be careful not to lose control of the class resulting in a correctional officer "gabfest" where various interesting war stories are told.

Information Outlets

What is exciting about jail training, especially over the span of my active duty career, are the various organizations and websites that training staff can go to for up-to-date information on jails and jail populations. Trainers should examine materials and seminars available through the ACA, the American Jail Association, the National Sheriffs' Association, and the International Association of Corrections Training Personnel. Also, many states have correctional associations or regional jail associations, many of which also offer conferences and training. Virginia is a good example, due to the existence of the Virginia Correctional Association and the Virginia Association of Regional Jails. Both have excellent conferences with a variety of seminars. Jail trainers who attend conferences and the seminars offered in them should be required to bring materials and information back to their respective agencies and present training on what they have learned.

Many websites about jail issues are on the Internet. Two of the most useful to me have been the U.S. Department of Justice, Office of Justice Programs at www.ojp.usdoj.gov, which links to many resources such as the Bureau of Justice Statistics. The other web site is The Corrections Connection at www.corrections.com. The blogs, feature articles, and news articles provide a broad range of information and are a treasure trove for the jail trainer. Also, the Corrections Connection has direct links to many professional corrections organizations.

Some websites stress one aspect of corrections, such as security, emergency response operations, restraints, and so forth. That is fine if the trainer's presentations are specific as to one subject. I recommend getting a more broad view of correctional issues. Also, trainers must be careful. Corrections agencies and facilities may not be popular in some circles. Trainers should use websites that are balanced in their content, factual in their reporting, and do not have a political or radical agenda negative to corrections.

Endnotes

[1] Gary F. Cornelius. 2008. *The American Jail: Cornerstone of Modern Corrections*. Upper Saddle River, N.J.: Pearson Prentice Hall, 302.

[2] Gary F. Cornelius, 2010. *The Correctional Officer: A Practical Guide, Second Edition*. Durham, N.C.: Carolina Academic Press, 49-51.

[3] Cornelius. *The Correctional Officer*, 52-53.

References

Cornelius, Gary F. 2008. *The American Jail: Cornerstone of Modern Corrections.* Upper Saddle River, N.J.: Pearson Prentice Hall.

Cornelius, Gary F. 2010. *The Correctional Officer: A Practical Guide, Second Edition.* Durham, N.C.: Carolina Academic Press.

About the Author

Lt. Gary F. Cornelius retired in 2005 from the Fairfax County, Virginia, Office of the Sheriff, after serving more than twenty-seven years in the Fairfax County Adult Detention Center. His career included assignments in confinement, work release, programs, and classification. He is an adjunct faculty member of the Administration of Justice Department at George Mason University, where he has taught four corrections courses. He also teaches corrections in-service sessions in Virginia, and has performed training and consulting for the American Correctional Association, the American Jail Association, and the National Institute of Justice. His new book, *The Correctional Officer: A Practical Guide, Second Edition* has just been published. He has authored eight other books in corrections. His most recent books are *The American Jail: Cornerstone of Modern Corrections,* 2007, from Pearson. The books he wrote for the American Correctional Association: *The Art of the Con: Avoiding Offender Manipulation, Second Edition* (2009) and *Stressed Out: Strategies for Living and Working in Corrections, Second Edition* (2005) are available from the American Correctional Association (800) 222-5646 ext. 0129. In 2008, he co-founded ETC, LLC: Education and Training in Corrections with Timothy P. Manley, MSW, LCSW. Gary can be reached at (571) 233-0912 or at adjinstructor@aol.com.

Training Issues in Corrections Administration: Interagency Collaboration in Shelby County, Tennessee

By Wayne J. Pitts and James Coleman

The correctional industry has evolved considerably during the past twenty years, and for correctional administrators the demands of the job are considerable. Correctional facilities are exceptionally intricate organizations. These facilities are expected to provide a full assortment of human services, including medical and mental health treatment, case management, recreation, religious programs, transportation, visitation, access to court and attorneys, meals, clothing, and laundry. Additionally, jail and prison administrators must meet the daily demands of securing the population while simultaneously adhering to the procedural guidelines and policies designed to meet the needs and personal safety requirements of an increasingly diverse inmate and employee population.

Although technological advances in equipment and more modern facilities have improved the efficiency and consistency of correctional activities, prisons and jails are increasingly expected to confine greater numbers of inmates, than ever before and must also deal with a broader range of special treatment needs and other issues requiring distinct consideration. Corrections is subject to more oversight and tighter restrictions than ever before, regarding both inmates and staff, and avoiding litigation associated with these demands is a top priority for administrators. This evolution in the field has challenged many correctional departments nationwide to re-evaluate their training programs to ensure that staff are well-qualified to address the shifts in the field.

Martin and Rosazza (2004) assert that staff training is one of the most powerful problem-solving interventions available to correctional administrators. Unfortunately, in many facilities, training activities are essentially segregated from the overall management strategy. In this scenario, training is not need-based but rather depends upon staff preferences, institutional culture, training capacity, and historical precedence. Thus, correctional administrators are charged with addressing policies and procedures that may have contributed to a situation of negligent hiring, training, management, and retention of underperforming staff.

Indeed, some departments are experiencing a situation that this article's authors refer to as "professional retardation," in which departments have underdeveloped training programs and have generally failed to train upper management to take advantage of technological, managerial, and administrative innovations in the field of corrections. Wardens, administrators, upper-level staff, and managers of programs and facilities sometimes lack the skills and training that are necessary to adequately perform the duties of their job. In many cases, these administrators may have limited management or administrative training or none at all. It is more common that top officials started at an entry-level position and worked their way to upper management through a series of promotions over a lengthy career (Finkelstein 1996). Thus, although these administrators may have an impeccable command of the day-to-day operations of the facilities, they may not have adequate training, education, or experience to perform optimally in upper-level management positions.

The Challenge of Correctional Administration: An Overview

Much can be done to improve the preparedness of correctional administrators and upper management. Identifying the key issues and shortcomings is the first part of solving the problem. Given the usual promotion practices of most correctional institutions, it is not uncommon for veteran administrators to have only limited specialized management training or expertise. Although there are many exceptional correctional administrators who do not possess advanced degrees or other correctional certifications, there are many benefits of their pursuing these qualifications. The main point here is that, given the vast diversity of responsibilities that upper-level correctional managers are required to address, advanced training beyond the skills able to be learned on the job is needed. Correctional administrators, especially newly promoted ones, must be prepared to tackle issues that they may not have been confronted with while they were moving up through the ranks.

The most important issues for new administrators can be grouped into four broad areas: issues of institutional culture, the internal environment, the external environment, and self-management (McCampbell 2002). With regard to culture, administrators must be aware of the institution's history and community relationships. Understanding the particular role that the institution has in the bigger picture will help an administrator in the performance of his or her job. In addition, it is imperative that administrators have a grasp of other cultural issues relating to the correctional facility itself. Having a working knowledge of both the staff and the inmate population is essential.

On issues of the internal environment, administrators should focus on the skills and knowledge necessary to lead the correctional facility from the inside. Management must be increasingly aware and adept at handling issues such as strategic planning, fiscal decision-making, human resource management, and internal personal relations.

Externally, public relations is an overriding concern, because the public's perception of the facility and the media presentation of the facility are important. Administrators must be able to communicate effectively with government entities at all levels, and developing a rapport with officials from other criminal justice agencies is essential. Finally, being able to separate the rigors of the job, the responsibilities of family, and social obligations is a challenging task. Administrators must recognize the power that comes with their positions and the impact it has not only on themselves and their families but on the institution itself. A correctional administrator faces the same types of stressors that managers in other industries face, and it is important that he or she take measures to minimize their effects (McCampbell 2002). To effectively address these issues, upper-level management should possess a combination of work experience, educational preparation, and vocational training.

With the ever-growing responsibilities of a correctional administrator, some have suggested that an education (or training) based on business administration would lead to greater success than a background in public administration (McCurdy 1978). Top administrators are required to oversee the training of subordinates, address staff retention, keep up with technological advances, monitor compliance with policies and procedures, and promote employee morale. Aside from these activities, top management must also be able to oversee budgets, track inventory, pay attention to shifting political climates, and competently deal with a range of public issues. Most of these tasks require specialized training and skills development.

Given the diversity of tasks and the consequences of undertrained administrators, it is imperative that correctional departments scrutinize the performance and capabilities of acting top administrators and address any areas of needed training. Moreover, today's administrators are responsible for fostering the development of the leaders of tomorrow. A more educated and diverse individual likely will make a better administrator in the long run (McCampbell 2002). In the following subsections, some of the most prominent issues affecting correctional administrators are addressed: training, human resource management, fiscal responsibility, and community relations.

Training Issues

At the heart of this chapter is the existence, or lack thereof, of adequate training for corrections personnel. Not only must facility administrators be extensively trained, but they also must be responsible for overseeing the management and training of other personnel. If administrators lack training and do not stress the importance of training, it undermines their effectiveness both as a manager and a leader. In some instances, the administrators of correctional facilities are promoted too quickly and are unable to make a successful jump from employee to manager or from manager to respected leader. Correctional administrators have reported that they feel competent in many areas but acquiesce to the fact that they lack training in many other important areas (McCampbell 2002).

Regarding training plans, researchers have noted the importance of training correctional officers so they are able to protect themselves and inmates while living and working in common areas (for example, Jurik and Musheno 1986, Pitts and Coleman 2006, Tartaro 2002). However, according to a jail survey, nearly 40 percent of respondents were offered six weeks or less of general training (Tartaro 2002). Even more disheartening is the fact that even less attention is given to training in communication; 36 percent of respondents indicated they received eight hours or less per year.

Perhaps most importantly, correctional administrators should have a system in place that accurately tracks the training progress of all employees and supervisors. At any given time, the administrator should be able to tell which employees have what training and how long it has been since they were trained in a particular area. Having future training plans set up and reviewed on a regular basis is also essential. There should be no doubt as to the training status of each employee of a correctional facility (McCampbell 2002).

Issues of Human Resource Management

Several items fall under the general heading of human resource management. Included in this category are stress management, personnel needs, recruitment, diversification, turnover, supervision, job satisfaction, and job autonomy (Lambert 2004). This list, while seemingly encompassing most human resource issues, is not exhaustive. Correctional administrators must be able effectively address these concerns.

Stress Management

Correctional administrators must be able to recognize the symptoms of stress and be able to react accordingly. Stress problems can manifest themselves in a multitude of ways, and it is important that they are identified early. Stress in a correctional setting is generally defined as "an employee's feelings of job-related hardness, tension, anxiety, frustration, worry, emotional exhaustion, and distress" (Lambert 2004). In most cases, the level of job stress is negatively related to job satisfaction. This indicates that the more job stress a correctional officer experiences, the less likely the officer is satisfied with his or her job. In the same vein, stress has a significant effect on the level of commitment one has to the organization, in this case the correctional facility. The more stress experienced, the less committed or loyal that employee is to the organization (Lambert 2004).

Numerous researchers have predicted that female correctional officers experience greater job-related stress than their male counterparts (for example, Patterson 1992, Savicki, Cooley, and Gjesvold 2003, Walters 1993). Female correctional employees face challenges on the job that are not likely to be experienced by men in the same position. Women are often the topic of sexual gossip and harassment. There is likely a difference in the methods used to block or cope with stressors on an individual level, and this difference may manifest itself more overtly for a woman than a man. Resentment expressed by their male counterparts is also a cause of stress for female correctional officers (Carlson, Anson, and Thomas 2003). It is important for upper-level management to be aware of important distinctions among staff they supervise.

The most feared result of stress is the possibility that the correctional administrator or officer will burn out and vacate his or her position. When the stress level reaches a particular point, it can be too much for the employee to bear. The employee may respond by acting out against peers or inmates, or taking the frustration out on others. Sources of stress may include long hours, difficulty in meeting financial obligations, lack of support and encouragement, and any number of outside factors such as family. Indeed, effectively addressing employee stress and other staffing issues may be one of the most challenging aspects of correctional management. It is imperative that correctional administrators be aware of employee job stress as well as their own. Identifying who is stressed and dealing with the problem is essential to maintaining an orderly and effectively managed correctional facility.

Personnel Needs and Recruitment

In addition to managing the stress levels of employees, a successful administrator must be able to manage personnel. Correctional administrators must be able to make good decisions regarding staff positions as well as be tactful in the process of making them. A correctional administrator must be able to intelligently forecast the personnel needs of the facility. The population of the facility, the desired standard of service, and the economic environment all affect the number of employees necessary to run a successful operation (Waldron and Altemose 1979).

It is important to recognize the need for diversity and to recruit employees from many different backgrounds. Obviously, an administrator must first and foremost hire those who are the most qualified. However, keeping an eye and ear open for opportunities to develop a staff comprising different races and backgrounds is essential. The Rhode Island Department of Corrections is a prime example. The agency revised its hiring practices to diversify its staff and make it more "reflective of the state's population" (St. Gerard 2004). By doing so, it possibly served to improve security, ease tensions among inmates, and give the agency more public credibility.

The idea is to create an environment within a correctional facility that fosters safety and respect. When officers and the administration can communicate with each other and with inmates better, it enhances the effectiveness of the facility. Problem areas can be identified before they escalate and any tensions can be handled more efficiently. Having bilingual staff members should be a key focus in the hiring practices of most correctional agencies. A mix of genders, races, skills, and languages can go a long way to promoting a successful correctional system. Supervisory employees should be at the forefront in ensuring that these types of hiring practices become more the norm rather than the exception.

Turnover

Given the levels of stress and inherent problems faced by employees in a correctional setting, it is no surprise that turnover is prevalent. In fact, turnover may be "the main problem plaguing correctional agencies nationwide" (Lommel 2004). Although compensation is often mentioned as a main factor behind turnover, several other factors have a hand in the ability to retain competent correctional employees. Some of them are demanding hours and shifts, inadequate benefits, burnout, and lack of understanding about the job caused by the use of inadequate hiring techniques. Issues of poor supervision, lack of career prospects, and other agency recruiting practices can also contribute (Lommel 2004).

Essentially, it is the job of the correctional administrator to do his or her best to retain the best personnel possible. It is important to retain current employees if at all possible due to the costs associated with training and replacing them with new ones. As veteran employees leave and new recruits fill their positions, the overall experience level of the staff declines as well. However, there are ways that this occurrence can be decreased and the other issues taken care of before they become too much of a problem.

The primary way to combat turnover is to take an active role in managing the employees. Simply boosting morale and offering incentives (both individual and group) to perform well on the job can go a long way to reducing turnover. Morale issues are more often than not the result of a clash between established standards and the differing views of supervisors and subordinates (Sullivan 2004). Therefore, properly introducing new employees to current staff members and providing good orientation programs are exceedingly important. The key lies in making all the employees feel wanted as part of a team. Hiring the right employees from the outset can also help to thwart problems later (Lommel 2004).

Involving staff as much as possible is the bottom line. Supervisors must promote an environment in which all staff members feel accepted and appreciated for the roles they serve. Administrators should provide a way to allow staff to provide suggestions and feedback—anonymously, if necessary. Avenues must exist for employees to call most any issue to the attention of whomever is next in the chain of command (Sullivan 2004). Because poor bosses are also reasons for turnover, anything the administrator can do to promote his or her support for the employees will go a long way to ensure retention (Lommel 2004).

Job Satisfaction

The level of job satisfaction is an important indicator of how effectively a correctional administrator is running a facility. Keeping oneself satisfied on the job and making sure employees are satisfied is essential for effectiveness as a supervisor in a correctional setting.

Levels of stress, autonomy, and job variety all help to determine job satisfaction. Autonomy is the degree of freedom employees have in making decisions on the job. Being able to make judgments without double-checking with higher-ranking officials makes employees feel needed, thus enhancing their level of job satisfaction. Job variety is simply the degree of variation within a job. Is the job repetitive and boring? An employee, including an administrator's level of job satisfaction, likely will decrease if either has a low level of job variety. Perhaps allowing employees to rotate within the correctional facility will keep the monotony to a tolerable level. Even if their actual job duties are not changed, by changing their physical assignment, the administrator is at least making an effort to provide some variety (Lambert 2004).

Effectively managing the levels of job stress, autonomy, and variety will help create a higher level of job satisfaction. In turn, employees will be more committed to their jobs and will be less likely to leave, thereby reducing turnover. Correctional administrators have a great deal to consider from a human-resource-management standpoint. The decisions they make and the policies they implement affect recruitment, turnover, and employee satisfaction.

Another challenge facing today's correctional administrators is labor management relations, especially in regard to correctional unions. Every administrator wants to have harmonious relations with his or her respective bargaining units; however, this relationship must be predicated around a few core values and shared beliefs. It is imperative for administrators and union officials to realize that:

1) Employees are the most valued resource in a correctional facility.
2) Management is responsible for the overall management of the agency.
3) Labor provides the resources to facilitate the smooth and efficient operations of the facility

Management and labor are not, and cannot be, independent of each other. Indeed, administrators and union members face a number of specific challenges. Each must have the ultimate goal of safety and security. Management and labor have to work together to reduce areas of excessive leave abuse and poor performance by employees. Labor and management must collaborate to provide working conditions that address the overall health of the labor force. While management and labor usually agree on the initial hiring requirements for new recruits and on physical training programs for basic recruit training, many agencies have failed to encourage employees to maintain the same level of fitness throughout their careers. Corrections in the twenty-first century cannot afford a "labor versus administration" attitude. Successful administrators must be able to create an appropriate and fair balance.

Fiscal Responsibility and Community Relations

Fiscal and budgetary responsibility is also important for an administrator in a correctional setting. Managing oneself and other employees is only one part of being a successful supervisor. Many correctional administrators are underqualified in areas of finance and business administration and thus may lack the competency necessary to have control over facility or system finances, which can be in the millions of dollars.

A correctional administrator is responsible for many of the expenditures relating to the facility that he or she is in charge of. Whether there is a financial officer who is dedicated to this area is irrelevant, because there must be some accountability from the person in the top position. Since much of the money used by corrections is provided through government tax dollars, it is essential that the supervisor have a working understanding of the budgetary process as a whole. Determining the areas where dollars can be shifted about to be more efficient is an administrator's responsibility. There may be particular areas that are underfunded. Is there a department that has a surplus of funds, and can those funds be transferred?

Payroll is another important area. Salaries are large expenses for any corporation. Determining how much is paid out on a weekly, monthly, or annual basis can help an administrator budget for the future. Also, having a grasp of the pay scale can help an administrator identify any instances where employees are being underpaid or overpaid for their respective positions.

Inventory and maintenance are other fiscal issues that must be taken into account. Housing and caring for hundreds, if not thousands, of staff and inmates requires day-to-day record-keeping. Good administrators will have a system in place to alert them to aging mechanical equipment and infrastructure. Additionally, it is important to accurately track inventory. Simple questions of how much inventory a facility has and where it is located must be answerable without hesitation. Those administrators with a background in accounting, management, or finance will be better equipped to institute such systems and be more successful in managing them. Knowing at a glance how much money is available and how best to use the resources at hand is necessary for a successful correctional administrator (McCampbell 2002).

Besides being fiscally responsible, a correctional administrator must be able to articulate his or her ideals clearly. Many times a public statement must be made through the media or other venue. Being able to get across a point succinctly and confidently instills trust in management. Correctional administrators must be outspoken in the community (city and county included) and show concern for how the facility is portrayed publicly. Making frequent community speeches and granting interviews is a good way to gain the confidence and approval of other criminal justice institutions as well as the public. Another way to increase public relations is to release frequent reports detailing any successes and acknowledging shortcomings. By doing so, the public will see that good things are being done to rehabilitate offenders and make the streets safer. Additionally, by acknowledging problem areas and highlighting a course of action, the public will see that the administrator is fallible but is working hard to remedy the situation (McCampbell 2002).

An Innovative Solution to These Issues

Aware of these issues, several correctional administrators with facilities in Shelby County, Tennessee, have established a working group known as the Training Advisory Committee, composed of representatives from the county, state and federal level and the Department of Criminology and Criminal Justice at the University of Memphis. The Shelby County Corrections Training Advisory Committee was created under the guidance of James Coleman of the Shelby County Sheriff's Office (Jail Division) in Memphis. Hired in 2001, Coleman recognized many training and other staff needs and sought an innovative, collaborative, and cost-effective strategy to address the concerns. To achieve these goals, Coleman invited the top correctional administrators in Shelby County to discuss the idea of a correctional command college. The focus of this initiative was to develop future leaders of the department but not to alienate or otherwise discount tenured employees. The advisory committee participants included representatives from the following four Shelby County correctional agencies:

- Federal Corrections Institute of Memphis
- Mark H. Lutrell Correctional Center (State of Tennessee Prison)
- Shelby County Division of Corrections
- Shelby County Sheriff's Office (Jail Division)

Representatives from the Department of Criminology and Criminal Justice at the University of Memphis completed the membership of the advisory committee. Each of the wardens and jail administrators included a number of relevant support staff on the committee.

The first meeting of the committee was held in August 2004 at the Shelby County Training Academy. The purpose of this initial meeting was for the various members to become acquainted with one another and to develop an understanding of how such a group could benefit the interests of the agencies involved. The most important result of the first meeting was the development of a self-administered survey questionnaire for all supervisory/management staff at each of the facilities. They also decided that the committee would meet monthly.

During the month following the initial meeting, one of the committee members from the University of Memphis worked to develop the survey. In mid-September, the career development survey was forwarded to Mr. James Coleman, the committee chair. A preliminary draft of the data collection tool was then presented to the entire committee for comment and review. By the end of September, the revised survey instrument was approved for distribution. The administrators distributed the confidential and anonymous surveys along with instructions for completing the forms. Respondents were directed to return the forms directly to the university for review and analysis within two weeks. A total of 133 correctional supervisors in three county facilities, one state facility, and one federal facility were surveyed regarding a variety of staff issues, including training, equipment, morale, job satisfaction/fulfillment, employment incentives, promotions, and other administrative issues. The results of the survey were compiled and analyzed and then distributed to the participants of the Training Advisory Committee. Readers interested in receiving a copy of the original survey or discussing the research design further may contact Wayne J. Pitts at wpitts@memphis.edu or by telephone at (901) 678-5662.

General Findings and Recommendations

The survey results showed that the surveyed administrators felt that they had limited specialized management training and experience. Most of the responding officers felt that they were not fully equipped to tackle the complex issues that arise both inside and outside the correctional facility. It is important to note that this finding is not meant (and should not be misconstrued) as an isolated criticism.

All correctional departments face these same challenges. Technological innovations in corrections have increased significantly during the past two decades. Besides the impact of these developments, correctional administrators have a wide array of obligations and job expectations. In some ways, securing inmates may be the easiest part of their job. Balancing the multifaceted management duties related to training, fiscal administration, human resources, and community relations is a complex assignment and one that requires an ongoing commitment to employee training and development. Based on the results of the survey, the report to the advisory committee produced several recommendations to improve and enhance the current training strategies with the goal of creating a more qualified staff at all levels.

A close analysis of the survey results showed that most officers felt undertrained to complete the various duties required by their job, and many respondents expressed an interest in receiving more targeted training. The advisory committee recommended the development of a partnership between local correctional agencies and the University of Memphis to develop an educational degree program tailored to meet the specific training deficiencies identified by the career development survey. As a result of this recommendation, a subcommittee of the Training Advisory Committee was created to make specific curriculum recommendations.

Based on the responses to the surveys and the consensus of the advisory committee, it was concluded that many current administrators would not be interested in pursuing a higher education degree. However, for these "less-aggressive" but valued employees, the committee decided that a certification program could be highly beneficial. The subcommittee was charged with developing a prospectus for two tracts: the degree program and the certificate program. Courses for academic credit were selected through available classes offered through the University of Memphis, University College, agency trainings, and the National Institute of Corrections.

The Training Advisory Committee identified several specific benefits of this partnership between local higher education institutions and the correctional agencies seeking to improve their training programs. Besides allowing current employees to achieve targeted vocational training, having a certification program could be a potential lure for prospective job applicants interested in further developing their skills and competency. The Training Advisory Committee also recommended that future staff promotions should be linked to competency levels as evidenced by the successful completion of certain tracks.

In other words, successful completion of certain certificate tracks would be listed as a prerequisite to staff promotions. Offering these types of classes to correctional employees would likely enhance the confidence with which they perform their duties and have the added benefit of providing incentives for motivated employees to advance their education. Perhaps completion of certain tracks could then be converted to academic credit for those employees who chose to pursue a bachelor's degree. Having a partnership with a local university not only could help administrators and employees reach their educational and training goals, but could also enhance the public's perception of (and respect for) the facility.

As a result of these recommendations, a proposal was developed in collaboration with the University of Memphis and presented to the advisory committee. The proposal was accepted and a new interdisciplinary degree program was established through the University College at the University of Memphis. The bachelor's degree program will allow students to receive a degree in corrections leadership and management.

Since the acceptance of the program by the university, the Training Advisory Subcommittee has been promoting and marketing this program to other correctional agencies throughout the state of Tennessee, including the Tennessee Board of Parole and Probation. Members of the Training Advisory Committee also made a presentation to the Tennessee Corrections Association. Since 2005, the new degree program has been promoted annually during the special events of National Correctional Officers' Week. Some employees have enrolled, although participation has been slower than originally anticipated. Participants from the advisory committee also have shared information about the new program at the statewide meeting of Tennessee Wardens and the Commissioners of Corrections.

Benefits

In short, the efforts and vision of the Shelby County Training Advisory Committee have led to an unprecedented level of collaboration in Shelby County corrections. The resulting degree and certificate program offered through the University of Memphis have been developed with amazingly quick turnaround, and information about the program has been widely disseminated throughout the state. Now that the model program has been developed, the Training Committee Subcommittee has begun to explore other educational and training options with other Memphis-area higher education entities, including Southwest Tennessee Community College, Christian Brothers University, and LeMoyne-Owen College.

The benefits of the collaborative effort have already extended beyond the original reasons for developing the advisory team. The association between the county, state, and federal correctional entities in Shelby County has allowed the team participants to share ideas and promote cross-agency development. Through the partnership, the three agencies came together during National Correctional Officers' Week and held a coordinated "corrections ball." The three partners also joined forces and held a Corrections Agency Olympics event, where teams from the agencies competed against one another in a variety of individual and team athletic events.

The unmatched partnership in Shelby County has improved communication about common training issues, and the benefits are already visible after just one year. Besides the development of the career development survey and the resulting bachelor's degree program in corrections leadership and management, the Training Advisory Committee has made local correctional institutions aware of training opportunities available within individual agencies. For example, the National Institute of Corrections conducted a recent training for Shelby County correctional employees, which state correctional staff also attended.

Shelby County correctional agencies have joined together to create a cost-effective and innovative approach to addressing shared correctional issues and concerns. Perhaps most important, this partnership is sustainable over time as long as the top administrators continue to participate at current levels. The Shelby County Training Advisory Committee for the correctional command college came together with a common problem and, through the commitment and innovation of the participants, developed a fresh new program and implemented it in less than one year. A similar strategy of collaboration may be expected to benefit other jurisdictions.

References

Carlson, J., R. Anson, and G. Thomas. 2003. Correctional officer burnout and stress: Does gender matter? *The Prison Journal* 83(3): 277-88.

Finkelstein, E. 1996. Status degradation and organizational succession in prison. *The British Journal of Sociology* 47(4): 671-83.

Jurik, N. and M. Musheno. 1986. The internal crisis of corrections: Professionalization and the work environment. *Justice Quarterly* 3(4): 457-80.

Lambert, E. 2004.The impact of job characteristics on correctional staff members. *The Prison Journal* 84(2): 208-27.

Lommel, J. 2004. Turning around turnover. *Corrections Today*, August, 66(5): 54-57.

Martin, M. D. and T. A. Rosazza. 2004. Resource guide for jail administrators. Washington, D.C.: National Institute of Corrections.

McCampbell, S. 2002. Making successful new wardens. *Corrections Today*, October, 64(6): 130-33.

McCurdy, H. 1978. Selecting and training public managers: Business skills versus public administration. *Public Administration Review* 38(6): 571-78.

Patterson, B. L. 1992. Job experience and perceived job stress among police, correctional, and probation/parole officers. *Criminal Justice and Behavior* 19(3): 260-85.

Pitts, W. and J. E. Coleman. 2006. Shelby County's training advisory committee: Developing a collaborative corrections training program. *LJN Exchange* (annual issue), July.

Savicki, V., E. Cooley, and J. Gjesvold. 2003. Harassment as a predictor of job burnout in correctional officers. *Criminal Justice and Behavior* 30(5): 602-19.

St. Gerard, V. 2004. Rhode Island recruiting more diverse staff. *Corrections Today*, August, 66(5): 12.

Sullivan, B. 2004. Can traditional work standards and contemporary employee coexist? *The Police Chief* 71(10): 99-102.

Tartaro, C. 2002. Examining implementation issues with new generation jails. *Criminal Justice Policy Review* 13(3): 219-37.

Waldron, R. and J. Altemose. 1979. Determining and defending personnel needs in criminal justice organizations. *Public Administration Review* 39(4): 385-89.

Walters, S. 1993. Gender, job satisfaction, and correctional officers: A comparative analysis. *Justice Professional* 7(2): 23-33.

About the Authors

Wayne J. Pitts, Ph.D., is an assistant professor in the Department of Criminology and Criminal Justice at the University of Memphis. James Coleman is the chief jail director of the Shelby County Jail in Memphis.

How Complex Is Change in a Jail System?

By William C. Lawhorn

On a daily basis, a jail's staff is challenged with emergent incidents of violence, medical distress, security breaches, and more. Although such incidents are anticipated, when a jail experiences a series of like events, such as a series of deaths or escapes in a short period of time, external stakeholders begin demanding that "something" change. Change in a correctional environment is neither something that comes naturally nor easily. However, change in corrections is inevitable and necessary, especially following a series of negative events or at times when laws and industry standards change, causing the profession to evolve. If one were to ask ten different jail administrators how to implement change effectively in a correctional system, the answers would no doubt be as varied as those answering.

Nevertheless, implementing change in a jail system is nearly identical to implementing change in any organization. The foundation of change rests on understanding the jail system's culture—mostly the culture of the system's staff, but also partially the inmate culture. Understanding why a system's culture exists and the influences that created it is necessary to implement an effective cycle of change. Although challenging, the cycle of change can be simplified in the following format: development, action, outcome, analysis, and revision. This chapter demonstrates how this simple format can be implemented in a jail system.

The Change Leader

Too often, new administrators, and even many experienced administrators, try overly hard to force change. Change happens over time. Change happens when the leadership and the recipients of change are both in agreement that something different is necessary. Administrators who try to force change through writing procedures that are inflexible or who resist input that alters their ideas are doomed to failure or, at the very least, are less effective in making change. A good administrator possesses strong leadership traits, traits that recognize the system's culture and empowers it to participate in change.

A change leader recognizes when repetitions in behavior that result in the same ineffective results are occurring and makes a conscious effort to amend the outcome by modifying the method by which change is being attempted. To do this, the administrator needs to not be self-focused but must obtain and sustain the confidence and development of those he or she is going to lead. An effective administrator must self-analyze and recognize when change is being forced. The change leader must learn what is effective for the system for which change is needed. According to Warren Bennis and Joan Goldsmith in their book,

Learning to Lead: A Workbook on Becoming a Leader, "The learning process is one that includes the pain of self-critical examination and the exhilaration of taking risks and reaching goals." Finally, an effective administrator must hold individuals accountable for their actions and inactions.

So, how does one induce change? Three elements of successful change in a jail system are alignment, empowerment, and endurance. Changing a jail system requires movement, movement from where it is to where the administrator wants it to be. The movement process is similar to that of moving a stationary five-foot, marble stone ball. If one were to start with such an object, symmetrically round, without imperfection, and move it to a specified destination, the planning, inception, action, endurance, and outcome would reflect the process necessary to change a jail system. Alone, the solid marble stone weighs more than 11,000 pounds. Moving it from point A to the region of point B, nearly 100 yards away, would demonstrate the challenges, mishaps, and alterations to direction experienced while accomplishing this goal.

Alignment

Before undertaking such an enormous task, the change leader should develop a structure or a plan for change. The plan should incorporate a common vision comprised of shared objectives and goals. According to Bennis and Goldsmith, "It has much to do with spirit and a team atmosphere." Planning for such a course of action must be strategically thought out and purposeful, taking into account where the system currently rests and knowing what direction the system needs to reach to be able to measure success. The planning phase should include an evaluation of the elements that may be impacted and those elements that could alter the course. A well-developed plan includes a vision and goals that the system's culture can relate to, measure, and aspire toward.

To develop the plan, the administrator must first establish a few key components:

- Identify leaders within the staff who can make change happen
- Establish a respectful and trusting relationship to instill confidence in the administrator's leadership abilities
- Gather staff ideas for change and incorporate them into the plan
- Identify the "playing field"—know the boundaries and obstacles
- Establish guidelines and boundaries through clear communications
- Define goals and benchmarks to gauge progress
- Establish a starting point and timeline.

The first three key components deal with those individuals in the jail system who can and want to effect change. Finding individuals who desire change and have the ability to influence others in the system are essential to the team leadership. The change leader should establish trusting relationships with these individuals, building confidence, and creating a respectful rapport. "The trust factor is the social glue that binds commitment and promotes action necessary to produce results. To trust other people, to have confidence in them, we need to see evidence of their competence," Bennis and Goldsmith noted.

Making decisions and giving valuable feedback that promotes individual thinking begins to build confidence in the relationship. Another part of relationship-building should include a process for the key players to insert their own ideas and merge them with the ultimate plan of action. The team members will value this ownership and will work harder to achieve the goals.

The remaining key components deal with implementing the mechanics of the plan. To get from point A to point B, a plan of action needs to be developed. Establishing a starting point and then developing a comprehensive, detailed plan that is clear to all involved is the first step in this process. The plan needs to include goals, objectives, and benchmarks. Both short- and long-term goals should be set to celebrate achievements and identify adjustments that need to be made. Analyze the "playing field" for imperfections and obstacles that could hinder or alter the course. Planning ahead and removing the obstacles or minimizing the hurdles will greatly increase the likelihood of success. It is necessary to set timeframes to achieve benchmarks and expect alterations. Prior to initiating any movement, the team needs to be fully prepared and familiar with the plan and the desired outcomes.

Empowerment

Bennis and Goldsmith discuss that empowering staff members has much to do with them obtaining a sense that they are at the center of the plan rather than on the periphery of the changes. Their ideas need to be acknowledged and factored into the overall plan. "Empowered individuals feel that what they do has meaning and significance. They have direction and obligations and live in a culture of respect," Bennis and Goldsmith stated. By having influence in the outcome of the plan, naturally, the staff will take that ownership and sell their ideas to those individuals with whom they have already established trust. This begins the rallying of staff to start the process. The change leader can assist in developing the ownership by holding accountable those who are responsible for action.

Once the plan is developed and relationships are established with the essential team members, the plan is ready to be implemented. Starting the ball rolling is one of the hardest aspects of implementing a plan. Imagine the 11,000-pound stone ball and the inertia necessary to make it start to move. Similarly, initiating change in a jail system requires the decision to move forward and the "big push" behind it. Too often a staff that is fearful of change or fearful of failure procrastinates and puts off the commencement of change. The administrator should step out as the leader and show confidence in the plan.

An effective change process requires adaptation to the inevitable along the way. As the plan is implemented, the administrator needs to anticipate and deal with obstacles in its path. As the administrator begins the process of change, those opposed to change will become obstacles or challenges. If allowed to interfere, they could deter the overall course. Other obstacles that will alter the course of change are the inevitable crisis incidents that jails experience—inmate deaths, escape attempts, natural disasters—as well as budget shortfalls, bargaining unit interference, and staff turnover.

One last potential obstacle in the path of change for the administrator to consider is the culture of the inmate population. Alone, the inmate culture is relatively negative due to the circumstance of incarceration. Though understood to be negative, a poor inmate culture could be reflective of a poor staff culture. High rates of violence, grievances, thefts, and rape are indicators that inmates are not being held accountable for their actions. These problems compound the difficulty of implementing change and make the change much more vital. Whatever the cause, the administrator should take a moment, review the original plan and make necessary adjustments to right the course of movement.

Endurance

In the course of moving forward, endurance and persistence are necessary. Over time, team members will experience frustration and exhaustion while continuing to push against seemingly constant resistance. As the leader, the administrator needs to keep his or her eye on the end result and encourage the staff involved to continue on with persistence—to keep the team enthusiastic and engaged.

Establishing milestones early on helps maintain the team confidence. As each milestone is achieved, small celebrations in recognition of the goal should occur to reassure the team members that the plan is moving forward. Benchmarks that are not reached need to be analyzed and the plan re-evaluated to determine why targets were missed. With each opportunity, the administrator should continuously involve the team members in problem solving to ensure buy-in continues. Similarly, as momentum appears to dwindle and exhaustion appears to take over, fresh ideas and new strengths help reassure the stakeholders that persistence is the key. Failures will occur and the ball will roll off course, but taking the time and effort to regroup and redirect the course puts the plan back on the right track.

In the original planning phase, the end goals were established in the "area" of point B as opposed to a specific location at point B. This allows for deviations in the plan and alterations in the course. In some instances, the deviation from the original course will be toward the path of least resistance. As long as the course remains steady and the end result is in the region of point B, the objective is still attained. To pinpoint a specific place for the jail to come to rest without the expectation of some deviation is not realistic.

For example, a jail system that suffers from a shortage of staff, budgetary constraints, overpopulation, high staff turnover, and/or significant security breaches cannot expect to be picture perfect just because a plan was written and implemented. However, realistic milestones at point B should be lessening each of these drains on the system. The successes of reducing each or any of these should be broadcast and celebrated, while also re-evaluating and starting the process over to further improve the system.

Although many individuals are comfortable with the way the world is, or at least the way the world they live in is, change in a jail system is inevitable. Resistance to change is often based on fear and a lack of trust in those implementing the change. However, change is necessary. As jail systems continue to increase the levels of professionalism in both operations and personnel, the more change is needed. When the right changes are made, the jail system will be better equipped to deal with the endless list of struggles. Although there are many different opinions and approaches to change, the essential mechanics are simple: develop a plan, implement the plan, evaluate the outcomes, revisit and revise the original plan, and start the cycle again. The primary elements of establishing relationships with those that need to make change happen and holding both the staff and leaders accountable are essential components of the cycle of change. Without the trust and respect of those who are leading change—and without accountability for actions or inactions—change is not likely to occur.

Reference

Bennes, Warren, and Joan Goldsmith. 1997. *Learning to Lead: A Workbook on Becoming a Leader*. Basic Books, New York.

About the Author

William C. Lawhorn is director of security, operations, and audits for the Vermont Department of Corrections.

The National Institute of Corrections: Serving Jails for More Than Thirty Years

By Virginia Hutchinson

Since 1976, the National Institute of Corrections has been the primary federal source of technical assistance, training, and information services to jails. The National Institute of Corrections provides services at no cost to the requesting agency.

Although jails may request services from various National Institute of Corrections divisions—such as the Community Corrections, Academy, and Transition and Offender Workforce Development divisions—most jail-specific services are housed within the Jails Division. The Jails Division works closely with other divisions on jail-related services, such as the Transition from Jail to the Community Initiative, which focuses on helping inmates successfully reintegrate into their communities after release.

Throughout its history, the National Institute of Corrections Jails Division has based its services on several key principles:

- Services must be of practical use to jails
- Services must be based on a thorough understanding of the issues facing jails
- Services are developed with recognition of the diversity among jails, in terms of, for example, size, age, resource levels, and operational philosophy
- Staff have a working knowledge of jail management and operations and are colleagues of the jail practitioners the National Institute of Corrections serves
- Staff work in partnership with jail practitioners to identify effective practices and share these with the field
- The Jails Division uses its limited resources as effectively as possible by addressing issues that are pervasive throughout jails, are critical to operations, and can be effectively addressed within its mission and resource constraints.

Based on these principles, the Jails Division currently provides training, technical assistance, and information services under four initiatives: Jail Administration, Inmate Behavior Management, New Jail Planning, and Jail Standards and Inspections.

Jail Administration

The Jail Administration Initiative includes training, technical assistance, and materials on a wide variety of topics related to jail management and operations.

Training Programs and Networks

The Jails Division offers training on critical elements in jail administration for small and medium-sized jails. It has recently revised both these programs—Administering the Small Jail and Jail Administration—to ensure their continued relevance and usefulness. This year, the division is developing a new program on administering jails with 1,000 or more beds. This course will take into account the administrative challenges unique to large jail systems. The division is working closely with a group of large jail administrators to shape its approach to the program and review the work as it progresses. The National Institute of Corrections will begin conducting this program in its 2011 fiscal year.

In addition, the Jails Division continues to conduct Jail Resource Management and Jail as Part of County Government programs as part of this initiative. It created Jail Resource Management in response to many requests from jail administrators for help with developing and managing their budgets. The program focuses on how to identify and track resource needs, present, and justify those needs, and manage the resources allocated to the jail.

Jail as Part of County Government addresses the often adversarial relationship between jail officials and their funding authorities. Its primary goal is to foster a more informed and productive relationship between the two entities. Jail officials attend with representatives of their funding authorities to discuss the role and functions of the jail, liability issues, jail resource needs, and the funding authorities' challenges in meeting competing demands for limited funds.

One of the National Institute of Corrections' largest and most active networks is the Large Jail Network, designed for the top administrator of jails with 1,000 or more beds. The Jails Division sponsors two network meetings each year and hosts an electronic community forum for members. The division encourages administrators of all large jails to join the network and benefit from the extensive information-sharing and peer training.

Documents and DVDs

The Jails Division has developed materials on various issues in jail administration, such as staffing analysis, budgeting, jail crowding, data collection and analysis, and criminal justice coordinating councils. These are available upon request and many can be downloaded from the National Institute of Corrections' website at www.nicic.gov. The division recommends, at a minimum, that jail administrators have the following materials.

Beyond the Myths: The Jail in Your Community—The Jails Division developed this twenty-three-minute DVD primarily as a community education tool. Public misconceptions about jails are widespread, and they often result in a lack of support for professional, effective jail operations. Many jail officials have used the DVD in their presentations to community groups; some have aired it in on local televisions stations; and some have placed it on their organization's website. Officials have also found the DVD effective in educating members of their funding authority and in introducing new staff members to the role and functions of local jails.

Jail Resource Issues: What Every Funding Authority Needs to Know—This publication was written for members of the local funding authority who know little about jails. It is a concise document that zeros in on the critical characteristics of a well-run jail and the role of the funding authority in ensuring its jail has those characteristics. Many jail administrators have shared this with their funding authorities as a basis for better-informed discussions about jail issues and resource needs.

Sheriff's Guide to Effective Jail Operations—This guide focuses on the sheriff's role in ensuring the jail is operating effectively. It is useful not only to sheriffs but also to chief executive officers who oversee jails not run by sheriffs.

Resource Guide for Jail Administrators—This basic desk reference includes sound practices in jail administration and operations. It also provides information on the role of the jail administrator, an operational assessment checklist, and references for further information on specific topics. This document is helpful to both new and veteran jail administrators.

The most recently published document under the Jail Administration Initiative is *A Guide to Preparing for and Responding to Emergencies*. This covers information on leadership during crises, prevention of jail emergencies, and emergency teams. It also includes self-audit checklists to help jails determine their level of emergency preparedness.

Technical Assistance

The Jails Division conducts technical assistance under this initiative on a broad range of topics identified by individual jails requesting this assistance. These have included general operational assessments, assessments of medical operations, assistance with developing criminal justice coordinating committees, reviews of security practices, and more.

Inmate Behavior Management

The Inmate Behavior Management Initiative includes services on direct supervision jails and assistance related to effectively managing inmates in any jail, regardless of the physical plant design.

Training

This year, the Jails Division is extensively revising its training programs on direct supervision. It is developing a new program on the administrator's role in ensuring that direct supervision principles are fully integrated into the design and operation of the jail. Additionally, the division is revising *How to Run a Direct Supervision Housing Unit: Training for Trainers* so that it addresses not only the role of the housing officer but also that of the first-line supervisor in supporting the officer. In fiscal year 2011, the Jails Division will begin conducting both these programs.

Several years ago, the Jails Division began to offer training on the key elements in effectively managing inmate behavior in any type of jail, regardless of design. The division's efforts in this area were substantially informed by its ongoing work with direct supervision, objective classification, and inmate supervision. The Jails Division recognized that, although direct supervision jails were highly successful in reducing negative inmate behavior, not all local jurisdictions had the opportunity to build a new direct supervision facility. Regardless of their jail's design, however, all local jurisdictions remained responsible for operating safe and secure facilities. To help all jails reduce negative inmate behavior and improve safety and security, the Jails Division identified six key elements in managing inmate behavior, then developed related training services. The elements are as follows:

- Assessing the risks and needs of inmates at various points during their stay for accurate inmate classification
- Assigning inmates to housing so they are placed where they can be managed most effectively
- Meeting inmates' basic needs
- Defining and conveying expectations for inmate behavior
- Supervising inmates
- Keeping inmates productively occupied.

The Inmate Behavior Management training program focuses on these elements, explaining how and why they work to improve inmate behavior, enhance safety and security, and help create an overall better working environment for staff and living environment for inmates.

Documents and DVDs

Jail administrators who would like to assess their implementation of the direct supervision principles may request the *Self-Audit Instrument for Administrators of Direct Supervision Jails* from the National Institute of Corrections Information Center. *Jails in America: A Report on Podular Direct Supervision* is a DVD that gives an overview of direct supervision and can be used to educate citizens and local officials. Many jails also use this as part of their staff training on direct supervision. This year, the Jails Division will publish a new document, *Direct Supervision Jails: The Role of the Administrator.*

The Jails Division recently published *Inmate Behavior Management: The Key to a Safe and Secure Jail*, which concisely explains the six elements to effectively manage inmate behavior. The division is also developing a set of documents that will help guide jail practitioners in implementing each of the elements. The first, *Programs and Activities: Tools for Managing Inmate Behavior*, was published in 2010.

Technical Assistance

The Jails Division provides on-site technical assistance to individual jurisdictions on direct supervision and on each of the six elements of inmate behavior management.

New Jail Planning

The National Institute of Corrections Jails Division has provided information, training, and technical assistance on the new jail planning process since the 1970s. The division has a continuum of services that coincide with the major components of the process. Through the years, many local jurisdictions have cited the benefits of this process in terms of cost-savings and in building a jail that meets the needs of their communities.

Technical Assistance and Training

Through on-site technical assistance, the Jails Division conducts jail and justice-system assessments for jurisdictions that are considering new jail construction. The jail is reviewed, and the policies and practices of the local criminal justice system are assessed for their effect on the inmate population (size, makeup, and length of stay). This gives local officials a foundation for further assessing system policies and practices and for more accurately determining their detention needs.

For jurisdictions that have made the commitment to build a new jail, the Jails Division offers a training program, *Planning of New Institutions: Taking Control of the Process*. This focuses on predesign planning activities and the need for local officials to maintain control of the early planning process to ensure that the jail meets their communities' needs.

Managing Jail Design and Construction is a training program for jurisdictions that are beginning to design a new jail. It covers the knowledge and skills participants need to ensure that the facility's design reflects their operational philosophy and will facilitate their desired operational practices.

For jurisdictions within twelve-to-eighteen months of opening their new jail, the Jails Division conducts on-site technical assistance to train selected staff members on activities required for a successful transition to the new jail. These include, for example, testing operating scenarios, writing policies and procedures, ordering equipment and supplies, determining the final staffing plan, developing and implementing a staff training plan, and planning the logistics of moving inmates and staff into the new jail.

Documents and DVDs

Local officials can get an introduction to the new jail planning process by reading the National Institute of Corrections' *Jail Planning and Expansion: Local Officials and Their Roles*. The division has also published documents on getting community support for a new jail, new jail site selection, jail design review, and how to make the transition to a new jail. The most recent document, published this year, is *Jail Capacity Planning Guide: A Systems Approach*, which discusses jail population forecasting and management within the larger framework of the policies and practices of the local criminal justice system. It describes a comprehensive strategy to identify, address, and manage the factors that drive the demand for jail beds.

This year, the division has added a DVD on the new jail planning process to its array of materials. The DVD is a twenty-minute informational tool that gives an overview of the process and stresses its underlying concepts: 1) effective planning; 2) control of the project by the jail's owners and operators; and 3) inclusion of a wide variety of citizens, local officials, and jail staff at various stages in the process. The DVD is useful in educating citizens, local officials, jail staff, and others about new jail planning.

Jail Standards and Inspections

The Jails Division continues to support the development and implementation of jail standards. Currently, thirty-three states have some form of jail standards. The standards vary widely among states, and not all of these states have inspection systems. In recent years, the division has seen some states abandon standards altogether, shift their standards from mandatory to voluntary, or maintain some level of standards but do away with inspection. Chief jail inspectors in states that have standards voiced their need for the National Institute of Corrections' support, and in 1999, the Jails Division responded by establishing a network for them. The chief jail inspectors meet once each year for information-sharing and peer training, and they are active in an electronic community forum. Biannually, the Jails Division also offers training for new jail inspectors on how to conduct a jail inspection.

Additionally, the division has published three documents related to standards. The first, *Jail Standards and Inspection Programs: Resource and Implementation Guide*, provides information on how to develop or update jail standards and inspections programs. The second, developed in conjunction with state jail inspection agencies, is *Jail Inspection Basics: An Introductory Self-Study Course for Jail Inspectors*. The third document, *Jail Inspection Basics: Supervisor's Guide*, helps supervisors work with their staff as they complete the jail inspectors' self-study course. Finally, state agencies or other organizations that want to develop or revise their jail standards and inspection systems may request technical assistance from the Jails Division.

For more information on how to obtain the National Institute of Corrections' services, documents, and DVDs, readers may visit the National Institute of Corrections' website at www.nicic.gov. To request hard copies of documents, readers should call the National Institute of Corrections' Information Center at (800) 877-1461. The Jails Division welcomes phone calls and e-mail questions about its services. Contact information for the Jails Division staff members, along with their program areas, is listed below:

Virginia Hutchinson, National Institute of Corrections Jails Division Chief
(800) 995-6423, ext. 75811
vhutchinson@bop.gov

Jim Barbee, Correctional Program Specialist
Jail standards and inspections, Inmate Transition from Jail to the Community
(800) 995-6423, ext. 40100
jbarbee@bop.gov

Robbye Braxton-Mintz, Correctional Program Specialist
Direct supervision jails, Jail as Part of County Government program,
Jail Resource Management program
(800) 995-6423, ext. 44562

Mike Jackson, Correctional Program Specialist
Jail Administration program, Planning of New Institutions program, jail and justice system assessments, jail crowding, Large Jail Network
(800) 995-6423, ext. 69565
mpjackson@bop.gov

Cheryl Paul, Correctional Program Specialist
Administering the Small Jail program, Managing Jail Design and Construction program, Transition to a New Jail
(800) 995-6423, ext. 69590
cmpaul@bop.gov

Fran Zandi, Correctional Program Specialist
Inmate Behavior Management program, inmate classification, mentally ill
inmates in jails, general technical assistance
(800) 994-6423, ext. 71070
fzandi@bop.gov

About the Author

Virginia Hutchinson has been the chief of the National Institute of Corrections Jails Division since 1998. She came to National Institute of Corrections as a correctional program specialist in 1988 from the Larimer County Detention Center in Fort Collins, Colorado.

They Don't Bite: Working with the Press to Build Public Confidence

By Timothy P. Ryan

We, in corrections, spend a great deal of our energy worrying about what the media is going to say about us, rather than recognizing that the press, whether print, audio, or visual, has its "job to do" and we are just part of that job. So, if their job is to say something about our job, let us spend our energy determining how we are going to tell our story that best meets our needs. When we simply try to do just that, our outcomes are better and the media can use their time to tell the story in the best manner they might without implying that "they found the story" or "that we are hiding something."

One of the characteristics of the process that we sometimes forget is that "we have the information" that the media needs. So, sharing the information in a format that the media likes really is something we can control.

We need to be sensitive to some of "their" constraints, such as time, but the meat of the story is in how we present it to the media. Therefore, our first obligation is to know the facts, then be able to convey them in a meaningful manner, and, in the end, respond to follow-ups with in-depth facts and more truth.

In his book *Winning with the News Media*, Clarence Jones provides us with the "Ten Commandments of News Relations," which are as follows:

1. Be open and cooperative—never lie
2. Personalize the organization
3. Develop media contacts
4. Take good stories to the media
5. Respond quickly
6. Never say "No Comment"
7. It is okay to say "I do not know" (but, I will find out)
8. If you screw up, confess and repent
9. Use the "Big Dump" (say it all now)
10. Prepare, prepare, and prepare

Although I do not believe that you can ever feel fully comfortable with the media, it has been my experience that if you are friendly, forthright, and responsive, you will gain much. And if you use Mr. Jones' foundation for "Winning," you and your agency will be as successful as possible with the media. With such an approach, the community receives the information it needs, and you and your agency become the credible source instead of an incredible barrier.

As one of the persons who taught me this business would sometimes say, "Always work to make chicken salad out of chicken (stuff), and the media will be pecking grain out of your hand instead of forcing it up your bottom."

About the Author

Timothy P. Ryan is the Director of the Miami-Dade, Florida, Corrections and Rehabilitation Department.

Section 2

Twenty-First Century Jail Issues

When Johnny or Jane Comes Marching Home and Changes One Uniform for Another*

By Art Beeler

Editor's Note: *The points of view presented in this chapter are those of the author and do not necessarily represent the position of the Department of Justice or the Federal Bureau of Prisons.*

When soldiers come home from war, it is inevitable that some will end up doing time. By self-report, about half of U.S. veterans will spend at least one night in jail.[1] However, the focus of this paper will be on those veterans who are confined as a condition of sentencing. The world has changed considerably since World War II. The same is true for incarceration policies. In the past thirty years, correctional policies and interventions have significantly changed in this country and have increased the population of correctional facilities to more than two million inmates.[2] Included in this population are more than 140,000 veterans.[3] The last definitive statistics on the veteran population in jails and prisons comes from a Bureau of Justice Statistics' special report, *Veterans in Prisons or Jail*, published in 2007. It notes that among male inmates there are 630 incarcerated males per 100,000, down from 937 per 100,000 in 1998.

When you look at the percentage of veterans against the whole of those confined, the number of veterans has declined from 12 percent in 1998 to about 10 percent in 2007.[4] Two environmental factors contribute to this: first, the end of the Cold War and the resultant decrease in the number of those serving, and second, the significant increase in confined populations during the same period.

The movement to an all-volunteer force may have played a role in the change in the rate of incarceration. The U.S. military ended the draft in 1973. Between 1985 and 1998, the number of male veterans dropped about 1 percent a year from almost 27 million to about 24 million.[5] For women, the number of veterans rose for this same period of time from about 1 million to more than 1.2 million.[6] During the same time, the number of female offenders increased but generally stayed constant as a percentage of the overall prison population—close to 7 percent.

Overall, in 1998, about one in four incarcerated persons in this country was able to claim veteran status, down from one in three in 1985.[7] Before delving into issues brought forth by the incarcerated veteran, here are some demographic highlights from the 2004 data:

This article was originally published in conjunction with the North Carolina Bar Association Foundation Continuing Education Program "Veterans' Rights: When Johnny and Jane Come Marching Home," October 5, 2006. Data was updated for 2010 using the report Veterans in State and Federal Prison *(Bureau of Justice Statistics, 2007.)*

- Thirty-eight percent of incarcerated veterans were not honorably discharged.

- Twenty-three percent of veterans saw combat duty during their tour of duty.

- In 1998, about 18,500 Gulf War I veterans were incarcerated.

- Approximately 57 percent of veterans in prison were convicted of violent offenses, versus 47 percent of the non-veteran population.

- More veterans are first-time offenders than non-veterans.

- Among violent offenders, veterans serve about thirty months longer than their violent non-veteran counterparts.

- Veterans were less likely than their counterparts to have used drugs at the time of offense.

- Veterans who had served in the army represent 46 percent of the veteran population; yet, they made up 56 percent of those incarcerated.

- Veterans were more likely to be white, non-Hispanic. For state prisoners, more than 50 percent were white, non-Hispanic compared to 31 percent of the entire population. For federal offenders, veterans who were white comprised 50 percent of the population compared to 26 percent of those confined.

- Veterans who are incarcerated are on average about ten years older than the non-veteran offender. The median age for veterans incarcerated was more than forty, while the median age for non-veterans is approximately thirty-three.

- Veterans were more likely to have been married; however, when looking at those currently married, the data is similar to that of veterans and non-veterans.

- Veterans report higher levels of education. Veterans where three times more likely to have attended some college versus non-veterans (33 percent versus 10 percent). Conversely, 40 percent of non-veterans had not achieved a GED or high school diploma; whereas, only 9 percent of non-veterans had not reached this milestone.

- Combat veterans are no more or less likely to have committed violent offenses than non-combat veterans.

- Forty-three percent of veterans reported past drug use. Veterans were more likely to have used intravenous drugs than non-veterans.

- Veterans were significantly more likely to have alcohol-abuse indicators than their non-veteran counterparts, and much more likely to have been involved in errant behavior associated with alcohol use, such as DWI, losing a job, and being involved in a physical confrontation.

- Incarcerated veterans were more likely to report mental illness than other inmates.

- Overall, incarcerated veterans were more likely than incarcerated non-veterans to have been employed and employed full time.

- Veterans were no more likely than non-veterans to have been homeless prior to confinement.

When looking at incarcerated veterans, it is very difficult to separate their needs from their non-incarcerated brethren. This becomes more evident when you look at the special needs presented by this population in general. In the past forty years, prisons have become an institution of last resort for many people with mental illness.[8] Veterans Affairs hospitals and clinics, likewise, have seen an increase in those who suffer from mental illness. From a numeric standpoint, between the years 1955 and 1985, the number of state mental health hospital beds dropped from 339 per 100,000 to 29 per 100,000.[9] If the number of mentally ill inmates is approximately 16 percent, those with special needs would approximate 336,000. This is five times the number of patients currently in state psychiatric hospitals.[10]

As indicated in federal prison, veterans report mental illness at about twice the rate of non-veterans[11] as shown in Table 1 on the next page. More surprising is the large variance in Axis I diagnoses in the *Diagnostic and Statistical Manual of Mental Disorders* (DSM-IV-TR). These diagnoses include psychiatric illnesses such as schizophrenia or bipolar disorder but do not include borderline personality disorder or antisocial offenders. Spoont indicates that the most common diagnoses are mood disorder (15 percent to 70 percent), anxiety disorder (60 percent), substance abuse disorders (34 to 44 percent), and post-traumatic stress disorder (6 percent to 70 percent).[12] The wide variance of Axis I diagnoses presents large problems for administrators challenged to meet the needs of this population.

Spoont goes on to report that a majority of incarcerated veterans have more than one Axis I diagnosis.[13] A study completed by McGuire, Rosenheck, and Kasprow in 2003 reveals that one in three incarcerated offenders had a diagnosis of mental illness and one in two currently abused drugs.[14] If this is extrapolated using available 1998 data, some 75,000 incarcerated veterans suffer mental illness to some extent and more than 112,000 currently abuse drugs. According to Black, in one of the only works published regarding incarcerated veterans of Gulf War I, veterans are three times more likely to report post-traumatic stress disorder (PTSD), nearly three times more likely to report dysthymia, and nearly twice as likely to report alcohol abuse, anxiety disorders, and asthma.[15] This study reveals that, when adjusted for variables such as education, income, mental health characteristics, and antisocial behavior, Gulf War combat veterans had a positive association toward incarceration.

Table 1. The Comparison of DSM-IV Diagnostic Rates across Several Studies

DSM Diagnosis	Natelson (2001) Community n = 76	Saxon (2001) Jail n = 129	McGuire (2003) Community and Jail n = 8,236	Spoont (2003) Veterans Affairs Medical Center n = 83	Bosworth (2004) Veterans Affairs Inpatient Unit n = 396	Lim[30] (2006) Community n = 67,441
Mood Disorder			15%	70%	16% Bipolar	28.6%
Anxiety Disorder				60%		
Psychotic Disorder			11%	5%	46%	12.3%
Somatoform Disorder				14%		
Substance Use Disorder			43% Alcohol 44% Other	34%		
Cognitive Disorder NOS				10%		
Eating Disorder NOS				2%		
PTSD	50%	39%	6%	70% - female 62% - male	38%	8.1%
Other Axis I				5%		
Axis II Disorders			2%	76%		

The rate of PTSD in the general population is 7.8 percent; for the incarcerated population,[16] several studies report a wide variance, between 6 to 70 percent. Saxon reports that trauma and PTSD generally precede drug and alcohol abuse problems, thus giving rise to dual diagnosis for this segment of the incarcerated cohort.[17] While this same group of veterans had greater instances of drug treatment, they had greater use of alcohol, heroin, and cocaine.[18] Additionally, those who suffer PTSD experience more psychopathology and more general health issues than non-incarcerated veterans. Depending upon data collected subsequent to Gulf War II and depending if the positive correlation with incarceration continues, this may speak especially to the development of post-incarceration programs for these offenders in hopes to prevent them from reoffending. The rate of PTSD is quite high in health care settings with veterans who have been diagnosed with chronic fatigue or idiopathic chronic fatigue.[19]

A recent study by Kubiak at Wayne State University examines the co-morbidity of substance abuse and PTSD on successful reentry into the community.[20] While this data represents a study cohort of incarcerated felons not differentiating for veterans' status, it warrants review. The hypothesis of the study was that for inmates who have co-morbid disorders of substance use disorder and PTSD, recidivism would be significantly higher than for those who had a substance abuse diagnosis alone. The conclusions of this study were mixed; however, for women with a dual diagnosis they were 22 percent more likely to relapse than those who had a single diagnosis, of substance use disorder (SUD).[21] Men with PTSD and substance abuse disorder were much more likely to recidivate (17 percent versus 6 percent), but this was not viewed as statistically significant. It is clear that the presence of co-morbid mental health disorders among the inmate population has to be viewed holistically in hopes to provide intervention and lessen the likelihood of recidivism.

Department of Veterans Affairs facilities are used by more than half of all veterans as their primary provider of care.[22] It is estimated that approximately 16 percent of males using Veterans Affairs' behavioral health service between 1994 and 1997 had also been incarcerated during this same period of time.[23] While the average incarceration rate for Veterans Affairs' patients was less than for patients at general service hospitals and state hospitals, the percentage presents continuing concern, especially as annual incarceration rates did not change from 1994 to 1997, although there were significant bed closures in the Veterans Affairs' system.[24]

Do veterans in custody receive Veterans Affairs' benefits? Title 18 CFR, Section 3.655 would provide a general answer—no. In the 1970s, statutes were passed to make certain that incarcerated offenders did not receive money from another government entity while confined. This not only occurred for Veterans' benefits but for Social Security and other government benefits, including in some cases, certain types of government pensions. But the general answer "no" is not as simple as it seems. Families, otherwise entitled to benefits, may continue to receive them to some degree while the offender is incarcerated.

Full benefits may be restored as long as they are restored within one year of release from confinement. Veterans Affairs may require the released veteran to attend a re-examination to ensure that the service-connected disability is still valid, and in some cases, it increase benefits because of recently enhanced benefits. It is incumbent upon the veterans to seek a reinstatement of benefits as part of their reentry into the community.[25] One issue, which often causes problems for incarcerated felons, is that somewhere a bench warrant has been issued in another jurisdiction and the matter has never been adjudicated. However, as long as the bench warrant remains active and is not closed, the veteran may have difficulty obtaining a reinstatement of benefits.[26] It is doubtful many released veterans or probation officers are aware of these nuances. The bottom line is—if a veteran has a service-connected disability, he or she should clean up all open charges and apply for reinstatement soon after release.

Also, a very small number of mentally ill offenders in custody may still continue to receive benefits. These are inmates who have been civilly committed as not guilty by reason of insanity or not competent to proceed to trial. Since these offenders are not sentenced, they may continue to receive Veterans Affairs' benefits while in custody. This represents a challenge for some because most people do not understand the difference between someone who is sentenced and someone who is confined.

A review of the literature reveals little in the way of specialized programs for incarcerated veterans. Two exceptions are the Outreach to Homeless Veterans in the Los Angeles County Jail program. This program targets efforts to keep released incarcerated veterans from becoming homeless.[27] Research regarding the establishment of this program is a public policy analysis of collaboration across agencies and demonstrates how to use economic models to overcome barriers. The research clearly says it is not possible to determine success in an empirical sense as there are not controlled populations or other programs to benchmark against.

A second program described in the literature involves the Incarcerated Veterans Program in the New York Department of Correction.[28] Since 1986, this program has existed to help incarcerated veterans have knowledge of entitlements, benefits, and community resources. This program, like the Los Angeles Jail program, relies on collaboration with other agencies. One of the most important aspects of the program is to educate veterans on what benefits are maintained even while they are incarcerated.

In June 2006, the Undersecretary of Health published an information letter, "Guidelines and Recommendations for Services Provided by VHA Facilities to Incarcerated Veterans Re-entering Community Living." These guidelines have been published as part of a renewed emphasis on offender reentry.[29] Any successful reentry plan will need to have a prison-based component, community-based transition, and community long-term support. If the one-in-four inmates being released within the next year can claim veterans' status, then almost 168,000 veterans will be released from state or federal prison. If society does not wish for them to recidivate, it must realize that simply turning them out the door with a gratuity and a suit of clothes is simply not enough.

Endnotes

[1] Mumola, C. J. and Margaret E. Noonan. 2007. *Veterans in prisons or jail.* Bureau of Justice Statistics Special Report. Available at www.ojp.usdoj.gov/bjs/pub/pdf/vsfp04.pdf

[2] MacKenzie, Doris Layton. 2006. *What Works in Corrections: Reducing the Criminal Activities of Offenders and Delinquents.* New York: Cambridge University Press.

[3] Mumola, C. J 2007.

[4] Ibid.

[5] Ibid.

[6] Ibid.

[7] Ibid.

[8] Lamb, H. Richard and Linda E. Weinberger. 1998. Persons with severe mental illness in jails and prisons: A review. *Psychiatric Services* 49 (April): 483-92.

[9] Lamb, H. Richard and Linda E. Weinberger. 1998.

[10] Weedon, Joey R. 2005.The incarceration of the mentally ill. *Corrections Today,* February, 67(1):16-20.

[11] Mumola, C. J. 2000.

[12] Spoont, Michele R., Nina A. Sayer, Paul Thuras, Chris Erbes, and Elizabeth Winston. 2003. Adaptation of dialectical behavior therapy by a Veterans Affairs medical center. *Psychiatric Services* 54(5): 627-28.

[13] Ibid.

[14] McGuire, James, Robert A. Rosenheck, and Wesley J. Kasprow. 2003. Health status, service use, and costs among veterans receiving outreach services in jail or community settings. *Psychiatric Services* 54(2): 201-07.

[15] Black, Donald W. 2005. Incarceration and veterans of the first Gulf War. *Military Medicine* 170(7): 612-18.

[16] Saxon, Andrew J., Tania M. Davis, Kevin L. Sloan, Katherine M. McKnight, Miles E. McFall, and Daniel R. Kiviahan. 2001. Trauma, symptoms of posttraumatic stress disorder, and associated problems among incarcerated veterans. *Psychiatric Services* 52(7): 959- 64.

[17] Ibid.

[18] Ibid.

[19] Natelson, Benjamin H., Lana Tiersky, and Jennifer Nelson. 2001. The diagnosis of posttraumatic stress disorder in Gulf veterans with medically unexplained fatiguing illness. *The Journal of Nervous and Mental Disease* 189(11): 795-96.

[20] Kubiak, Sheryl Pimlott. 2004. The effects of PTSD on treatment adherence, drug relapse, and criminal recidivism in a sample of incarcerated men and women. *Research on Social Work Practice* 14(6): 424-32.

[21] Ibid.

[22] Bosworth, Hayden B., Patrick Calhoun, Karen M. Stechuchak, and Marian I. Butterfield. 2004. Use of psychiatric and medical health services by veterans with severe mental illness. *Psychiatric Services* (55)6: 708-10.

[23] Rosenheck, Robert A., Steven Banks, John Pandiani, and Rani Hoff. 2000. Bed closures and incarceration rates among users of Veterans Affairs mental health services. *Psychiatric Services* 51(10): 1282-85.

[24] Ibid.

[25] Cartner, Barry. August 4, 2006. *Incarcerated veterans*. Personal communication to Craig Kabatchnick.

[26] Ibid.

[27] Nakashima, John. 2006. Outreach to homeless veterans in Los Angeles County Jail: The Veterans Affairs Greater Los Angeles Healthcare story. *LJN Exchange*. P. 11-20.

[28] Conly, Catherine B. June 7, 2005. *Helping inmates obtain federal disability benefits: Serious medical and mental illness, incarceration, and federal disability*

entitlement programs. Research report submitted by Abt. Associates Inc. to U.S. Department of Justice.

[29] Perlin, Jonathan B. June 27, 2006. *Guidelines and recommendations for services provided by VHA facilities to incarcerated veterans re-entering community living.* (IL 10-2006-07). Washington, D.C.: Department of Veterans Affairs, Veterans Health Administration. Available at www1.va.gov/VHAPUBLICATIONS/ViewPublication.asp?pub_ID=1445.

[30] Lim, Sabina, Wesley Kasprow, and Robert A. Rosenheck. 2006. Psychiatric illness and substance abuse among homeless Asian-American veterans. *Psychiatric Services* 57(5): 704-06.

The Davidson County Jail for Females:
A Modern-Day Crisis Center

By Kristy Kummerow and Ruby Joyner

The Davidson County Sheriff's Office Correctional Development Center for Women in Nashville, Tennessee, functions like a twenty-four-hour-a-day crisis center, open seven days a week. Women from all walks of life, accused of crimes from trespassing to murder, are housed at the center. The Correctional Development Center for Women routinely stays just under state capacity. Managing the care, custody, and control of women more often than not includes managing mental illnesses, addiction issues, dental disease, and a host of other health issues from lice to gynecological problems that have gone untreated for months and sometimes years.

Jails house a fairly transient population, so if a female stays in custody long enough, many of her medical issues are addressed before she gets out the door. Most times, however, a woman will come to jail and be released before practitioners have a chance to begin any real treatment or recovery regimen. If an inmate is not treated while she is in custody, the likelihood that she will follow up on care (without some sort of case management/counselor intervention) is slim to none.

The Davidson County Sheriff's Office's correctional health services are provided by Nashville's public health department through a contract with Correct Care Solutions, a for-profit correctional health care management company. Of particular challenge to the Correctional Development Center for Women's correctional health providers are gynecological and obstetrical health issues. Women in this population have sex in high-risk circumstances, compounded by a background of mental health problems, substance abuse, and inadequate health care. The results include higher rates of unplanned pregnancies, sexually transmitted diseases, and children born with significant health problems into broken families.

All-Too-Familiar Circumstances

A twenty-seven-year-old black female inmate recently came to the jail and reported that she was ten-weeks pregnant. She admitted that this was her eleventh pregnancy. Without facial expression, any inflection or emotion in her voice, she said: "If I lose this one, I have seven others so I'll be fine." Four of her children had already died either before birth or shortly thereafter. She had her first child at age thirteen. Of her seven living children, she has custody of none of them. She has been in and out of the adult system since 2004. Sadly, many women in custody can tell a similar story.

According to research conducted in 2007 at the Correctional Development Center for Women, of the inmates who had been pregnant at least once, 86 percent had at least one unplanned pregnancy—some had as many as nine. On average, 68 percent of female inmates' pregnancies were unplanned, which is significantly higher than the national average of 49 percent.[1] Furthermore, the majority—54 percent—of female inmates stated that all of their pregnancies had been unplanned.

The effects of unprotected sex are tremendous, and the risks may be even greater for female inmates, who are often charged with drug-related offenses.[2] These women are more likely to have had multiple sexual partners in exchange for drugs and to have had unprotected intercourse while under the influence of drugs and/or alcohol. Of greatest concern for the women and society are sexually transmitted diseases, especially HIV/AIDS, and unplanned pregnancies.

According to the Centers for Disease Control and Prevention, correctional facilities consistently report higher rates of HIV, Chlamydia, gonorrhea, and syphilis than the general population.[3] In fact, more than 20 percent of HIV-infected people in the United States passed through a correctional facility in 1997.[4] HIV/AIDS is of particular concern because it is chronic, life threatening, and costly to treat. A 1996 study done in a San Diego jail found that the average daily cost of care for an HIV-infected, injection-drug-using inmate was $51.40, while care for a noninfected, noninjection-drug-using inmate cost only $4.10 per day.[5] Black women, who are disproportionately represented in correctional populations,[6] constituted 72 percent of newly reported cases of HIV infection.

Another potentially negative effect of unprotected sex is unintended pregnancies, which can pose significant risks to both the neonate and the mother, especially when they occur under the high-risk circumstance of substance abuse. These risks include higher infant mortality, higher rates of preterm deliveries, lower birth weight, fetal alcohol syndrome, birth defects, and pre-eclampsia, which is a life-threatening condition for the mother.[7]

Unintended pregnancies among this population also threaten the lives of the children once they are born and the stability of society in general. In a 1999 survey, 2.1 percent of minor children in the United States had a parent in prison. This amounts to 1.5 million children with an incarcerated parent—a 50 percent increase from 1991, when a previous survey was conducted. The increase is attributed to the increase in the number of female offenders, a number that has steadily risen.[8]

Data is not available for parents incarcerated in jails, but these numbers likely compare, as jails and prisons house a similar population of individuals. Based on an informal survey at the Correctional Development Center for Women, most women report that their children are staying with a relative or are in custody of the Department of Children's Services. A few have children who stay with the child's father.

Children can be negatively affected by their parent's incarceration. Boys who were separated from a parent due to the parent's incarceration were found to exhibit more antisocial behavior and delinquency in adulthood than their peers, registering greater incidences of criminal convictions, substance use, self-reported delinquency, and problems in interpersonal relationships. These negative impacts can be partially attributed to the stigma of having an incarcerated parent, as boys who were separated from their parents for other reasons exhibited less antisocial and delinquent behavior than those who were separated due to parental incarceration.[9]

The challenges of unplanned pregnancies and sexually transmitted diseases among female inmates have a direct economic impact on correctional institutions, governments, and, ultimately, society. The pregnant inmate discussed earlier experienced pregnancy complications that required a five-day stay in the hospital. She lost the baby and a dilation and curettage had to be performed to remove the contents of her uterus. Prenatal care was financed by the county health department, while her in-hospital care and procedure were provided at Nashville's public hospital. Her care, like that of most other pregnant inmates, has been financed by Davidson County taxpayers.

The Correctional Population and Contraception

The Correctional Development Center for Women's 2007 study[10] identified some major reasons that women in the correctional population do not use contraception. The three most common reasons offered by women indicate a lack of education. Fifty out of ninety-six women (52 percent) reported that they did not use a method of contraception because they had a consistent partner or they were in love. Women must be educated that there is a place for using contraception, including condoms, even within monogamous and loving relationships, to prevent unplanned pregnancies and sexually transmitted diseases. Concern regarding side effects was a reason given by 39 percent of female inmates surveyed for not using contraception in the past. Finally, 20 percent became pregnant at a time when they did not think pregnancy was possible. Thus, women require more education regarding the low incidence of negative side effects among people who use contraceptives and more individual counseling regarding their personal risks for pregnancy.

There was also a significant correlation between women who responded that they were "very likely" or "somewhat likely" to have unprotected sex within three months of release from jail and women who responded that they "felt sex would be less exciting if birth control was used" and "felt that using birth control would make sex unnatural" as reasons why they had not used birth control in the past.[11] These perceptions must be addressed when educating women about birth control.

Another major factor in the pregnancies and sexually transmitted diseases with which female inmates present is substance use. In 40 percent of the 221 unplanned pregnancies characterized in the 2007 study at the Correctional Development Center for Women, women reported that they were high on drugs at conception. In 27 percent of the unplanned pregnancies, women reported being drunk at conception.[12] This makes sense, given the high rates of substance use among incarcerated women. Arrests of women account for 18 percent of total (men and women) drug-related arrests. Almost one in three women incarcerated in state prisons report that they committed the offense for which they are incarcerated "to obtain money to support their need for drugs."[13]

Mental illness is another factor that may initiate or complicate the course of substance addiction, and may also independently effect women's decisions regarding contraception and prophylaxis. According to Jeff Blum, mental health coordinator for the Davidson County Sheriff's Office, about 25 percent of female inmates are being treated for a mental illness with psychotropic medication. Almost all of these women also have a substance use disorder.

Although women did not report this information during the 2007 survey, some staff members at the Correctional Development Center for Women speculate that another major reason that women fail to protect themselves is that they have sex in desperate situations. They deal with the "here and now" and address basic needs as they arise—by any means necessary. For many, sex may be a means to an end. HIV, pregnancy, and sexually transmitted diseases are issues that they will deal with if and when they arise.

Educating Women in Correctional Development Centers

How can a correctional institution combat these significant physical, mental, and psychological barriers to female health and mindful conceptions with better lifelong outcomes? Based on the previously mentioned data and observations, potential solutions include education, satisfaction of women's physical needs, and empowerment of female inmates to set and work toward goals for the future, including preventing unplanned pregnancies and contracting of sexually transmitted diseases. Correctional institutions can serve a critical role in arming inmates with these much-needed resources and tools.

Methods of intervention include offering general medical and mental health treatment and rehabilitation for substance abusers; facilitating beneficial relationships between inmates and community-based service providers; and educating women about sexually transmitted diseases, pregnancy, and contraception. A network of programs at the Correctional Development Center for Women, in collaboration with community organizations, aims to provide these essential resources.

To address the significant problem of substance addiction, the Correctional Development Center for Women offers New Avenues–Healing Journey, an alcohol and drug treatment program that is supported by a four-year grant from the Edward Byrne Memorial State and Local Law Enforcement Assistance Grant Program. The program was the first licensed alcohol and drug treatment program for women in jail in Tennessee, and women eagerly participate.

To address educational needs and physical needs such as food and shelter, the county health department employs a correctional health services liaison who links inmates with community clinics and other health care resources that they may use upon release. Women receive this information in multiple settings—in groups during informational presentations, one-on-one during release planning sessions, and in their release packets. The liaison also coordinates numerous educational presentations by members of community organizations on topics such as contraceptive services, HIV/AIDS support services, cancers that commonly affect women, and application processes for health insurance programs. These educational sessions take place within the women's housing areas so that the information is accessible to all women present.

Beyond offering assistance with "here and now" needs, the Correctional Development Center for Women offers an array of programs aimed at empowering women to plan for the future and to make future-oriented decisions. Women voluntarily participate in GED preparation courses, faith-based initiatives, and classes on personal hygiene and self-esteem, culinary arts, and parenting skills. Recognizing that women with mental illness are particularly vulnerable, The Davidson County Sheriff's Office offers "Mind, Body, Spirit," a holistic educational program for women in the special needs pod that addresses issues of physical, mental, and spiritual health.

Two significant lessons have been learned from this research and these initiatives. First, many stakeholders are involved in improving these complex reproductive health problems, from the women themselves to the correctional facilities, government funders in the criminal justice and health sectors, and all members of society who support these institutions with their tax money. Second, correctional institutions cannot single-handedly address these issues. The ongoing growth of collaborations with outside agencies is critical to the Correctional Development Center for Women's efforts to bridge the many gaps in resources and services, ensuring that women leave jail better equipped to handle future crises.

Endnotes

[1] Finer, L. B. and, S. K. Henshaw. 2006. Disparities in rates of unintended pregnancy in the United States, 1994 and 2001. *Perspectives on Sexual and Reproductive Health* 38(2): 90-96.

[2] Greenfeld, L. A. and T. L. Snell. 1999. *Women offenders.* Washington, D.C.: U.S. Department of Justice, Bureau of Justice Statistics.

[3] Centers for Disease Control and Prevention. 2006. *Sexually transmitted disease surveillance 2005: Persons entering corrections facilities.* Available at www.cdc. gov/std/stats05/corrections.htm.

Maruschak, L. M. 2007. *HIV in Prisons*, 2005. Washington, D.C.: U.S. Department of Justice, Bureau of Justice Statistics.

Centers for Disease Control and Prevention. 2006. *Trends in Reportable Sexually Transmitted Diseases in the United States*, 2005. Atlanta: CDC.

Centers for Disease Control and Prevention. 2007. *HIV/AIDS Surveillance Report* 2005. Atlanta: CDC.

[4] Hammett, T. M., M. P. Harmon, and W. Rhodes. 2002. The burden of infectious diseases among inmates of and releasees from US corrections facilities, 1997. *American Journal of Public Health* 92(11): 1789-95.

[5] Ray, R., K. Stafford, M. Hewett, R. Hernandez, and N. Williams. 1996. Medical care costs associated with jail incarceration of people with HIV/AIDS. Paper presented at the International Conference on AIDS. July 7-12 in Vancouver, British Columbia.

[6] Greenfeld, L. A. and T. L. Snell. 1999.

[7] Clarke, J. G., C. Rosengard, J. Rose, M. R. Hebert, M. G. Phipps, and M. D. Stein. 2006. Pregnancy attitudes and contraceptive plans among women entering jail. *Women and Health* 43(2): 111-30.

[8] Greenfeld, L. A. and T. L. Snell. 1999.

[9] Murray, J. and D. P. Farrington. 2005. Parental imprisonment: Effects on boys' antisocial behaviour and delinquency through the life-course. *Journal of Child Psychology and Psychiatry* 46(12): 1269-78.

[10] Kummerow, K. L. 2008.Circumstances of pregnancy among women at an urban jail. Poster presented at the national Convention of the American Medical Student Association, March 14 in Houston.

[11] Ibid.

[12] Ibid.

[13] Mumola, C. J. 2000. *Incarcerated Parents and their Children.* U.S. Department of Justice, Bureau of Justice Statistics.

About the Authors

Kristy Kummerow is a graduate student at Vanderbilt University. Ruby Joyner, MSW, is an administrator at the Davidson County Sheriff's Office Correctional Development Center.

Service Learning: A Partnership That Works

By Karen Kennedy Schultz, Jason Walgrave, Jessica McNeil, and Julie Dilorio

W hat is the recipe for a successful public-private partnership? In Winchester, Virginia, it takes a combination of a three-credit university-level service-learning course, energetic doctoral pharmacy students who want to make a difference, and a detention center supervisor and team who are open to trying something new.

This public-private partnership between Shenandoah University's Bernard J. Dunn School of Pharmacy and Northwestern Regional Adult Detention Center in Winchester provides a learning opportunity for students and inmates alike. Through time and devoted service, seven students initially paved the way by working side by side with the detention center's staff in programs, medical services, and GED preparation.

The idea of including the detention center in the service-learning course began five years ago when Associate Professor Karen Kennedy Schultz and Superintendent Fred Hildebrand discussed ways of increasing understanding and communication between health care students and the incarcerated population. Both students and inmates had much they could learn from one another through a formal educational setting.

Approximately fifty inmates have benefited from the dedicated pharmacy students through tutoring, medication assistance and explanations, and discussions dealing with anger management, substance abuse, and financial management (such as how to balance a checkbook). Since the number of incarcerated adults with increased medical needs, particularly in mental health, continues to grow, it is imperative that doctoral pharmacy students have first-hand knowledge of the challenges of meeting these medical needs. Both the university and the detention center had staff willing to mentor and supervise the pharmacy students, so it was clear that great potential for growth of understanding and service could occur at the detention center through the service-learning course.

Concept

Students of the Dunn School of Pharmacy participate in service learning as part of their curriculum during their first year. The service-learning course has been in place since the pharmacy school's inception. It includes twelve nonprofit sites from which the students can choose to spend three hours per week for a semester working with and learning from diverse populations. Once a student chooses a site, he or she spends the entire semester there, developing relationships and working on projects. The service-learning project at the detention center provides students an extraordinary opportunity to see the inner workings of a jail system and to work face to face with inmates. This effort allows students the opportunity and experience of integrating with an underserved portion of the community to better use their knowledge for the education of those who are incarcerated.

Service learning is becoming increasingly popular as a way to involve students in their communities while concurrently enhancing learning objectives.[1] Service learning involves dedicating one's time and energy to benefit another individual or the community to which he or she belongs. The insight and knowledge gathered from the experiences are unique opportunities that cannot be captured in a textbook or classroom alone.[2] The concept of community-based service learning can be applied to any correctional facility because of the corrections health care component.

One of the main principles of service learning activities is that both the student and the community should be equal beneficiaries. The service-learning experience engages students in the community and the civil sector, leading to opportunities where students can affect real and lasting social change.[3] Student reflection is a critical aspect of the service-learning experience. Reflection allows students to consider the time they have spent providing service and how it applies to the community needs and the students' own educational experiences. Community advocacy and a sense of responsibility and ownership in the community grow within the student. Reflection may take the form of structured journal entries, group discussions, oral presentations, production of videotapes, art projects, or reflective essays. It has been found that service-learning students become better citizens, are more committed to lifelong community service, and learn at least as much, if not more, course content as students not engaged in service learning.[4]

Benefits

When Director Hildebrand first heard that service-learning students actually wanted to come to the detention center, he was extremely surprised. In establishing the partnership, Hildebrand wanted students to gain two things from their experience: first, for students to experience working with a sub-population of the community with whom most people never have contact, and second, for students to see the many dedicated people who work in the hidden, and sometimes unrecognized, corrections profession.

Hildebrand said that students at the graduate level bring professionalism, research capabilities, and eagerness to the table—an eagerness to make connections with the inmates. This allows the organization and the students to benefit equally from the time spent participating in service learning. Because of its twofold benefits, Hildebrand has discussed the service-learning collaboration with other corrections professionals with the hope that other facilities will gain interest in similar service-learning partnerships.

Case Studies

Pharmacy student Jason Walgrave spent the majority of his time at the detention center tutoring inmates in the GED program in math and science. Most inmates who participate in the GED program show a desire to better their lives. However, Walgrave said, "They lack skills that you or I may take for granted." These include family support, a high school diploma, a drug-free lifestyle, and the motivation to create a better life. Walgrave said, "As a student, this is where I was able to play a key role."

There was one inmate in particular with whom Walgrave had the most positive interaction. The inmate was a young Hispanic man who had little mastery of English and needed help in both reading and writing English. Because Walgrave spoke Spanish, the director of the GED program partnered him with the inmate. The duo worked together for an hour each week for five weeks.

"After the first meeting, I began to see a difference in his English," Walgrave said. "He looked forward to seeing me every week because I was the only one who was able to communicate with him and teach him effectively." Walgrave, who had not used his Spanish in several years, was able to practice and improve, much like his mentee. "The time we spent together benefited not only him but me as well."

This interactive education goes to show what service and learning paired together can achieve. Walgrave emphasized what a great feeling it was to help his mentee attain a GED. "I no longer look at this as a class assignment or a course credit, but as an opportunity to better the community in which I live," Walgrave said.

Pharmacy student, Jessica McNeil, also helped prepare inmates to take the GED by tutoring them in math and science. For some inmates, the goal is simple: They just want to get their GED so that they will be able to get a job that will help them support their family. Others simply want to prove to themselves that they are able to finish something they start. "This is where service-learning students come in," McNeil said. "We help them to achieve this goal."

McNeil had the opportunity to work with an eighteen-year-old inmate who had recently been arrested for stealing an automobile and for possession of drugs. All he wanted was to be able to go back to high school. During their time together, McNeil tried to impress upon him that he still had amazing opportunities ahead of him that he could achieve if he would make a plan for his future and follow through with it. "I have gained as much knowledge from the inmates as they have from me. I have learned of their desire to tell their story and, for some, their drive to make their life and the lives of those around them better," McNeil said.

Keys to Success

The partnership between Shenandoah University's Dunn School of Pharmacy and the Northwestern Regional Adult Detention Center continues, as the service-learning course has been successful in bringing together doctoral pharmacy students and inmates. The students have participated in panels and conferences to encourage other institutions to adopt this philosophy in teaching and learning.

The keys to success of this collaboration are as follows:

- A commitment from the faculty member at Shenandoah University and the superintendent and his staff to communicate and dedicate the proper personnel to mentor students in an unfamiliar environment;
- The proximity of the detention center to Shenandoah University, which allowed for convenient student travel;
- Ongoing communication between university faculty and the mentor/preceptor of the students to evaluate the experience of the inmates, students, and detention center personnel so that adjustments could be made by both institutions, as needed; and
- Realization that both the university and detention center were meeting their missions in developing this partnership.

Opportunities like this are not only valuable to this school and this detention center, but could also benefit others around the country. It is hoped that this experience can serve as a guideline for others to take advantage of the resources found within colleges and universities.

Many students spent their time tutoring inmates at the Northwest Regional Detention Center to help them obtain a GED. In turn, students gained communication and leadership skills, opportunities to learn about diverse populations, a sense of caring for others, self-confidence, and much more. Learning continues to be a strong, two-way street, benefiting doctoral pharmacy students, inmates, detention center personnel, and university faculty. It is an educational community partnership and a vibrant community-collaboration effort.

Endnotes

[1] Community-Campus Partnerships for Health. 2003. Service-learning in the health professions: Advancing educational innovations for improved student learning and community health. *CCPH Seventh Annual Introductory Service-Learning Institute Proceedings*, June 21-24, Leavenworth, Washington.

[2] Barner, J. 2000. First-year pharmacy students' perceptions of their service-learning experience. *American Journal of Pharmaceutical Education* 64 (Fall): 260-71.

[3] Ibid.

[4] CCPH. 2003.

About the Authors

Karen Kennedy Schultz, Ph.D., MBA, is an associate professor in the Bernard J. Dunn School of Pharmacy at Shenandoah University. Jason Walgrave, Jessica McNeil, and Julie Dilorio received their doctorate of pharmacy degrees in May of 2009.

Sheriff's Department Reforms Special Management Unit

By Richard J. McCarthy and Thomas W. Connor

T he Hampden County Sheriff's Department serves the urban area of Springfield/Holyoke, Massachusetts, and is part of the Large Jail Network, a collaborative of large urban jails throughout the country. Although the count has gone to more than 2,000 in the past, there are currently 1,576 sentenced offenders and pretrial detainees in custody. Sentenced individuals are usually serving time for crimes with sentences of two and a half years or less, such as drug charges, burglary, larceny, driving under the influence, domestic violence, and assault. Those awaiting trial are often charged with felonies such as murder, armed robbery, and rape.

In many states, those sentenced to one year or more are sent to state prison, so Massachusetts' sheriffs have many inmates in their sentenced population who would (in other states) be sent to state prisons. In that sense, Massachusetts' sheriffs are "hybrids," whose experience is applicable to both county jails and state prisons throughout the country.

Up until January 2008, the Hampden County Sheriff's Department maintained a Special Management Unit (aka disciplinary and administrative segregation unit) that was similar in many ways to other twenty-three-hour-a-day lockdown units in jails and prisons throughout the country. Although its segregation unit was never intended to be a long-term, filled-to-capacity major housing unit, it had become one over the years. The unit was a repository for inmates who were difficult to manage in regular housing units—an out-of-sight, out-of-mind jail within a jail. Because segregation's isolating environment may actually worsen the mental health of some inmates, this resulted in increased behavioral problems in segregation, throughout the institution and, eventually, in the community.

Identifying the Problems

In January 2008, Hampden County Sheriff Michael J. Ashe, Jr. formed a working staff committee with representatives from every security level and satellite facility throughout the department and from various areas of operations such as security, classification, human services, and forensics. Uniform and nonuniform personnel worked together to develop and submit a proposal. Their goal was to make the Special Management Unit a more positive and productive environment, where inmates were given the challenge and opportunity to change their behavior.

The committee identified a number of problems in segregation that worked against the goal of establishing a positive and safe environment for both staff and inmates. Use of segregation as a first response to troublesome and bothersome inmates, rather than as a last resort safe-housing unit to contain otherwise unmanageable, dangerous, and disruptive inmates, could lead to chronic and severe crowding in segregation. This crowding could amplify the existing oppositional disorders, mental health pathologies, denial systems, and criminal thinking patterns of inmates, increasing the possibilities for negativity and nonproductivity. Some inmates even actively sought segregation so they could "veg out" or escape from the demands and expectations placed on them in general housing.

Moreover, there were only two privileges that could be earned: limited access to phones and noncontact visits. Though important, they were not sufficient to serve as an effective behavior-management tool.

While emergency mental health services were provided, correctional programming was very limited. Segregation was not the corrective action unit that the sheriff envisioned. Improvements to the segregation unit programming were needed to reduce the likelihood that inmates would leave segregation angrier, more embittered, unchanged, and more likely to return after having caused yet another, possibly greater, problem for the safe operations of the larger institution.

After many months of teamwork, inspiration, and perspiration, the committee came back with a balanced and sensible plan for changes that were largely approved by the sheriff. Implementation began in November 2008.

Classification Changes

The first step in the plan was to reduce the population in segregation by instituting classification changes. There would be new encouragements for staff to deal with inmates in the regular living units and new protocols to assure that inmates who could be managed on regular living units were kept on those units. Classification changes would reduce the segregation population through intermediate sanctions in living units, early graduation from segregation for good behavior, and retention in step-down units after segregation.

Previously, for example, anyone with a ten-day or more disciplinary lockdown would be sent to segregation; that has now been changed to fifteen days or more. Inmates would stay in segregation for only as long as their disciplinary board ruling stipulated; until behavioral issues were resolved; or as necessary, to assure the safety, security, and order of the facility. During their stay in segregation, inmates would be oriented and guided by a written corrective action plan developed by the general housing or lower security unit from which the inmate came. This plan would identify benchmarks for expected behavior, and compliance would determine privileges and early exit from segregation.

The results of these classification changes were measurable after the first six months. "Double bunking" was eliminated, lessening the potential for assaults. The total number of individuals sent to segregation, as compared to a six-month period before the classification changes, was reduced from 590 to 423. The mean length of stay was reduced from 24.06 days to 13.52 days.

Positive Behavior Reinforcement

Beyond reducing the numbers in segregation, changes were made to alter its climate. A behavioral program was introduced by which inmates are given a pass/fail grade daily by line officers working in segregation. Grades are based on the inmate's cooperative attitude, cleanliness of cell, and avoidance of actions or noise that is assaultive to others. Segregation inmates who consistently achieve a certain grade are given extra time out of their cell, one at a time, in a cell that was converted into a "wellness area."

This wellness area was designed with the safety and security of staff and inmates, as well as with budget restrictions, in mind. All furniture was removed from the cell and 3/8th-inch-thick rubber matting was put on the floor. Exercise equipment in the cell includes a stability ball, a rack of five medicine balls varying in weight and size, a foam roller, a stationary bike, and a mini-stepper. Free weights and a chin-up bar are not considered as options because of risks associated with the safety of officers or risks of injury to the inmate. Just this seemingly small "carrot" of an exercise cell was partially responsible for more than 200 segregation inmates earning the highest weekly behavior grade.

For those with a sustained high weekly grade, opportunities for group recreation outside the unit are provided. In the first six months after the changes, more than eighty segregation inmates were granted this earned opportunity for recreation outside the segregation unit, and not one rule violation occurred.

What these results showed is that the kind of "carrot" and "stick" behavioral philosophy that characterized the rest of the institution should not stop at the doors of segregation. Simply put, inmates in segregation were already experiencing the "stick;" what was needed was a "carrot" to encourage good behavior. As with anywhere else in the institution, a certain percentage of inmates responded to this positive behavior reinforcement.

Access to Programs

It was also believed that facilitywide extensive and intensive program efforts should not stop at the doors of segregation. A substance abuse group; educational outreach, such as individual education plans; and release planning, including pre-employment and housing counseling, were brought to the unit. Mental health counseling and intervention were also made more proactive on the unit.

Corrections officers assigned to segregation, along with the primary captains of the main institution's three 500-bed general housing towers and administrative, clinical and program staff meet weekly to review every segregation inmate. Inmates who are mentally stable, free of any safety issues, and who are willing to engage in programming, are allowed to participate in small program groups and in individual counseling sessions on site. Clinical staff provide tactical guidance to segregation staff as to how best to interact with inmates to prevent escalation, enhance safety, and motivate compliance.

To counter the mental deterioration that can take place on lockdown units, in-cell correctional programming is offered on a voluntary basis through the use of a wireless headphone system. In addition, five hours a day of soundscapes—sounds from nature and peaceful music—is pumped into cells through the vents. These soundscapes are not an effort to make a stay in segregation pleasant, but rather to help assure that it is not mentally debilitating to the inmate, resulting in problems for the individual, the institution, and society.

Return to General Housing

The primary captains of the main institution and the lead counselor of the segregation unit meet each week to determine the appropriateness of moving an inmate back into the general population sooner than expected. This is determined by looking at the inmate's graded level of rules compliance, resolution of behavioral issues, mental health status, program participation, awareness of wrongdoing, and commitment to change. Inmates not cleared for early step-down to general housing units remain in segregation pending a further review.

As an additional safeguard, certain offenders are classified as special management inmates and are referred to the institution's weekly central classification meeting for authorization to step down from segregation to general housing. These inmates include: validated members of security risk groups, such as gang members; those who are charged with or convicted of high profile crimes, such as murder, home invasion, and sex offense; those who are identified as too dangerous for medium security; or those with chronic discipline problems.

The corrective action plan is continued once the inmate steps down to general housing from segregation, whether through early release or not. Staff hold a reentry session with the inmate to discuss his or her plan, expectations, and support services available for transition to general housing. It cannot be overemphasized how essential face-to-face contact with the inmates is to establish their "buy-in" and to enhance their chances for successful avoidance of segregation in the future. Indeed, a lack of this connectedness to others is a primary reason why so many failed to get out—and stay out—of segregation in the past.

The Hampden County Sheriff's Department is in the business of corrections and realizes there are those who think that the changes to its segregation unit represent a "watering down" of its effectiveness—a softer, weaker approach to unacceptable behavior in the institution. Sheriff Ashe answers this quite simply: "Even with all these changes, inmates in our segregation unit spend twenty-one to twenty-three hours a day locked alone in a cell. Try doing that yourself if you think segregation has become too easy."

Results

The changes in the unit include a less negative, less combative, psychologically healthier segregation population, resulting in fewer assaults on staff, not only in segregation, but also in the larger facility. Between January and July 2009, not one officer used chemical spray to incapacitate an inmate on the segregation unit—a fairly regular occurrence under the old model. In the general population, a similar pattern of improving safety emerged. Comparing the second half of 2008 to the first, throughout the institution, fights dropped 45 percent, gang activity decreased 42 percent, and threats against staff fell 46 percent, implying the segregation reforms had a multiplier effect. A 12 percent reduction in inmate census in the whole institution explains some, but obviously not nearly all, of this reduction in violence.

Further signs of progress included a drop in the average daily segregation count from seventy-two inmates, or 3.8 percent of the main institution's inmate count, in November 2007, to twenty-six inmates, or 1.6 percent of the main facility count, in April 2009.

In conclusion, the Special Management Unit at the Hampden County Correctional Center has become what it was meant to be: a place to address and improve problematic and pathological behavior, rather than a place to give it a home.

Any other facility or department wishing to learn more about the specifics of any or all of the changes that have been put in place in Hampden County is welcome to call Assistant Deputy Superintendent Tom Connor at (413) 547-8000 ext., 2221, or to e-mail him at Tom.Connor@sdh.state.ma.us.

About the Authors

Richard J. McCarthy is former assistant superintendent of Hampden County Correctional Center. Thomas W. Connor is assistant deputy superintendent for classification for Hampden County Correctional Center.

Section 3

A Look at A Successful Jail: Alexandria Detention Center, Alexandria, Virginia

**Photos by
Shoshana Frishberg,
ACA Intern**

In 2010, Alexandria Detention Center, in Alexandria Virginia, graciously provided access to its facility and staff so our intern, Shoshana Frishberg could come in and take photographs illustrating the operation of a well-run facility.

The control center at Alexandria Detention Center is a busy place, with staff viewing those coming in and carefully watching the activities happening throughout the facility.

The watch commander plays an active role in the proper operation of the facility.

In the booking area, a correctional officer checks fingerprints and other information about inmates.

At the entrance to the pods, an officer keeps track of what is occurring.

Entrance to the more secure areas is through a separate locked door.

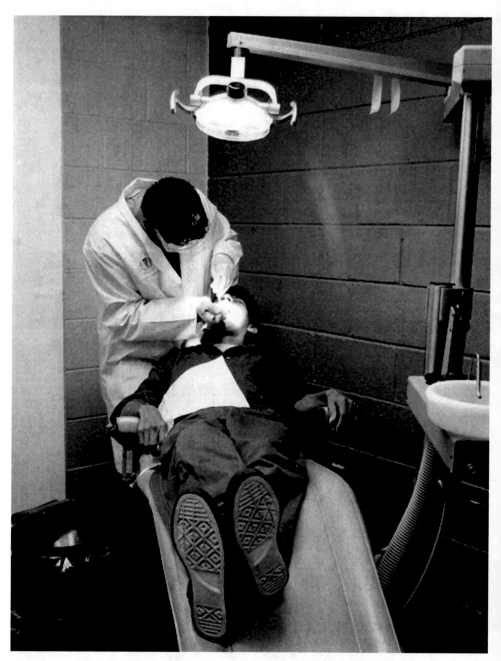

Attention to medical and dental needs is important. Many inmates have neglected their health and their teeth, so they have greater need for dental care.

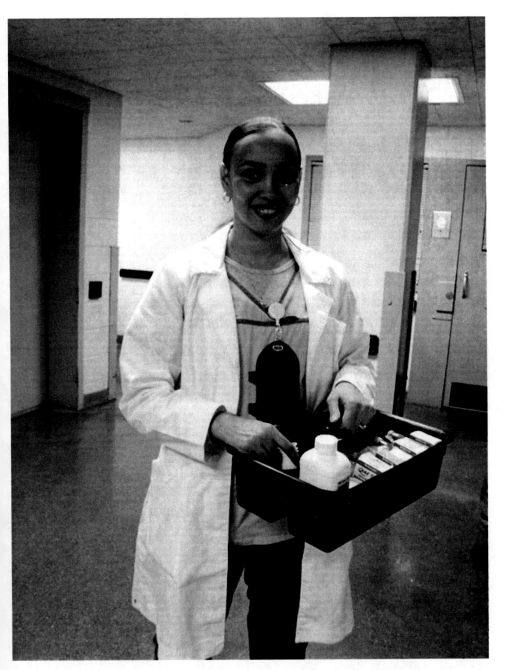

Pill distribution is a vital function to insure the health of the inmates.

Inmate workers are employed in a variety of kitchen duties, which may help them secure employment on their release.

Inmates in the honor dorm operate in a therapeutic community. Here they are emphasizing adherence to the steps of Alcoholics Anonymous. Men in this area have greater freedom of movement than those in other areas. Inmates live on the second tier and have a dayroom on the first floor.

Some inmates have creative talent, and the jail operates an area for arts activity. An inmate artist created a credible likeness of the President and is preparing a backdrop for an inmate play.

Visiting is vital to reentry. Here is the secure visiting area where inmates may converse with their visitors behind a wall.

Section 4

Jail Technology

The Best Professionals Partner with the Best Technology

By Daron Hall

D avidson County Sheriff's Office employees strive daily to make our agency a model for others to follow. Of course, setting the goal of being the best makes every day a challenge. Taking assistance wherever one can is important—and necessary. Technology is an area about which we have learned a great deal through the years. Hopefully, sharing our best practices will help others advance toward being the Best in the Business.

It was about twenty years ago when I heard the saying, "I've never seen a camera jump off a wall and help anybody." I think our profession has learned that technology can play a vital role in the world of corrections, so long as staff exhibit the utmost professionalism. No matter how good the technology, people are what make facilities safe and secure.

Technology certainly will never replace a correctional officer, but it can enhance an officer's ability to do his or her job. The same cameras that can't jump off the wall, can be mounted in strategic locations that may help defend an officer in a lawsuit or may encourage staff to act appropriately in difficult situations. In addition to enhancing security, technology can track inmate movement and statistics, reduce paperwork, and make inmate institutional history easily available for classification purposes.

The Davidson County Sheriff's Office has come a long way since our jail management system was implemented in 2001 and our first security electronics system came online in 2005. We just completed installation of another security electronics system (three facilities in two years), and because of what we learned previously, this installation went much smoother. We learned that when implementing technology in a correctional setting, it is necessary to consider five areas:

1) ***Determine needs to match the resources available.*** When determining your needs, it is important to distinguish between critical needs and the "nice to have" items. In other words, do you really need a Mercedes when a Chevy will do? Once you establish your budget, you can determine how you can best meet those needs with the resources at hand. When starting a technology project you should first determine what your essential criteria are and if you have the resources—in terms of funding and staff—to implement and maintain the system you choose.

2) ***Research and select a reliable vendor with a proven product.*** It is important to select a vendor who will provide a technology that has been proven in the correctional setting. Some questions you may ask are the following: Who else is using that product? Does the vendor have a history of supporting their technology in a correctional environment?

3) ***Select a knowledgeable internal coordinator.*** One area often overlooked is the role of the internal coordinator. The internal coordinator bridges the gap between the world of technology and the operations of corrections. He or she must identify and prevent breakdowns in communication, keep the project on task and on time, and ensure the technology meets the needs and expectations that you initially defined. When selecting this person to coordinate between the vendor and the jails, you should look for someone who understands the technology, communicates well, works without constant direction, and understands the needs of a correctional environment.

4) ***Be flexible throughout the implementation. Expect change and react positively.*** How you handle changes will have enormous impact on your project. In the middle of implementing an electronic security system in our largest jail, we were surprised to find that the floor plan on our touch screen system—displaying door locations, intercoms, and cameras—did not completely match the building layout. Operations had chosen to move two doors, which were not reflected in our documentation or in the software. We did not panic or complain; we talked with operations, who informed us that this was a valid and necessary change that better suited their workflow. We assessed the cost to our budget and timeline and moved forward.

5) ***Plan for support after implementation.*** Now that your system is in place and your users are trained, life is good. Suddenly, the phone rings at 2 a.m. Your technology is broken. This is the wrong time to be thinking about how to repair and support your new technology. Support has to be addressed at the same time you are identifying your needs and resources. The level of support you need (whether it is next-business-day or twenty-four/seven) will depend on how critical the system is to your operations. You may choose to contract with your vendor for support or to educate your in-house staff, depending on the cost.

Technology is, for the most part, a behind-the-scenes tool that assists all of us daily.

About the Author

Daron Hall is the current ACA president. He is Sheriff of Davidson County in Nashville, Tennessee.

Data-Driven Management Systems Improve Safety and Accountability in New York City Jails

By Martin F. Horn

"If you don't measure it, you can't manage it." That is the mantra of the New York City Department of Correction. In 1995, when the department first began to carefully track such incidents, there were more than 1,000 "stabbings and slashings" in the city's jails. In calendar year 2006, there were just nineteen, and for the twelve months of fiscal year 2008 that ended July 1, there were once again only nineteen incidents in which an inmate slashed or stabbed another. Furthermore, as the city's jails have become safer, analysis of other data shows that staff have become more confident in their work and safety. For example, the use of sick leave by officers was cut in half during the 1995-2008 period, indicating this confidence in their safety.

Clearly, these operational improvements did not happen by chance, nor were they solely the result of having fewer inmates. The drop in jail violence has dramatically outpaced changes in the city jail's inmate population. Instead, the improvements and many others like them are the result of aggressive data-driven management and a renewed culture of accountability coupled with a firm belief that keeping staff and inmates safe is the department's preeminent responsibility.

Management Systems

New York City jails are not the only incarceration system to have adopted such principles, nor is the Department of Correction the only New York City municipal agency to have done so. In fact, the aggressive use of data to guide management and policy in New York City government dates to about 1994, when the New York Police Department instituted its COMSTAT (Computer Statistics) program. Under the much-heralded COMSTAT approach, New York Police Department's borough commanders and unit managers were called periodically before a "management tribunal" headed by William Bratton, the commissioner at the time. There, New York Police Department management reviewed crime rates, arrests, and other trends; identified high crime areas; and then allocated resources accordingly. The process was rigorous, to say the least. The pressure was intense, and careers were launched and terminated in the COMSTAT conference room. However, combined with the administration's adoption of the "broken windows" theory, enforcement of "quality-of-life" laws would lead to reductions of other more serious crimes; the COMSTAT management tool was given much of the credit for New York City's initial, historic reductions in crime.

The city's Department of Correction operates under a similar principle and program, known as TEAMS (Total Efficiency Accountability Management

System). Incarceration management is a complex world, where policies, the procedures, and practices to implement them, proliferate by the day. Often, the courts dictate and even monitor daily practices under consent agreements. And bad things happen most often when procedures and best practices are not followed. In such a world, this much is certain: Managers cannot succeed without two tools—a data-based system for constant measurement of performance against key metrics and a culture of accountability. The two reinforce one another. While TEAMS is not the only management tool the New York City jails use, it is certainly at the center of the success New York has had in turning its jails from violent places into the safe places of confinement they are today.

Prisons and jails operate relatively violence free with the consent of the inmates confined inside them. On any given day, there are far more inmates than staff, and they follow instructions because they respect the fact that jail managers have their welfare at heart. However, the rules must be reasonable, fair, and understood. That is what is meant by "firm, fair, and consistent"—an instruction given to New York City correctional officers from their earliest days of training. And that is how officers derive what academics refer to as "legitimacy," the process by which jails maintain the ability to operate without constantly resorting to force. History has demonstrated that when a prison or jail administration loses legitimacy, inmates let them know by riot, gang activity, escape, or assaults on staff. History has taught us that people cannot and will not live in an unsafe setting; instead, they will do whatever it takes to make themselves safe. For these reasons, the measurement, maintenance, and management of safety are always foremost in the minds of New York City jail managers.

Recent studies show that America's prisons are safe and getting safer. In their recently published book, Bert Useem of Purdue University and Anne Piehl of Rutgers University observe, "Critics of the prison buildup were certain that the country had embarked upon a self-destructive course. . . . The prison system would collapse under its own weight because of the flaws inherent to prisons . . . . We now know they were wrong. The prison buildup has been associated with a sharp decline in chaos behind bars. ... Prison riots have become rare, the homicide and suicide rates have declined dramatically, and a smaller proportion of incarcerated persons are held in segregation and protective custody."

The challenge of corrections administration is the challenge of leadership. According to political scientist John Dilulio, "Prison management may be the single most important determinant of the quality of prison life." Leadership determines what happens inside a prison. An institution as separate and self-sustaining as a prison or jail, left to its own devices, can become dangerous and corrupt. In a 2004 *Pace Law Review* article, James Jacobs wrote, "Professional correctional leadership is the key to establishing and maintaining humane prisons. Well-run prisons are not brought into being by good philosophy, good laws, or good lawsuits . . . . Even lawsuits on unconstitutional conditions of confinement that result in sweeping remedial orders can only succeed if there are professional prison personnel willing and able to carry out court-mandated reforms." Useem and Piehl conclude that "the data are consistent with the position that political and correctional leadership made the institution more effective," and "a substantial body of evidence, based on in-depth case studies, shows that level of order depends crucially on the quality of political and correctional leadership."

Looking again at New York City's experience, leadership without accountability is merely cheerleading. Early COMSTAT models focused on an inquisition effect. However, the department has moved beyond that because accountability is more than punishment. In New York, management data does not belong to headquarters. It arises from and is "owned" by each jail's command team. Facility managers are expected to come to TEAMS meetings each month prepared to tell a story based on what their data tells them. In TEAMS, the only crimes are not paying attention to the data, not being aware of what the data says about a facility, or not doing something about it. Managers are expected to relay how they interpret the data, describe the scale and causes of the problems they have identified, and explain the steps they have taken to fix them. Managers are told "don't bring us problems, bring us solutions." It is fine to speak at TEAMS sessions about a success story, but it is unacceptable to cast blame.

Accountability means the assumption of responsibility for the failures as well as the claim of credit for successes. When a problem surfaces, the proper TEAMS answer is, "That is my responsibility and I will fix it." Yet, simply accepting responsibility is not enough; there must be relentless follow-up. There is a clear expectation that the following month will show a discernible improvement in the relevant indicator. One bad performance at TEAMS is not a "career ender." However, not knowing what the numbers mean or failing to correct a problem once it is identified may well be the death knell for an otherwise promising warden.

TEAMS in Action

Late in 2006, the number of stabbings and slashings in New York City jails (something that is tracked daily) was on the rise. Stabbings and slashings are considered the "gold standard" in measuring jail safety, much as the FBI looks at murders and car thefts to measure crime nationally. Reducing the number even further is a matter of no small pride in the department. So in January 2007, city corrections officials convened a special TEAMS session to look specifically at the rise in stabbings and slashings. The analysis showed that thirty-two of thirty-seven slashings and stabbings in 2006 occurred in just three of the city's twelve jails. After further analyzing many factors—specific location of each incident, the types of housing units in which they took place, the housing units of the involved inmates, the day of the week and time of day of each attack, inmate backgrounds, charges and gang affiliations, inmate motives, the kinds and sources of weapons used, the experience levels of the staff on the scene, and other factors— they fashioned some solutions.

While every manager in the department owns a share of the work to make it better, each of the three wardens understood that it was their responsibility to address the problem. Slashings and stabbings in calendar year 2007 dropped by about half from 2006, and the department achieved a twelve-month low of only nineteen stabbings and slashings. Staff did it by using the data; developing strategies for prevention such as tactical searches, jail intelligence, and inmate separations; and holding themselves accountable for the results.

Other Data-Driven Management

Jail violence is by far not the only topic to which the department has applied data-driven management and accountability. It tracks data on more than 600 large and small aspects of the day-to-day life of the city's jails. These aspects range from escapes and homicides, to the number of inmates regularly attending religious services, and the length of time inmates must wait before they are seen for medical care in the clinic. The department measures the time it takes to process and house a newly admitted inmate and counts searches, contraband finds, days lost to sick leave, overtime, maintenance order backlogs, and hundreds of other metrics. Knowing that information is management power. The department even measures the cleanliness of its showers and toilets, and here too, data management and accountability have produced positive results.

In 1974, New York City was sued in a federal court case regarding conditions of confinement. *Benjamin v. Horn* still exists. It is the oldest case on the docket of the District Court for the Southern District of New York, and it has lingered for thirty-four years. However, with information management tools like TEAMS, the department is determined to resolve and close the case during its tenure. One of the most difficult issues in the case is that of sanitation, and for years, the plaintiffs have argued that the city's jails are not clean. Admittedly, the facilities are old—and they look it—but they are clean. So, to clear *Benjamin v. Horn*, the department needed to prove it to the court's monitors and to ensure that whenever and wherever monitors visited, they would find clean showers and bathrooms.

One problem was that all previous measures of sanitation had been subjective. The department changed that, adopting the City Health Department's sanitation standards for the public shower rooms, gyms, and health clubs that it inspects. It gave those criteria to the wardens, and through TEAMS, it began to inspect and track the more than 400 shower areas every month. The department established shower cleanliness ratings as a TEAMS' indicator, and it challenged the wardens, reminding them that if they could reduce stabbings and slashings from more than 1,000 per year to just nineteen, then surely they could keep their showers clean. Management gave them the resources to do the job—steam cleaners, money to pay inmates to clean particularly difficult areas on the night shift, better cleansers, and training for inmates and staff—and it held them accountable for the results.

The results were dramatic. When the effort began in 2006, barely half of the shower areas were at the highest cleanliness level. Today, more than 75 percent are rated at the top level of cleanliness. In 2006, thirty-nine showers were deemed slightly dirty. Only three are labeled slightly dirty today.

In management accountability, expectations are everything. The administration believes that if it fails to have expectations for its managers, they will not know what is expected of them, and that will lead to a loss of morale, confusion, and ultimately a loss of legitimacy. On the other hand, the department recognizes the efforts managers make when they understand what is expected of them, that performance is measured, that performance is recognized, and failure is identified. Hard working managers want top management to know who delivers and who does not. If the administration is determined to promote based on merit, there must be commonly accepted measures of merit, and TEAMS provides that.

Energized, empowered managers make all the difference between a well-run correctional facility and one that is poorly run. In a technological era when any data is easily stored and just as easily accessed, it would make little sense for correctional managers not to make use of the data to run their businesses. At the same time, the United States must operate its prisons and jails with transparency sufficient to satisfy the community. The public must know that the deprivation of liberty that corrections exercises in their name is done according to the values of the constitutional democracy. Measurement systems like TEAMS are a step in that direction.

References

Dilulio, John. 1987. *Governing Prisons*. New York: The Free Press.

Jacobs, James B. and Elana Olitsky. 2004. Leadership and correctional reform. *Pace Law Review* 24(2): 477.

Useem, Bert and Anne Morrison Piehl. 2008. *Prison State: The Challenge of Mass Incarceration*. New York: Cambridge University Press.

About the Author

Martin F. Horn, at the time of writing this article, was Commissioner of the New York City Department of Correction. He is currently a professor at the John Jay College of Criminal Justice in New York.

Coordinating Jail Workflow and Information in Your Facility and Beyond

By Sean Fawell

Typical jail management systems functionality begins and ends with the arrival and eventual departure of the offender. In reality, effective jail management involves offender processing, information exchanges, and viable connections with entities beyond the walls of the facility. This chapter explores one agency's progress in combining a comprehensive jail management system with biometric technology, an affordable IT infrastructure, and interagency cooperation. The goal: streamline the process from arrest to release, save money, maximize resources, and reduce liability.

Any sheriff would say that of all the varied public safety services he or she provides, jail operations tops the list in terms of civil liability, staff-intensive complexity, and the ravenous consumption of ever-shrinking budgets. The typical county jail operation serves as the critical workflow hub and clearinghouse for all aspects of local or regional criminal justice activities. Courts, probation, district attorney, public defender, state parole, and street and highway patrol elements all rely upon and filter their "work product" through the county jail. Take a county jail out of service and watch as the many and varied cogs and gears of law enforcement and criminal justice grind to a sudden and chaotic halt.

Running a safe and efficient county jail involves managing diverse operations in an environment of self-contained chaos. In a truly twenty-four/seven operation that accommodates the static bureaucracy of a nine-to-five court system, ensuring every inmate is where, when, and how, they are supposed to be is a challenging undertaking in the most optimal of circumstances. Inmates must be classified, housed, fed, and medically cared for in a secure environment. Their day-to-day activities, clothing, property, and money must be accounted for. Their mail, visitors, education, and contact with the outside world must be managed. Their progress through the adjudication process must be coordinated and continue unimpeded. This requires a highly trained and professional staff, adequate facilities, and a scrupulously managed budget.

Nonetheless, declining levels of funding, staff, and resources do not relieve any sheriff of the responsibility to operate a jail in accordance with the Constitution, statute, case law, court orders, and, in many instances, consent decrees. At all odds, a sheriff must operate the jail efficiently, humanely, economically, legally, and with precision. Furthermore, (and here is the trick) a sheriff must be able to prove this operation with readily accessible reports.

Enter the Jail Management System

Whether created "in-house" or supplied by a vendor, be it simple or complex, a jail management system can be found in almost any county jail. At a minimum, a typical jail management system will electronically record, store, and display information about inmates. It seems simple enough, but most jail managers wish they could replace their existing jail management system, while simultaneously dreading the prospect of replacing it. Having been through three jail management system replacements since 1991, this author readily identifies with the paradoxical conundrum of jail-management-system purgatory.

The Ideal Jail Management System

A jail management system should be flexible so that it complements, accommodates, and enhances the workflow of the jail. Agency IT staff should be able to modify the jail management system to accommodate changes in workflow. In addition, the ideal jail management system should:

- Empower jail staff to do their work efficiently and provide a means for the agency to prove the work was completed correctly.
- Create and store a chronological history of every inmate's relationship with the facility.
- Generate informative and customizable reports on demand
- Ensure that a newly arriving inmate is positively identified and appropriately classified
- Readily convey and receive data from the external systems used by other agencies, medical staff, courts, and so forth
- Ensure that jail managers can demonstrate stress-free and timely compliance
- Provide affordable maintenance and modifications
- Mitigate the impact of fiscal uncertainty

Doing more with less money and reduced staffing is nothing new to the Contra Costa County, California, Office of the Sheriff. Like other law enforcement agencies in the United States and around the globe, this San Francisco Bay area agency of more than 1,000 employees perpetually seeks creative and cost-efficient ways to fulfill its mandate to serve more than one million constituents.

Sheriff Warren Rupf and his Custody Service Bureau of 308 sworn and 123 general employees run a pre- and post-sentence detention operation with more than 2,050 inmates across four facilities. In fact, the Martinez facility is the country's first direct-supervision jail and processes between sixty and seventy inmates a day and has around 23,000 bookings a year.

In 2004, the agency assessed its needs thoroughly and sought a jail management system that could quickly and accurately identify inmates and control workflows while accommodating the flow of arrestees and inmates throughout all its facilities. In 2008, the agency implemented a creative solution that has reduced operational costs and ensures accurate identification of subjects throughout the incarceration process with a new jail management system and integrated iris-recognition technology.

Contra Costa County's Quest for the Ideal Jail Management System

The computerized jail management system first emerged as an innovation with an aim to eliminate or reduce paper and streamline jail operations. Contra Costa County first transitioned from pen-and-paper booking almost thirty years ago with a home-grown jail management systems called OSCAR—Operating System (for) Corrections and Records. OSCAR occupied two refrigerator-size, second-hand Data General mini computers. Each had a whopping 1 megabyte of random-access memory (RAM) and cost more than $1 million. Although OSCAR did the job and converted a lot of handwritten paper into even more dot-matrix printed paper, deputies, along with other jail and IT staff, contended with duplicate data entry errors, a disjointed workflow, and difficulty in customization. OSCAR basically did three things: booking, charge and/or hold updates, and release. Housing logs, movement lists, classification procedures, and just about everything else was achieved with pen and paper.

During the next ten years, the advent of affordable desktop personal computers (PCs) made it possible to expand the number of functional terminals in the facility. Vendors such as Oracle/Sun Microsystems began producing database applications and associated server hardware systems, and a growing number of jail management system applications came on the market.

In 1991, Contra Costa County purchased and installed Premier Jail Management System. This DOS-based client system was subsumed in 1999 by the Windows-based Premier Inmate Management System. Although these systems featured a module for almost every aspect of jail operations, modifying any aspect of its functionality or reporting formats was very costly. Economics constrained vendors to build one-size-fits-all systems.

In fact, during the ten years the Inmate Management System was in use, Contra Costa County spent nearly $300,000 on necessary modifications. This was over and above the $130,000 for the maintenance agreement, not to mention the $70,000 for the Oracle, Mugshot, and Terix maintenance fees. When a needed modification was not in the available budget, staff were forced to work around a system that should have been working for them.

The importance of entering accurate data into a jail management system database is matched only by the need to get that data out. Extracting what is needed in the format required for a specific purpose involves the creation of a report. Many critical programs that generate revenue from state and federal sources require detailed reports submitted with regular timeliness.

Many of the required reports must be configured with the use of third-party business intelligence applications, such as Crystal Reports. This excellent product yields a dazzling report in the hands of a skilled user with adequate training. At $300 per user license, these qualifications limited the number of report writers to just an overworked handful.

Other operational headaches that predicated the decision to seek alternatives included:

- Inmate funds were tracked using Quicken; accounting glitches and clerical labor to fix them made a clear case for a jail management system.
- Incident reporting was accomplished on a basic reporting tool in the jail management system, and incidents that amounted to a reportable crime required a standard crime report. This often resulted in two staff members writing two different reports about the same incident.
- Inmate/arrestee identification became one of the most technically vexing and, because of the inherent liability, most critical issues facing the Contra Costa Jail and IT staffs. Making certain that an offender is accurately matched to a true identity, mug shot and fingerprint is not difficult; performing that task 30,000 times annually with 100 percent accuracy during the intake and release process is a challenge. Moreover, the time required for the state to return confirmation of Livescan fingerprints often exceeded the time that inmate could stay in the intake area of the facility. This backlog was a contributing factor in many misidentification errors.

Information and data requirements of outside agencies proliferated at an alarming rate. The sheer quantity of information about inmates and offenders was overwhelming, and it became apparent that selected portions of the jail management system should be installed in locations outside of the facility to start processing earlier.

Budget cuts and reduced staff levels were a harsh reality in 2004 and have since become a genuine crisis. Greater levels of automation and secure access, wherever possible, were a must.

Recidivism in Contra Costa County hovers in the 70th percentile. The county saw an opportunity to take advantage of this storehouse of available data and minimize, if not eliminate, workflow redundancies for jail staff and for local agencies.

A Fresh Start

During the past decade, the number of routine law enforcement functions that have been automated via computerization has multiplied exponentially. With each conversion comes the requisite software and hardware. These are typically accompanied by a hefty purchase price and an annual maintenance contract.

By 2004, the sheriff's Technical Services Division, IT, and sworn staff had adopted the practice of building applications in-house through the cooperative collaboration of a willing software developer. Based in part on the notion that a product designed in accordance with the specific needs of an agency would yield a better application, several key law enforcement functions are now automated by the most economical and stable systems in use:

- Automated Regional Information Exchange System (ARIES)
- Automated "Probable Cause" Declaration System
- Automated Report Writing System (Precynct)
- Automated Court Call-off system

All of these systems are used or shared by agencies throughout Contra Costa County. They save money and increase efficiency. Wherever possible, these systems use the economical and user-friendly Microsoft SQL Server platform. So, it was in the autumn of 2004, that Contra Costa Country decided to build a system in collaboration with a local company, Securimetrics (now L-1 Identity Solutions).

Breaking Down the Incarceration Process

As part of its evaluation process, Contra Costa County sheriff's IT, records, central ID, and jail staff broke down the critical components that precede, involve, and follow the incarceration process and analyzed each individually and collectively. Possible enhancements were identified in the following areas:

Field arrest and prebooking. Saving time and money earlier in the booking process is possible with the added capabilities of instant identification and prebooking on the street. A jail management system paired with a mobile biometric identification solution to instantly identify subjects on the street can offset the lengthy and time-consuming process of transporting potential offenders for fingerprinting to determine identification.

A jail management system that has prebooking and remote booking interfaces that are accessible via a police cruiser's terminal for prepopulation of demographic, arrest and medical questionnaire information prior to arrival at the sallyport eliminates much needless waiting during peak hours. Booking officers find that this reduces the potential for errors, especially in comparison to handwritten forms, which might be illegible or incomplete. The prebooking and remote booking interfaces also reduce the need for duplicate data entry by the intake staff.

Subject identification. With recidivism rates in most correctional facilities at or more than 70 percent, most offenders have been in the system before and, therefore, have valuable arrest and personal information already contained within their arrest records. To take advantage of this data, iris devices were installed at the booking and release stations of all facilities.

Beginning in 2004, all currently housed inmates were scanned with the iris devices. Surprisingly, the inmate population cooperated with the mass enrollment. The data, along with the associated iris images, were stored in a server while the new jail management systems was designed and written. Meanwhile all new bookings included an iris enrollment. All releases were verified with an iris scan. By the time the new jail management system came online in 2008, several hundred thousand records resided in the system.

Intake. After an inmate has been identified and processed through the pre-booking workflow, the more extensive job of intake begins. These processes include property collection and storage, classification, sentence calculation, inputting arrest and charges information, scheduling initial court appearances, assigning housing, issuing jail clothing, setting up inmate accounts, and assigning and transporting the inmate to his or her housing location. Often, these processes are wrought with inefficiencies and costly mistakes.

Most other jail management system solutions are either incapable or prohibitively expensive to integrate with other third-party systems. This lack of data communication forces deputies to manually enter data into multiple systems, such as a mug shot repository, Live Scan, and California Law Enforcement Telecommunication System (CLETS) search, which results in costly staffing charges and errors due to data reentry. Contra Costa County deputies were committed to having an integrated jail management system capable of eliminating redundant data entry through a single, consistent user interface across all of the various systems and modules.

Operations. After the extensive intake process is completed, offenders must be housed and maintained on a daily basis. Many jail management system solutions can be frustrating and inefficient to use as offenders are scheduled for and transported to court dates, grievance hearings, work programs, housing, and medical visits, among other activities. In many cases, these interfaces and systems are disparate and do not communicate with one another, resulting again in duplicate entry and updates. This was especially prevalent in the custody alternatives process. Many legacy jail management system solutions typically restrict jail staff from viewing and fully comprehending the progress and status of inmates in the process. Finally, non-electronic or paper-based systems, that is, the handing off of paperwork, files and folders from one function to another during the processing and movement of the inmate through system and facility, were too cumbersome.

Release. The release process includes dismissing or clearing charges; releasing property; conducting a final check of the local, state, and federal wants and warrants system; notifying any victims, codefendants, or foreign embassies; and manually confirming the inmate's identity with a visual check of paperwork and/or an ID wristband and exit questions. This process is often slow and inefficient due to a lack of a consolidated data system and electronic communication with the wants and warrants system. Sometimes an inmate steals another inmate's wristband to impersonate him/her to escape. These incidents can be significantly minimized with the introduction of a biometric identification system.

Building the System

Once critical components were analyzed, software engineers and programmers from L-1 were "embedded" with jail staff where they viewed all aspects of facility operations, state criminal and correctional information systems, procedures, and systems.

All of the various components of the L-1 system were designed to look and feel the same for ease of use. Moreover, modification became a simple process and the system allowed the user to pause and save an inmate's information at any point in the booking process without allowing the individual to become lost in the shuffle.

During the next three years, iris devices were tested in patrol settings. All of the jail desktop PCs were upgraded with increased RAM to both accommodate the new system and allow upgrades in other systems not related to the jail management systems. The vehicle sallyport was equipped with two workstations that allowed submission of probable cause declarations to the court and was programmed to facilitate remote prebooking.

As completion neared, in-house training of jail staff and function testing commenced. Preparations for the migration of existing jail data from the old system to the new one was under way, as was modification of the ARIES system so that it could read and share Omni jail management system data elements with other ARIES user agencies. L-1 and the county reached an agreement for annual maintenance of the new system.

Benefit and Outcome

In July of 2008, the new jail management system went live. The transition required forty-eight hours of manageable disruption to the weekend operations of the three facilities involved. In contrast with the previous Inmate Management System/jail management system installs and a CAD/RMS install several years ago that amounted to multiweek nightmares, the transition to Omni Jail Management

Systems was comparatively painless. All changes and modifications made to accommodate workflow preferences or changes in reporting needs were accomplished in-house and, therefore, free of additional cost.

Within months, a significant reduction in intake and booking times and errors, including elimination of duplicate data entry for nonintegrated systems, was realized. This yielded an estimated annual savings of clerical staff time equivalent to one full-time position. Inmate monies are now managed within the jail management system rather than a home version of Quicken. Additionally, the new system facilitates the automation of inmate commissary procedures at an estimated annual savings of $50,000.

Several agencies have begun using the remote booking function. Officers who use this feature gain a "head of the line" privilege, thereby further reducing the time it takes to book an arrestee. The Omni Jail Management System application is now available in all of the 120 patrol mobile data computers, as well as any of the 600 or more desktop PCs and laptops throughout the agency. At present, iris scanning devices (at several thousand dollars each) are too costly for agency-wide deployment in patrol cars. Eventually, perhaps through a countywide Mobile Identification project now underway, a handheld biometric device could be used to further augment the remote booking process.

With a jail management systems based on an SQL Server, the county saves nearly $70,000 annually in Oracle and related system maintenance that is no longer needed. This applies to the huge Sun Microsystems servers that housed the previous jail management system. All of this takes less space and energy when compared with the two slim Dell servers that house the Omni Jail Management System. As an alternative to the costly Crystal Reports, the SQL reporting tool that is included in the price of the SQL Server can be used by anyone and everyone willing to learn it.

Unlike its ungainly predecessors, the SQL Server does not hog up precious network bandwidth and is easily serviced in-house. Most of the sheriff's systems are SQL-based. Eventually, when all of them are so equipped, IT staff can avoid the burden of mastering disparate database systems.

The three database specialists assigned to the Technical Services Division each spend about one-third less time addressing jail-related issues such as report creation and data mining. This recouping of a functional position amounts to time now dedicated to creating a SQL Server-based Sheriff's Personnel Administrative Record Keeping System.

The incident reporting system looks and feels more like the existing crime report system. Whether assigned to patrol or custody, deputies need only learn one way to document an incident. If the report in question is a crime that requires state and national reporting, and/or district attorney prosecution, it is routed accordingly with an appropriate case number.

The transition has not been free of some growing pains. While the iris technology works with precision and lightning speed, some patrol officers had difficulty obtaining a usable iris image from subjects in bright sunlight. L-1 is addressing this issue and has a mobile fingerprint feature coupled with some of their iris devices. Either way, the iris images are National Institute of Standards and Technology compliant and may well be part of a regional implementation of the statewide mobile identification initiative. As time and budget permits, use of the iris devices can be expanded to streamline the admittance of jail visitors.

Compliance with the state-mandated DNA sample verification initiative will involve the use of a positive identification device added to the beginning of the booking process. The necessary modifications to the Omni Jail Management Systems application will not involve a costly purchase from L-1.

For varying reasons, a number of local agencies have yet to take advantage of the mobile booking functionality. Increased workflow efficiency in the jail has mitigated the kind of backlog that otherwise might cause local agencies to demand remote booking. Furthermore, the economy has had a deleterious effect on the affordability of booking and prosecuting offenders. Since 2007, bookings in Contra County have declined 20 percent, from an annual average of 29,000 to just 23,000 in 2009. Meanwhile, recidivism increased, from an average of 70 percent to 75 percent in 2009.

Reductions in staffing have affected local agencies and to reduce or avoid booking fees, they cite and release whenever it is prudent to do so. Similar pressures on the Office of the District Attorney result in fewer case filings. Eventually, and with certainty, this downward trend will change. In response to a federal court order, the state of California must reduce its prison average daily population by as many as 40,000 inmates. Last year, legislators reduced parole supervision for low-level offenders and approved taking up to six weeks off prison terms for inmates who complete rehabilitation programs.

Meanwhile, in terms of feedback and response to tweaks and bug fixes, L-1 has been very responsive to the needs of the Office of the Sheriff. The Omni Jail Management System works very well. It has never crashed nor has it failed. Teams of four database experts oversee the care and feeding of the new system. They are part of the Office of the Sheriff's Technical Services Division team of twelve IT professionals. Although they work during normal business hours, members of the IT team share on-call responsibilities. The annual maintenance for the L-1 system is $130,000 and is equal to the fee charged by the previous vendor.

Four years of perseverance and teamwork up front has certainly spared the office headaches and lost productivity downstream. The importance of a solid jail operation extends beyond the facility walls, and its role as the informational centerpiece of all local law enforcement operations cannot be understated. Herein are the keys to making bearable the burden of not only doing more with less but doing more accurately for less.

About the Author

Sean Fawell is a captain and twenty-year veteran of the Contra Costa County Office of the Sheriff. He is currently assigned to the Technical Services Division.

Philadelphia Prisons Go Green: Solar Hot Water System Installed in Philadelphia Prisons

By Robert Eskind

Barely four months after Philadelphia unveiled its first jail-based solar panels for water heating, officials at the city's large urban jail system took steps to replicate the money-saving initiative at the Curran-Fromhold Correctional Facility, the system's largest jail. The prototype at Riverside Correctional Facility, with forty-five solar panels heating fifteen storage tanks, provides domestic hot water for 768 inmates; the proposed project (with an estimated fifteen-month duration) would raise 248 solar panels to the roofs of Curran-Fromhold Correctional Facility's four housing buildings, providing domestic hot water to more than 2,500 inmates. Regardless of whether the project goes forward, it is borne of the enthusiasm and know-how that came out of Philadelphia's first solar jail-based rooftop array, installed last winter.

On a brisk but bright December afternoon, with sunlight streaming in from the south, Philadelphia Mayor Michael A. Nutter joined prison and solar project staff on the roof of Riverside Correctional Facility to celebrate the installation of forty-five solar panels to provide hot water for the inmates below. "Making Philadelphia the 'Greenest City in America' is a hallmark challenge of my administration," Nutter announced, and praised the initiatives coming from the Philadelphia Prison System.

Philadelphia Prison System's Riverside Correctional Facility is the first large urban jail in the country to install such a system. It will provide energy savings of 20 to 25 percent annually during the anticipated twenty-five-year life of the system, saving an estimated $1.1 million and one million pounds of carbon emissions.

"This is an investment in our future, reducing our energy usage and saving us money," Nutter said in December. "Philadelphia is actually one of the sunniest cities in the world at our latitude and solar power represents a huge opportunity for us. With this project, we are leading by example to demonstrate to our citizens and businesses the benefits of tapping the sun's energy."

With the successful installation of the solar panels at Riverside Correctional Facility, the relative simplicity of the project and the immediate impact on energy costs, it was clear to all parties that a similar project would yield a comparable benefit at Curran-Fromhold Correctional Facility. Because the proposed project at Curran-Fromhold Correctional Facility would introduce dual-fuel boilers, Philadelphia Prison System would be eligible for a reduction in the rate charged for natural gas usage from the local utility company. The utility benefits because it can count on Curran-Fromhold Correctional Facility switching to diesel in the event of a critical shortage. (Riverside Correctional Facility already had dual-fuel boilers, so no further reduction was available). The water heating system at Riverside Correctional Facility was centralized in one boiler room. At Curran-Fromhold Correctional Facility, four separate housing buildings—each like a jail unto itself—would support sixty-two solar panels apiece, heating water in four separate boiler rooms.

"We had recurring failures with our water heaters at Riverside Correctional Facility," said Prisons Commissioner Louis Giorla. "U.S. Facilities came to us with a long-term solution that will save us money and put us in the forefront of solar applications. We are very pleased that they took the initiative on this innovative approach, led us through the development stages, and, with the other project partners, helped bring it to completion." U.S. Facilities has held the contract for facility maintenance at Curran-Fromhold Correctional Facility and Riverside Correctional Facility since 1995 and 2004, respectively.

It was a happy marriage of necessity and opportunity; the jail's continuously fired conventional boilers—three 1,000 gallon vertical-tube direct-feed boilers, which ran on fuel oil and natural gas, were exhausted and had to be replaced immediately. "The pressure vessels were still covered under warranty," project manager John Carroll explained, "but the installation cost wasn't covered, and that ran about $25,000 each."

"To find a long-term solution, we partnered with the Herman Goldner engineering firm to review the possibilities," said Carroll. "We settled on a durable and efficient Scotch marine boiler feeding external indirect storage tanks. Once that system was agreed upon, we realized there was the potential to add solar, because the tanks had that built-in capacity."

The indirect storage tanks would be dual-coil Buderus tanks—one coil to handle heat transfer from a conventional boiler, a second coil to connect with a solar heating system. The insulated tanks preserved water heated to 260 degrees, with a reported heat loss of only 0.5 of one degree per hour.

U.S. Facilities approached the Riverside Correctional Facility's administrators with a proposition: make full use of the Buderus tanks' dual capacity, invest up-front in the solar panels, and reap the financial rewards down the line. The dual capacity would also allow facility managers to meet one of the basic challenges of the project: to provide uninterrupted service while the installation was ongoing.

Cities are not known to be nimble-footed when it comes to capital projects, but in this case, fast action was motivated by compelling necessity of heat, light, and safety. Hot water is a fundamental expectation for a correctional program. The prison administrators were sold, but the cost of the project exceeded the available funds in the maintenance budget. The city's Capital Budget Office jumped on board immediately and it brought in the managing director's office and the city's new Office of Sustainability.

The opportunity to move forward came from the Office of Sustainability, which signed on to help fund a demonstration project that would serve as a model for future system upgrades. Not only did the Office of Sustainability provide cash (from a small fund of "seed money" to promote green projects throughout the city), it provided the persuasive analysis of the project's viability, and fast-tracked the process of approval.

In the meantime, U.S. Facilities was pulling out the old boilers. One of the challenges of this project was the transition from oil- and gas-fired water heaters to solar heat without any interruption of water service to Riverside Correctional Facility's staff or its 800 inmates, who need access to hot water for personal hygiene, laundry, cooking, and cleaning. "While we were doing this, the third boiler was starting to fail," said Carroll. "We were under pressure to not only get the job going but to get it going before the final boiler failed. We had to phase in the new boiler and storage tanks while we phased out the old."

While the rooftop array of forty-five solar panels provides the key visual for this project, the installation of the water storage tanks and heat transfer pumps into the limited existing boiler-room space was the primary engineering challenge. Within that fixed footprint, engineers had to install the new boiler, fifteen indirect storage tanks, piping, and control systems. The system also includes a mile of piping for the closed system that circulates propylene glycol from the solar panels through the roof, through the second floor to the ground-floor boiler room.

The final work on the system included balancing, purging, and synchronizing controls—balancing the temperature in the storage tanks (they should all be the same); purging air out of the system, as in a radiator system; and synchronizing the controls so that temperature and draw down from the tanks is equalized.

Prior to installation, Riverside Correctional Facility consumed between $4,000 a month (in the summer) and $34,000 a month (during the cold of winter) in natural gas, but not all of that went to produce hot water. Natural gas also fuels the facility's heating system, and both heat and hot water are on the same gas meter. The solar-panel system is expected to reduce the fuel used for hot water on average by 20 to 25 percent.

Philadelphia Prison System's Background

The Philadelphia Prison System is a large urban jail system serving Philadelphia. It managed more than 35,000 new admissions a year, with an average daily population of more than 9,200 inmates in fiscal year 2008. Most of the inmates are held pre-trial, for an average length of stay of ninety-two days. There are six major facilities on the campus, located in northeast Philadelphia.

The Riverside Correctional Facility was completed in 2004 at a cost of $38 million and was dedicated in July of that year. It serves as the central intake facility for all women who are incarcerated in Philadelphia, providing housing, admissions, diagnostic services, classification, treatment, and case management to an average daily population of 800 inmates.

Designed by Vitetta Architects/Engineers, Riverside Correctional Facility has a three-story housing building, and a connected administration and program center that offers medical and mental health offices, admission, and release services for 4,000 women a year. The building's mechanical infrastructure is isolated in the administration building. The housing building includes four 64-bed units on the first floor and four 128-bed units on the upper floors. There is one shower for every eight inmates on the housing units, plus four showers in the receiving room for a total of 100 shower units. Additional hot water demand comes from cleaning, laundry, and scullery chores.

Even in 2002, when construction designs were under review, no one urged the contractors to build "green." Mark Alan Hughes, director of the Office of Sustainability, sees the initiative as part of the administration's ongoing drive to change the way the city does business. "When Mayor Nutter opened the new green roof on the Free Library in the fall [of 2007], the city announced our commitment to building energy efficiency. When the mayor opened the new solar thermal system at Riverside Correctional Facility in December, the city showed we intend to stay in the game and play big. . . . Buildings account for more than three-quarters of our city government energy use and we're aggressively moving to lower our costs while improving performance."

The fact that the boiler room was well-separated from inmate traffic reduced security concerns about a project that involved a lot of roof access by outside contractors. Under U.S. Facilities' management, contractors from Herman Goldner could work without interruption or hindrance. The deployment of correctional staff to insure security during construction was constant, but minimal. Careful scheduling and coordination of deliveries and contractors' access coupled with an established relationship of communication between maintenance and Riverside Correctional Facility Warden Kenneth Brown's staff assured that traffic was controlled, orderly, and on time.

What is Next?

Prisons and jails are huge consumers of electricity, natural gas, and, potentially, diesel (the back-up generators rely on reserve tanks of diesel). Examining energy use, water use, waste-water, food waste, and office waste are all important elements of a green plan for the Philadelphia Prison System. Like all city departments, the Philadelphia Prison System is aggressively looking for ways to reduce spending during an economic downturn. That does not foreclose the opportunity to invest in energy savings; the Philadelphia Prison System proposal to replicate the solar rooftops at Curran-Fromhold Correctional Facility is under review.

While Philadelphia city offices began recycling in 1994 (by executive order), the Philadelphia Prison System did not effectively implement this program until 2008. With incentive programs driving collection of recyclables in inmate housing areas (paper only), and effective promotion of the program among staff (yielding office paper and plastic, predominantly), the Philadelphia Prison System now generates five tons of recyclables a week, reducing landfill use and tipping fees.

Composting food waste is a related initiative. The challenges include collection and cold storage of the waste for routine pick-up by a contracted partner who would then sell the food waste to a local farmer. The savings are very real, both in tipping fees reduced, and reduction of water use. Again, the Riverside Correctional Facility is expected to be the test pilot for this initiative, with expansion eyed for Curran-Fromhold Correctional Facility. All of this is under review by Philadelphia Prison System's recycling coordinator.

Other initiatives under review include energy performance contracting and participating in the local electric utility's Demand Response program. Universities and other large organizations have turned to energy-performance contracting, in which private companies make the up-front investment, contract the work, and share in the energy savings. Some of the low-hanging fruit has already been picked; the installation of energy-efficient lighting and movement sensors in office space to turn off lights is one example.

Demand Response offers savings (similar to those in dual-fuel price reductions offered by natural gas providers) in which the rate charged for electricity is substantially lowered if Philadelphia Prison System agrees to use back-up power generation for its facilities in a power emergency. The Philadelphia Prison System has the back-up generation capacity in place, and would realize savings even if it is never used.

There is the promise of new technology; the obligation to do better; the incentive of cost savings; and the challenge of finding the investment dollars to achieve these goals. The Philadelphia Prison System is operating in a complex environment, where new technologies and their promoters offer cost savings, energy savings, reductions in the system's carbon footprint, reductions in landfill use, and cleaner air and water. At the same time, like all city departments, the Philadelphia Prison System is challenged to exploit the opportunities available by finding incentives and investment dollars up-front in tough economic times. Riverside Correctional Facility has begun to meet these goals.

About the Author

Robert Eskind is the public information officer for the Philadelphia Prison System.

Section 5

Jail Security

National Institute of Corrections Offers Security Audit Training

By BeLinda Watson

Security is the top priority of a correctional institution, ensuring that the institution is providing a safe environment for inmates, staff, and the public. Many times because of the routine of the daily tasks associated with the operation of a correctional facility, staff can become complacent or operate outside of guidelines. Taking shortcuts, relying too much on technology, and neglecting to update operating procedures can result in dangerous outcomes if operations are not periodically checked or reviewed. Loss of jobs, property, or even life may also occur when there is no check and balance for ensuring procedures are current and staff are following them. External and objective reviews of security practices and procedures are one way to decrease the likelihood of those incidents occurring.

The National Institute of Corrections offers a thirty-six-hour training program three times a year for individuals who have the responsibility of auditing security operations at either the institution or agency level. Conducting Prison Security Audits' participants must apply with endorsement from their agencies as part of a three-person team to be accepted. They must also provide a brief narrative that describes their correctional experiences, their current assignments and responsibilities related to security, and the security level and size of their facilities or agencies. The class includes eighteen participants composed of three-person teams representing a maximum of six different states, municipalities, or the military who will who have a hands-on, on-site experience of auditing out-of-state institutions of various security levels and missions.

The six state teams are then divided up between three different institutions that the host agency has identified to be audited. No two team members from the same state go to the same institution, which enables each state team member to have varied experiences during the audit process. The faculty is primarily comprised of present or former wardens, who have held positions commensurate with that of an agency security manager. Participants receive four hours of classroom training regarding auditing protocol prior to the audit process and a tour of their assigned facilities.

Throughout the training, they are guided by their team leader who is a faculty member. They work both individually and with a team member or the team leader on reviewing areas of security that are assigned. As they conduct the audit, team members focus on skills in security auditing, become more familiar with the essential elements of a sound security program, and assist the host agency in identifying steps that may be taken to enhance their security operations and audit program. A verbal and a written report of the observations and recommendations of the audit team are presented to institution and department officials at the close of the seminar. There are twenty-one points of inquiry either in procedure or in a specific area of the institution that are addressed through the audit such as armory/arsenal, inmate counts, control center, key control, inmate movement, hazardous materials, post orders, and physical plant.

The program is voluntary on the part of the correctional agency, and an agency must apply to host the program. When an agency hosts the program, it is only responsible for transportation of the program staff and participants throughout the session and providing a workspace for the audit team while on-site. The National Institute of Corrections provides all training materials and covers all costs for travel and housing for the facilitators and participants. To ensure the audits are objective, hosting agency staff can only be involved as liaisons and are not involved in the actual auditing process or training.

However, after receipt of the written reports, the host agency can request, through technical assistance, to train up to thirty of its staff on security auditing procedures. The National Institute of Corrections will provide funding for three facilitators to return and conduct a thirty-six-hour training program for the host agency staff. The follow-up training is one of the National Institute of Corrections' Prisons Division's areas of Targeted Technical Assistance, which are areas that have been identified to be critical in correctional operations or are emerging trends in correctional practice.

The National Institute of Corrections has also collaborated with large jail systems to train staff in security procedures that may be similar in the jail setting. There are operational procedures in prison and jail settings, such as inmate counts, inmate movement, key control, and control center, which overlap and provide a venue for shared training among staff in both settings. As a result, the National Institute of Corrections has been able to involve large jail systems in this particular training.

"Conducting Prison Security Audits" continues to be one of the classes prison personnel apply to most. Since 2000, the National Institute of Corrections has audited twenty-eight different state and large city prison systems and trained additional staff in twenty-five out of twenty-eight of those systems. The classroom session has also been offered at the Correctional Security Network's annual security conference in Cincinnati. The National Institute of Corrections' goal is to build capacity for security auditing in as many jail and prison systems as possible by providing training in this critical part of daily operations, as well as to provide thorough audits of the host facilities.

About the Author

BeLinda P. Watson, M.Ed., is chief of the National Institute of Corrections' Prisons Division.

Reducing Exposure in Use-of-Force Litigation

By Jeffrey A. Schwartz

The author recently testified as an expert witness in a jury trial involving use of force in a jail. The jury returned a verdict for $170,000 against the jail staff involved. That amount included $50,000 in punitive damages against the sergeant who was present during the incident, $25,000 in punitive damages against each of the four deputies involved in the incident, and $20,000 in compensatory damages. Interestingly, jurors indicated after the trial that the compensatory damages were not awarded because of medical injuries the plaintiff had suffered but, according to various jurors, because "They chained him to a grate like a dog; he's human." They awarded the damages because of the plaintiff's emotional trauma and because their decision was "constitutional." In the aftermath of the verdict, the author reflected on how unnecessary the entire situation had been and how frequent use-of-force litigation is in prisons and jails.

It began routinely enough. The plaintiff had a car accident, failed a breathalyzer, and was booked into a large county jail on a variety of charges. After a verbal confrontation in the booking area and concern on the part of a deputy that the plaintiff might become assaultive, a sergeant and several deputies escorted the plaintiff without incident or resistance to a padded safety cell adjacent to the booking area. The plaintiff was told not to yell or to hit or kick the cell door. The plaintiff was bleeding from a broken nose suffered before he reached the jail, and the evidence suggested that the jail may not have sought the required medical clearance from a hospital prior to admitting the injured prison to the jail.

Jail policy required medical screening upon placement in a safety cell, but the records indicated that did not occur. After two hours of sitting or standing quietly in the safety cell, the plaintiff was increasingly upset with the lack of medical treatment and by the amount of blood he was swallowing from his broken nose. He went to the cell door and yelled and began to kick or hit the cell door to draw attention. A deputy admonished him that he had been warned not to do that, and then a sergeant and several deputies entered the safety cell, took the plaintiff to the ground, applied handcuffs and leg irons in a hog-tied position, and chained the plaintiff on the floor by his restraints to a metal grate in the center of the dry safety cell. That grate serves as the drain when the cell is washed down, but it also serves as the toilet for prisoners who need to urinate, defecate, or vomit. Testimony suggested that the cell and the grate were not cleaned when there was a change of occupancy.

The plaintiff alleged that he was beaten when the deputies and sergeant entered the cell to put him in restraints and that one of the deputies used a "bar arm" hold to choke him out. A day later, when the plaintiff was released from jail, he did need surgery to repair a crushed larynx. The county denied using excessive force, but none of the five staff members had any memory of going into the cell, placing the plaintiff in restraints, or "grating" him, including the deputy who had had the initial verbal confrontation with the plaintiff and had a detailed memory of that initial interaction. Further, there was no report of any kind on the use of force within the safety cell.

The county had a number of other problems with this case. The jail had camcorders for "planned" uses of force, such as cell extractions, but no camcorder was used for this situation. The safety cell had a built-in video surveillance camera, but the videotape from that camera was lost, recycled, or destroyed.

The center of the county's defense was that an inmate who was hitting or kicking the cell door might injure himself and that staff were obligated to restrain the person because he had demonstrated he was a danger to himself. However, staff were unable to explain how "grating" an individual would prevent the person from intentionally or unintentionally injuring himself by hitting, kicking, or banging his head on the steel grate.

There were one or more Prostraint chairs available in the jail. Those are, of course, specifically designed to restrain someone in a manner that will prevent self-injury. The jail had policy and procedure on the Prostraint chair, and the deputies involved had received training on its use. On the other hand, there was no policy, procedure, or training on "grating" a prisoner. It was easy to conclude that the jail staff "grated" the plaintiff rather than using the Prostraint chair because grating was seen as punishment whereas the Prostraint chair was not. It seemed that the jury had no trouble finding that the sergeant and the deputies had impermissibly engaged in corporal punishment.

After the verdict, the sheriff said that the practice of "grating" inmates had been discontinued more than a year before the trial. He said that once an inmate was in a padded safety cell, "nothing they can do can harm themselves," the exact argument the plaintiff's attorneys used at trial.

The verdict made statewide news and was covered on at least one national internet review service. None of the publicity was helpful to the sheriff's office. All of this was because of a practice the sheriff's office itself recognized as inappropriate and unnecessary after giving it serious consideration. This paper, then, is an exploration of ways in which a correctional institution or department can reduce its exposure in use-of-force litigation.

Poor Practices

The case summarized above illustrates the single largest problem for the defense in use-of-force litigation. If actual practices are poor, defending those practices in court is an uphill battle. A jail or a prison that regularly uses physical force as punishment (corporal punishment) will likely be held accountable in court. Sometimes a practice involves a relatively low-level use of force, which seldom results in serious injury. The practice is not scrutinized because it has been commonly used for a long time and because there is a rationale that is accepted without real thought or analysis.

A good example is the use of chemical agents against an inmate who is "mouthing off" or refusing an order ("get away from the bars") but is locked in a cell by himself. The chemical agent spray is not used as part of a cell-extraction procedure; it is simply punishment for behavior that has already taken place. The rationale that "he was inciting other inmates on the unit" (who were also locked in their cells) or that "we had to maintain the good order of the institution" will not stand muster but is frequently used.

When management ignores or actively condones such practices, it constitutes a ticking time bomb. When such practice finally results in death or permanent injury, the jail or prison wins the trifecta: terrible personal tragedy, horrible publicity, and a big-time payday for plaintiffs in the litigation that is certain to follow. Use-of-force policies and practices have also been a frequent focus of the U.S. Department of Justice's Civil Rights Division investigations of jails and prisons, under the authority of the Civil Rights of Institutionalized Persons Act (CRIPA). When a Department of Justice investigation finds unconstitutional use of force, changes can be mandated and the correctional agency may find itself working with an appointed monitor.

In jails and prisons, uses of force will occur and some of these incidents will result in litigation. However, the frequency of use of force is not a given nor does it "come with the territory." Although uses of force may be much more frequent in a jail's booking area than in its general population medium-security housing unit, and they may be extremely infrequent in small minimum-security state prisons, there are also major differences in frequency of uses of force when comparing similar institutions or units. That is, relatively frequent uses of force are simply part of the culture in some jails and prisons, a culture affecting inmates and staff alike. In other institutions, the opposite is true. In the author's experience, there is a distinct correlation between the frequency of use-of-force incidents and the occurrence of unnecessary or excessive uses of force.

Reports and Documentation

The second major area that leads to unnecessary exposure in use-of-force litigation concerns record keeping and documentation. It is no secret that some use-of-force litigation is based on false allegations by inmates. In too many of these cases, the correctional institution has difficulty defending its actions not because staff acted inappropriately, but because the lack of thorough records and reports prevents the institution from corroborating that staff did what they say they did.

A review of all of the common flaws in record keeping and report writing is beyond the scope of this paper. However, a few examples may illustrate the issue. When several staff are involved in a use of force, some agencies fail to require individual reports from each staff member involved in or witnessing the use of force. Thus, instead of several first-hand reports, the agency receives a single summary report, sometimes prepared by a supervisor who was not actually present during the use of force. Sometimes reports are not detailed and omit exactly the kind of information that would allow a judge or jury to decide whether the force used in a situation was appropriate, such as describing the inmate's resistance or assaultive behavior or detailing which staff physically did what to bring the inmate under control. Vague and incomplete reports are sometimes signed off by a supervisor as if they were perfectly reasonable. When the underlying incident reaches trial, no one has any explanation of why the staff involved did not follow the department's policy or their training on report writing, or why the supervisor claimed that the report was acceptable.

The author also has experience with situations in which the involved staff members did write separate reports but, on examination, it was obvious the reports were not based on that staff member's personal knowledge or memory because the same paragraph (or more) could be found verbatim in several of the individual reports. There is little that can be done at trial to rebuild a staff member's credibility if he or she has copied portions of someone else's report verbatim and then presented it as his or her own description of events.

Another prime example of inappropriate record keeping has to do with the logs used to document fifteen-minute checks on inmates on suicide watch, or perhaps thirty-minute or one-hour security or welfare rounds on an entire unit. When there is litigation, most often concerning a suicide or a cellmate-on-cellmate assault, the unit or cell logs are among the first documents to be requested in the discovery phase of the litigation. If the department policy requires documented welfare checks every thirty minutes and the relevant log at the time of the incident reflects welfare rounds completed at exactly 2 a.m., 2:30 a.m., 3 a.m., and 3:30 a.m. and so on, there is a serious problem.

Common sense argues that welfare checks were not completed every half hour, on the half hour, to the minute. The staff member who completed the log will be forced to admit under oath that the log is knowingly inaccurate, that no attempt was made to record the actual times of the welfare checks, and that the staff member is unable to testify as to the actual times of the welfare checks (that occurred closest to the incident that is being litigated). Although these kinds of problems may not by themselves determine the outcome of litigation, they can erode the credibility of the department, its staff, and the trial defense.

The responsibility for these kinds of problems with record keeping lies with the management of the institution or the department, not during trial preparation but in day-to-day operations. When sloppy or inappropriate record keeping goes unexamined or is condoned by supervisors and managers, the practice may come back to haunt the department in the midst of a high-profile and potentially very expensive lawsuit.

Some practices with regard to documentation and record keeping are much more egregious. The author has, on more than one occasion, toured a correctional institution and reviewed a unit log or a suicide cell check log to find that the log had been completed in advance for the remainder of the shift, with entries indicating that there was no problem. If a consultant can spot those kinds of blatant falsification of records during an informal tour, what does that say about the effectiveness of supervision and management in that facility? Those are not the issues anyone wants spotlighted in the midst of civil litigation.

Code of Silence

Everyone with more than a bit of experience in law enforcement or correctional work knows the meaning of the term "code of silence." Historically, and with few exceptions, the code of silence has been an integral part of the culture of correctional agencies. However, there is no question that some agencies have worked hard or are working hard to eliminate the code of silence and to replace it as a cultural anchor with a commitment to professionalism and integrity.

Where a code of silence continues to operate, it affects use-of-force situations perhaps more frequently than any other kind of incident. A code of silence can make a court case on use of force more complicated and more challenging for plaintiffs, but the attempt at cover-up is not undertaken without great jeopardy for the defense, whether officers are actively lying or whether they are passively failing to report actionable behavior to protect one another. There is always the risk that under pressure someone will "come clean."

What may begin rather simply as describing an incident inaccurately to a supervisor (or not describing the incident) gets a bit more difficult for the staff members involved when they must write reports. If there is an internal review or investigation of the incident, the stakes are raised substantially because lying to an investigator is grounds for termination in most correctional agencies. If there is litigation over the incident, the risk is ratcheted much higher when those same staff must testify at depositions under oath. Testifying in court under oath is even worse. The officer who "only was doing what was expected" and trying to help out a co-worker now realizes that this seemingly innocent action could result in the officer serving time for perjury. Thus, the code of silence is a slippery slope and there is always the risk that some individual will decide to get off the slope prematurely.

The defense is in a troublesome predicament in a use-of-force case within an institution where the code of silence is alive and well. Attorneys on both sides share a distaste for surprises during litigation. If a defense witness or one of the defendants becomes scared and starts to tell the truth, the defense case may collapse even if the actual use of force in the litigation was compliant with both the law and department policy. Even if no one "breaks," the judge or jury may recognize the code of silence for what it is. In a complicated situation with many reports and other documents and a great deal of testimony, it can be almost impossible to invent false testimony that is consistent with all of the other elements in the case.

The answer to this potential problem is much the same as it is with use-of-force practices. This is something that should be assessed and fixed before some potential seven-figure case goes to trial. If there is a pervasive code of silence in a correctional institution, management either knows or should know, and the former is almost always the case. Also, if a code of silence exists, management can root it out if they are fully committed to doing so: it is a matter of leadership rather than a technical challenge.

Use of an Expert Witness

The author has served as an expert witness on both the plaintiff's side and the defense's side (in fact, while the author was a plaintiff's expert in the case described at the beginning of this article, his two prior cases were as an expert for a state department of corrections). From that perspective, a number of issues seem clear regarding the use of experts in correctional use-of-force litigation; some of these "lessons learned" apply equally to other kinds of correctional litigation.

An expert can be helpful. That is true whether the litigation is against the agency or against individual staff members, and whether the issues litigated are policy, procedures, or simply the appropriateness of force used.

There is a tendency to believe that the judge or jury (the finder of fact) must determine questions such as whether the force used in a situation was excessive, and thus to dismiss the use of a correctional expert as unnecessary or irrelevant. However, questions almost always arise about options available to staff, the interpretation of policy, commonly accepted correctional practices, and much more. In many ways, a lawsuit alleging excessive force is analogous to a claim of correctional malpractice. In a legal malpractice case or a medical malpractice case, it is widely accepted that expert testimony will be required to inform a jury about accepted practices and to help the jury interpret technical issues in the case. (In fact, a judge may dismiss a legal or medical malpractice lawsuit simply because plaintiffs have failed to identify an expert witness.) A use-of-force case in corrections may not be very different. If the case is about injuries suffered by an inmate during a cell extraction, how many jurors know anything about cell extractions? How will the jury decide if the training was adequate? How will the jury understand optional approaches that may have been available to the department or to the staff involved, or the risks to those staff?

While these are just examples and the work of an expert must be dictated by the specifics of a given case, most of the testimony a jury hears is from the plaintiffs, the defendants, or fact witnesses who are clearly supporting the story of one side or the other. Although an expert witness is hired by one side, the expert witness' obligation is to provide an independent analysis to the court. Quite apart from situations everyone has seen involving "dueling" expert witnesses, and the cynical view that you can obtain any expert opinion you are willing to pay for, in numerous cases, the verdict is largely determined by expert testimony and which experts may be more credible to the judge or jury than the parties in the case.

An expert witness' analysis may also be helpful in prompting an overall reevaluation of the case itself. The author has been involved in several cases in which he declined the case after a review of a fact-situation summary and explained to the party wishing to retain him that there were serious flaws in the case. That led either to a decision by the defense to attempt to settle the litigation out of court or to a decision by the plaintiff's attorneys to dismiss the lawsuit.

Scope of an Expert's Work

With expert witnesses, as with so many other things, timing may be almost everything. If an expert witness is to be retained in a case, that expert should be identified and retained early on. That is often not the case. Although federal court and various state courts may differ markedly on the deadlines for identifying experts, there is always a deadline. Far too often an expert is contacted within weeks or even days of the deadline for identifying the expert to the court and to the other side.

When an expert is hired very late in a case, discovery may be closed or almost completed and the attorney or attorneys in the case have long since committed to a general strategy and identified their major issues. However, an expert's analysis can lead to much more than testimony from that expert. The plaintiff's attorneys may be inexperienced with use-of-force cases or with correctional litigation in general. That is not usually the case with the defense, but even then, defense attorneys often have no knowledge of practices in other jurisdictions or the broader scope of what is generally accepted in American corrections.

If an expert is retained early, that individual's analysis may identify problems with either side of the case that might have otherwise gone unrecognized. He or she may identify documents that should be requested in discovery, and those may lead to important evidence. The expert's analysis may add to or change the focus of depositions. Some or all of this will be lost if the expert is identified late in the proceedings.

Choosing an Expert

If an expert is to be employed on a use-of-force case, it is obviously important to carefully consider how to choose the "right" expert. From the author's perspective, it is fascinating to be on one side of a case and to review the history and qualifications of the expert on the other side and then to actually read that expert's testimony, usually in the form of a report and/or a deposition. Some "opposing" experts have seemed bright, knowledgeable, and strong while others have seemed, well, just silly.

One surprisingly common defense tactic is to identify an expert who is a staff member of the agency involved in the litigation. This raises obvious questions about the independence of the opinions of the expert, and the credibility gap may be widened by questions from the plaintiff's counsel such as, "If your professional opinions in a case like this were that your department had acted wrongly, and those opinions led to a large financial judgment against your department, would that have the potential to affect your career or your professional relationships within the department?" or "How many times have you been asked to testify as an expert for your department and then reviewed the specifics of the case and refused to testify because you thought your department was wrong?"

A related question has to do with identifying an expert who only testifies for the defense or, conversely, for plaintiffs. That, too, can go directly to the credibility of the expert. If an expert has been retained in 100 cases but in each of those cases it was the plaintiff who retained the expert, the next question should be, "How many plaintiff's cases have you been offered but turned down because you thought the actions of the defendants were right and correct?"

At the end of the day, the expert witness chosen should have deep, specific knowledge about the issues being litigated and solid integrity. The author was an expert on the defense side on a case involving an escape from a correctional institution. The plaintiff's expert, who did not visit the institution, wrote a report saying that everything from security procedures to emergency plans to supervision and management at the institution were wrong. It turned out that he had been hired on another case by the same institution as a defense expert and had, eight or ten months before his current report for the plaintiffs, written a report saying that everything at the institution from security procedures to emergency plans to supervision and management were being done correctly. The case settled, and he was spared explaining his diametrically opposed opinions in court and under oath.

That expert also worked full time as an expert witness and had done so for years. That is another dimension that may be considered when choosing an expert witness. Will it compromise the expert's opinion if he or she is a "professional" expert, meaning someone who does nothing other than expert witness work? There may be advantages to using an expert who works in the field, is engaged in other professional activities, and does expert witness work part-time rather than full-time.

Almost without exception, correctional agencies are interested in reducing exposure to liability in use-of-force situations. That goal is achievable if agencies are willing to revise or eliminate poor practices, ensure thorough contemporaneous reports and documentation, work aggressively to eliminate the code of silence, and maintain a rigorous management review and investigation process. Finally, when use-of-force litigation does occur, and it will, careful attention should be paid to the choice and use of expert witnesses.

Specific Recommendations for Decreasing Exposure in Use-of-Force Litigation

- Arrange an independent evaluation of the department's use-of-force policy and use-of-force practices.
- Ensure that use-of-force practices conform in detail to use-of-force policies, changing one or both, as necessary.
- Identify and, where possible, change controversial use-of-force practices before they are at the center of difficult litigation.
- Audit the types of records and other documentation that will be available for defense and discoverable by plaintiffs if a use-of-force situation results in a serious lawsuit.
- Candidly evaluate whether a "code of silence" exists and, if it does, eliminate it.
- Consider whether an expert witness will be necessary or helpful.
- If an expert witness is to be used, retain that individual as early as possible.
- When choosing an expert witness, consider factors such as the expert's independence from the agency being defended, the expert's record of testifying for both the plaintiff's side and the defense's side, and consider whether expert witness work is the individual's only professional activity.

About the Author

Jeffrey A. Schwartz, Ph.D., is president of LETRA, Inc., a nonprofit criminal justice training and research organization in Campbell, California.

Core Jail Standards

Jeannelle Ferreira and Kathy Black-Dennis

> A performance standard is a statement that clearly defines a required or essential condition to be achieved and maintained. A performance standard describes a "state of being," a condition, and does not describe the activities or practices that might be necessary to achieve compliance. Performance standards reflect the program's overall mission and purpose.
> *From* "Performance-Based Standards Explained,"
>
> *Core Jail Standards, 1st Edition* (American Correctional Association, 2010)

For almost forty years, the American Correctional Association has designed professional standards to make correctional facilities safer for inmates and corrections professionals. With the revision of *Performance-Based Standards for Adult Local Detention Facilities, 4th ed.* (2002), facilities gained guidance on ACA best practices that were generally applicable to jails. ACA accredited 130 jails under these standards. For many jails, especially smaller ones, a more tailored solution was needed; the result was the *Core Jail Standards*, published in Spring 2010.

These new core standards are suitable for jails of all sizes that are seeking to implement standards. ACA's new *Core Jail Standards* provide a practical and reasonable means to improve conditions in all jails. These national minimum standards were developed through several years' research of ACA in collaboration with the National Institute of Corrections, the Federal Bureau of Prisons, the U..S Army, the National Sheriffs' Association, and the American Jail Association. The standards were designed to guide those facilities for which ACA accreditation is not immediately feasible.

The need for standards applicable for all jail facilities, from small rural jails to large city jails, has gone unmet until now. Thirty-two states do have minimum standards for jails, but these are largely voluntary; some states do not have a protocol in place for jail auditing or inspections. Core Jail Standards Certification is now available for all jails—at the request of larger jails' managers, ACA has not restricted the certification process by size. ACA urges agencies that had not previously considered accreditation to examine and implement the new set of core standards.

Of the 138 standards, forty-five are mandatory. These include such items as sanitation; water supply; emergencies; fire safety; and special management inmates. Other mandatory standards involve use of force; weapons; key, tool, and utensil control. Additional mandatory standards concern dietary allowances;

food service facilities; health protection; access to care/clinical services; pregnancy management; communicable disease and infection control program; chronic care; health screens; mental health program; suicide prevention and intervention; detoxification; pharmaceuticals; and health authority. More mandatory standards cover provision of treatment; personnel qualifications or credentials; confidentiality; informed consent; use of restraints; sexual assault; inmate death; work and correctional industries; and training and staff development.

ACA began field testing the core jail standards in May 2009, assisted by the National Institute of Corrections and the U.S. Army, which lent procedural expertise and sample policies. The Mackinac County (Michigan) Jail tested the draft standards for feasibility and reported back to the Standards Committee. Facility staff took on the challenge of implementing the core jail standards with the goal of completing a compliance audit by August 2009. Mackinac County's commitment to the project is all the more impressive when one learns that the Michigan minimum standards for jails encompassed only 24.3 percent of ACA's proposed core jail standards. In July, Mackinac County Jail was subjected to a rigorous two-day audit process by David Haasenritter, assistant deputy of corrections oversight for the Army Review Board, and ACA Standards and Accreditations Director Mark Flowers. The jail gained accreditation in August 2009, the first to do so under the new core standards.

At the 139th Congress of Correction, the *Core Jail Standards* were unanimously approved by the ACA Standards Committee. Thanks to the personnel of the Mackinac County Jail, who spent three months engaged in the arduous process of testing, rewriting, and clarifying the standards for use in the field, the 138 core standards are ready for adoption and implementation across the United States. In his foreword to the first edition, ACA Executive Director James A. Gondles, Jr., CAE, said "I am particularly pleased with this manual's relevance to small-to-medium-sized facilities. . . I encourage jails of all sizes to adopt these core standards, subject themselves to independent assessment to ensure compliance, and seek certification." In August, 2010, at the 140th Congress of Correction, the Etowah County, Alabama jail was celebrated as the first jail to complete the certification process.

Any agency that operates a jail may participate in certification, which is similar in scope and practice to ACA's longstanding accreditation process. ACA will provide the application materials, policy and procedure manuals, and an organizational summary. For more information on implementing ACA's *Core Jail Standards* in your facility, or to learn more about the eligibility criteria and certification process for jails, contact the Standards and Accreditation and Professional Development Department at (800) 222-5646 or visit us on the World Wide Web at www.aca.org/standards . Accreditation is available for agencies that wish to comply with the full set of *Performance-Based Standards for Adult Local Detention Facilities* (ALDF), on which the *Core Jail Standards* are based. Copies of the *Core Jail Standards* or the ACA standards manuals are available by calling (800) 222-5646 ext. 0129 or by logging into www.aca.org/store.

About the Authors

Jeannelle Ferreira is an associate editor for ACA. Kathy Black-Dennis is the director for the Standards, Accreditation and Professional Development Department.

Positional Asphyxia

By Holly Mathis, M.S.N., R.N., ANP-BC and Melanie Wahl, R.N., CCHP

The authors describe acute psychotic delirium, define positional asphyxia, compare and describe the physiology of normal and abnormal respiration, describe who is at risk for positional asphyxia, and identify measures to reduce the incidence of positional asphyxia.

Delirium is an acute and often fluctuating disturbance in level of consciousness and thought processes (cognition). It develops over a short period of time, and observers may note significant change from an individual's previous functioning. Attention, concentration, speech, memory, or perceptions may be impaired. There are two subtypes of delirium, *hyperactive* (for example, agitated), and *hypoactive* (for example, quietly confused). The American Medical Association and American Psychological Association do not recognize "excited delirium" as a medical or mental-health condition, but the *DSM-IV-TR* lists Acute Psychotic Delirium—also "excited delirium" or "acute excited state."

The cause of excited delirium is as yet unknown. This serious medical emergency may result from a neural-chemical imbalance in the brain, or an excess of adrenaline. It may also be induced in users of cocaine. There is now no definitive way to prove a person died as a result of excited delirium. However, it can prove lethal. Nearly all reported cases of excited delirium occur in persons having an altercation with police. Victims display extraordinary strength and endurance when struggling, apparently without fatigue. Officers see bizarre and alarming behavior, which they most often perceive as strictly a control-and-arrest situation.

Such incidents occur under very consistent circumstances. Law enforcement professionals respond to a property damage or unusual behavior call and find an individual displaying bizarre behavior, often partially clothed or naked, speaking incoherently or in gibberish. The suspects may be yelling or screaming, behaving in a disoriented way or hallucinating, foaming at the mouth or drooling, sweating profusely and apparently uncooled by their perspiration. Because of diminished pain sensation, these individuals—usually males in their early thirties, influenced by cocaine or alcohol use—resist confinement, are aggressive, and may even run into traffic.

The logical thing for an officer to do is to restrain the delirious individual, but breathing is the very thing that is restricted by restraint. The body eliminates carbon dioxide through breathing. Failure to eliminate carbon dioxide results in a buildup of waste carbon dioxide in the body's cells—acidosis. If the body is restrained and the airways are not patent (unrestricted), a cycle begins that invariably ends in fatality. Asphyxia, or failure to breathe, leads to decreased blood-oxygen levels (hypoxia), which increases CO^2 in the blood and tissues (hypercapnia). This leads to failure of the respiratory center in the brain (the medulla oblongata) and irreversible cell injury.

Positional asphyxia is insufficient intake of oxygen as a result of body position that interferes with one's ability to breathe. In adults, a common cause is restraint *asphyxia*, which occurs during the process of subduing and restraining an individual in a manner causing ventilation compromise. Restraint in a position that could reasonably result in impaired breathing ability leading to death is considered homicide.

Clinical studies in the 1990s and early 2000s demonstrated conflicting results. Some showed no respiratory compromise. Others demonstrated significant compromise. Autopsies often list asphyxiation related to body positioning as evidenced by cerebral hypoxia and petechiae. In general, those who exhibited prolonged struggle prior to restraint, hypothermia, evidence of substance abuse, or obesity and poor conditioning were most likely to suffer positional asphyxia. Individuals who abuse substances place their cardiac status at risk because of the physiologic action of these drugs on the heart. Obesity itself results in decreased lung capacity (restriction). Prone position reduces lung capacity in even non-obese individuals. Obese individuals in a prone position may suffer from obstructed airways as well, a situation compounded with pressure from the restraining officer. Individuals' past medical history and conditioning may also put them at positional-asphyxia risk. Respiratory and cardiac conditions such as asthma, emphysema, cardiomegaly, and arrhythmia are all risk factors for positional-asphyxia victims.

- ✓ **Hog-tying** refers to the restraint of a person in a prone position with his/her wrists and ankles bound together behind the back—a distance of less than 12 inches
- ✓ **Hobble tying** refers to restraint of ankles and/or hands
- ✓ **Prone containment** is the brief physical holding of an individual prone, usually on the floor, for the purpose of effectively gaining quick control of an aggressive and agitated individual
- ✓ **Prone restraint** is the **extended restraint** (either physical or mechanical) of an individual

The authors will construct a hypothetical situation as a prelude to discussion of *Cruz v. Laramie* (Wyoming 2001). A person exerts energy during an escape, or an arrest. Exertion increases the body's need for oxygen; the natural reaction to oxygen deficiency is increased agitation or restlessness. Responding officers then apply more compression to subdue the individual. Physical and diaphragmatic exhaustion (respiratory muscle fatigue) develops. Hypoxia/hypercapnia and acidosis ensues. The resultant cardiac arrhythmia leads to death.

A man, later identified as Cruz, was running around naked near an apartment complex. The first officer on scene found Cruz on a stairwell landing on the exterior of the apartment complex, "jumping up and down, yelling, and kicking his legs in the air." A second officer arrived, and upon seeing Cruz, immediately called for an ambulance. The officers tried to calm Cruz and persuade him to come down the stairs. Cruz initially refused, but at some point started toward the officers, who were at the bottom of the landing with batons at the ready position.

Cruz attempted to pass the officers, was wrestled to the ground face down and was handcuffed; yet, he continued kicking and flailing about. A backup officer decided after assessing the situation to shackle Cruz' ankles using a nylon flex-cuff and then attach the flex cuff to the handcuffs with a metal clip. (Evidence presented by the parties in this case did not agree as to the distance between Cruz' hands and ankles as a result of this hog-tie [or maybe hobble-tie] restraint.) Cruz calmed down markedly following the use of this restraint. In fact, just prior to the arrival of the ambulance, one of the officers noticed that Cruz had "blanched."

CPR was immediately begun; however, Cruz was pronounced dead on arrival at the hospital. Autopsy results indicated that Cruz had a large amount of cocaine in his system at the time of his death. During the ensuing court case, two experts disagreed. One said Cruz died from positional asphyxia, the second said he died from cocaine. The U.S. Court of Appeals for the 10th Circuit asserted:

> The conduct at issue involves the tying of the decedent's arms behind his back, binding his ankles together, securing his ankles to his wrists, and then placing him face down on the ground. We note that while sister circuits may characterize the hog-tie restraint somewhat differently; we understand such to involve the binding of the ankles to the wrists, behind the back, with 12 inches or less of separation.
>
> We have not heretofore ruled on the validity of this type of restraint. We do not reach the question whether all hog tie restraints constitute a constitutional violation per se, but hold that officers may not apply this technique when an individual's diminished capacity is apparent. The diminished capacity might result from severe intoxication, the influence of controlled substances, a discernible mental condition, or any other condition apparent to the officers at the time, which would make the application of a hog tie restraint likely to result in any significant risk to the individual's health or well-being. In such situations, an individual's condition mandates the use of less restrictive means for physical restraint.

The court looked at the facts of this particular case and determined that the officers had clear notice of Cruz' diminished capacity. The court pointed out that one of the officers on the scene called for an ambulance prior to Cruz' restraint based upon observations of his condition. After concluding that a constitutional violation had occurred, the court granted qualified immunity to the officers since prior to this decision, the law on hog tying of persons with diminished capacities had not been clearly established.

Three criteria were established to determine whether the cause of death is related to restraint asphyxia.

- All other causes of death must be excluded
- A person was held in position that might compromise breathing at time of death
- The person was clearly unable to escape the position

The following can help reduce instances of sudden death by restraint asphyxia in custody: avoid hog-ties completely; apply restraints to extremities separately; use a wall, not the floor, to assist in the process; avoid pressure to the chest, back, lungs, diaphragm or stomach, and avoid obstructing the airway. As soon as the person is restrained, move him or her to a side-lying or sitting position (if alert). Do not leave the individual unattended.

Assign an "observer" to note the situation and pay attention to the patient's symptoms, especially respiratory compromise, until an ambulance is called and arrives. Monitor the person carefully during and after restraint for breathing problems or loss of consciousness. Notify the receiving facility of conditions surrounding the apprehension and any medical history elicited.

Develop a plan for your institution in advance. Train with emergency medical services on how individuals should best be placed on and secured to a stretcher. Train officers and dispatchers to recognize excited delirium potential, and send sufficient officer back-up from the start. Alert dispatchers to send emergency medical services at the same time and to stand by at a safe distance. Do not approach the individual until several officers for backup and medical personnel are there on the scene. Contain the subject in an environment that offers maximum possible safety for all, and get the subject under control as quickly and safely as possible

Train and practice in working together on multi-officer techniques. Empty-handed, mechanical techniques are most effective, but require advanced training as a multiple-officer takedown team. Pain-based takedown techniques rarely work on those in excited delirium or other altered states of consciousness. If conducted-energy devices (Tasers) are used, avoid multiple firings, which are associated with increased mortality. Avoid "push" or "stun" modes, which are pain-reliant, and instead elect to use one Taser firing in "probe" mode. This should be followed by effective takedown and restraint techniques that do not impair respiration. Hand the restrained individual off to medics as soon as control is achieved, as quickly as possible. Do not transport subjects in a van or car unless emergency medical services are absolutely unavailable. The subject should be asked about recent drug use, health conditions, asthma, bronchitis, emphysema, and recent cardiac or respiratory disease.

Another option is to use the Total Appendage Restraint Procedure (TARP). Responder #1 talks to the violent subject while other responders station themselves at 45 degree angles to the subject's position. This first responder is to maintain the subject's attention, and is responsible for protecting the subject's head, as well as giving any cues to begin the restraint procedure. Front responders, #2 and #3, are responsible for the subject's arms. Two responders to the rear, #4 and #5, are responsible for the subject's legs.

References and Resources

http://www.charlydmiller.com/CLASS/positional.html

http://www.ha.uci.edu/anatomy/histo/files/6%20Cell%20death%20-%20Schreiber.pdf

http://patc.com/weeklyarticles/asphyxia.shtml

http://www.emsresponder.com/print/EMS-Magazine/Excited-Delirium/1$9165

http://www.policeone.com/columnists/Force-Science/articles/119828-10-training-tips-for-handling-excited-delirium

http://www.npr.org/templates/story/story.php?storyId=7608386&sc=emaf

Ann Price, et al. Plaintiffs v. County of San Diego et al. defendants, 990 F. Supp 1230 (S.D.Ca), 1998.

Chan T. C., G. M. Vilke, T. Neuman, J. L. Clausen. 1997. Restraint position and positional asphyxia. *Ann EmergMed* 30(5): 578-86, Nov.

Di Maio, T. G. *Excited Delirium Syndrome: Cause of Death and Prevention.* CRC Publishing, September 2005.

EMS.gov, National Emergency Services Advisory Council, Draft Standards.

Gardner, John. *Institute for the Prevention of In-Custody Deaths,* 2007 Annual Conference, Las Vegas.

Miami-Dade Fire Rescue Medical Operations Manual. 2007. Electronic Control Device, Protocol 33, June.

Peters, Dr. John. 2006-2007. Roll Call Mini Poster. Institute for the Prevention of In-Custody Deaths Incorporated. http://ipicd.com/

Reay D. T., C. L. Flinger, A. D. Stillwell, J. Arnold. 1992. Positional asphyxiation during law enforcement transport. *American Journal of Forensic Medicine and Pathology* 13(2).

TARP, RIPP Restraints Training Program, 1996.

About the Authors

Holly Mathis is the Disease Case Manager at Correctional Medical Services in St. Louis, Missouri. Melanie Wahl is the Director of Correctional Medical Services in St. Louis, Missouri.

Section 6

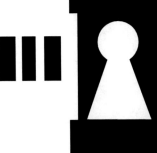

Jail Health Care

Defining Penal Harm Nursing and Deliberate Indifference

By Victoria Scotti, M.S.N., R.N., CCHP

Correctional health care staff must be able to recognize the dangers associated with penal harm nursing. The ability of the correctional nurse to recognize the specialized needs of this patient population in a nonjudgmental manner is essential for eliminating the risks associated with penal harm nursing in a correctional environment. The curriculum outlined in this chapter will identify behaviors associated with penal harm nursing and provide strategies to assist in avoiding this behavior.

Challenges

With the rising jail and prison populations, nurses and other health care workers are increasingly exposed to individuals accused of or convicted of a crime. The difficulties encountered by nurses in correctional environments include limitations related to the provision of health care in nontraditional settings. The primary mission of correctional facilities is to contain and punish criminals. This mission is in direct conflict with the traditional caring environments of health care facilities. Part of this challenge lies in creating an environment conducive to the provision of patient care while adhering to the safety and security needs of the restrictive environment of a correctional facility.

One of the main limitations placed upon correctional nurses is the constraints placed upon the nurse in developing a caring, therapeutic relationship in this traditionally non-caring correctional environment (Weiskopf 2005). This is a significant obstacle. Correctional health care workers are faced with balancing the clinical and cultural needs of the patient with the security needs of the jails and prisons that currently hold more than two million people in the United States.

The inmate-patient population is getting older and sicker. We are seeing increased rates of serious chronic, physical, and mental illness in our jails and prisons. There are challenges associated with staffing correctional health care units. Part of the challenge lies in attracting staff to work in a less attractive environment than traditional health care settings. Health care staff may face potential stigma from peers by working in jails or prisons and have been perceived as less competent or unable to get "real" health care jobs. Correctional settings have higher nurse-to-patient ratios and correctional health care may not always financially compensate staff as well as in the traditional hospital, private-sector environment. Finally, yet as important is the value society places on prisoners. If society does not value prisoners, then why should or would they value those who take care of them?

Deliberate Indifference

Adequate health care is mandated by the Eighth Amendment. In 1976, *Estelle v. Gamble* set the standards for medical care in jails and prisons. This case identified and defined the term deliberate indifference. *Deliberate indifference* is a complicated legal concept, however, a basic definition is "the conscious or reckless disregard of the consequences of one's acts or omissions" (Lectlaw n.d., par. 1). It is exactly what it says. You know about it but do not care. Deliberate indifference is not the same as medical negligence or malpractice.

To be deliberately indifferent to an inmate patient's serious health care needs is to violate that individual's civil rights. Deliberate indifference shocks the conscience. From a health care perspective, deliberate indifference falls under the Eighth Amendment, as cruel and unusual punishment.

Estelle v. Gamble

Gamble was an inmate injured during a work detail in a Texas prison. He alleged that he was subjected to cruel and unusual punishment in violation of the Eighth Amendment for inadequate treatment of this injury. Per his medical record, he was seen on seventeen occasions during a three-month span and treated for his injury and other problems. Because of this case, the courts found that the government had an obligation to provide medical care for those being punished by incarceration. They also stated that inmates, due to incarceration, cannot care for themselves and rely on the system to treat their medical needs. Failure to meet those needs could cause unnecessary pain and suffering.

In the end, the court did not enter a judgment in favor of Mr. Gamble but did find that deliberate indifference to serious medical needs of prisoners constitutes "unnecessary and wanton infliction of pain." They also stated this was true whether the indifference is manifested by health care staff in their response to the inmate patient's needs, or by detention staff in intentionally denying, delaying access to care, or intentionally interfering with the prescribed treatment.

Penal Harm Nursing

Penal harm nursing is a belief system that allows for punishment, pain, and suffering and rationalizes these behaviors as permissible because the behavior involves inmates who deserve the punishment. Penal harm nursing is evident when nursing staff supports the harm through either their actions or lack of intervention (Maeve and Vaughn 2001). Often, this behavior goes unrecognized, especially when medical staff closely aligns themselves with detention staff. An environment that promotes penal harm eventually becomes the acceptable standard of operation.

Case Studies/Discussion

During the 1960s, medical personnel were implicated in the torture of inmates at the Tucker State Prison Farm in Arkansas. Doctor A. E. Rollins, the prison doctor, invented the Tucker Telephone. Inmates were undressed and strapped to a treatment table and an electrical generator from a "ring-type" telephone was then connected by way of electrodes to the inmate's big toe and penis. An electrical charge was sent into the inmate's body. The prison doctor then would "ring-up" the inmates five or six times until they were ready to pass out. This facility was alleged to take prisoners "designated for elimination," and place them in the prison hospital, where the prison doctor allegedly "put them to sleep." Death certificates indicated they died naturally.

Martin Lee Anderson was a fourteen-year-old juvenile in a Florida panhandle boot camp. Seven guards and one nurse were criminally charged with his death.

In January 2004, two nurses were charged in the death of Omar Paisley, seventeen, who was pleading for medical attention at a juvenile lockup. Paisley died June 9 of a ruptured appendix after begging for three days for medical attention. The grand jury also cited, "the utter lack of humanity demonstrated by officers." A supervisor scolded Paisley to "suck it up" and "ignore the pain" while a nurse declared "ain't nothing wrong with his ass" (Miller 2004).

In October 1999, a county was accused of negligence for failure to provide CPR. Media reports indicated the sheriff's department allowed a mentally ill man to die in its custody. Unnecessary restraints and delayed CPR were cited. It took fifteen minutes before a jail doctor realized no one had attempted CPR and began doing so. The supervising nurse was forced to resign for violating department policy by not ensuring a nurse was present when he was placed in restraints. She also pleaded no contest to a misdemeanor for falsifying a report (Riccardi 2001).

Calvin Moore, eighteen, died in February 1996 after serving only a few weeks of a two-year burglary sentence. He lost more than fifty pounds in less than a month and suffered symptoms of severe mental illness, dehydration, and starvation (Allen and Bell 1998).

Charles Guffey, thirty-nine, died of a perforated ulcer in October 1997 after nurses allegedly ignored his pleas about severe abdominal pain. Jailers said a nurse told them to return Guffey to his cell and "let inmate justice take its course." He had been booked into the jail after failing to appear in court on drug charges.

Nancy Blumenthal, a seventeen-year-old, committed suicide in May 1996 in a county jail after the jail psychiatrist took her off an antidepressant drug following a twenty-minute interview, even though she was suicidal. Blumenthal had been jailed for robbery and for threatening her mother with a kitchen knife (Allen and Bell 1998).

Diane Nelson, a forty-six-year-old mother of three, died of a heart attack in March 1994 after three nurses ignored her repeated requests for heart medication prescribed by her doctor. Nelson had been arrested for slapping her teenage daughter. As Nelson collapsed, a nurse yelled, "stop the theatrics" (Allen and Bell 1998).

How Does this Occur?

The sole purpose of a correctional environment is to detain or punish; therefore, the potential for penal harm nursing exists within any correctional facility (Maeve and Vaughn 2001). Correctional health care staff works in an environment where the organization's primary mission has nothing to do with the mission of health care.

Jails and prisons house individuals from all racial, ethnic, and religious backgrounds. There are three distinct social groups within a correctional environment: inmates, detention staff, and medical staff. Detention and medical staff work closely with each other in the correctional environment. Although detention and medical staff interact and identify with each other, they are two separate groups with differing missions. While the development of positive working relations with co-workers is desirable, the individual staff must not lose sight of their individual purpose.

The mission of the detention staff is to provide care, custody, and control of the inmate population. Correctional health care staff provides health care, teaching, and discharge planning. Medical staff must be aware of the dangers involved with aligning themselves too closely with detention staff. This behavior can confuse the medical mission with the detention mission. Socializing medical staff to a detention model that values a penal-harm-custody mission diminishes the medical provider's ability to embrace the medical mission.

Ethical Relativism

Ethical Relativism is the "belief that ethical standards are not universal but malleable depending on the context" (Vaughn and Smith 1999). This takes place when the lines between the custody and medical mission are blurred. It is inhumane to be cruel, but is it okay if you are a prisoner? What if the prisoner is a terrorist? Look at the happenings at Abu Ghraib.

Natural Caring versus Ethical Caring. Natural caring is a core component of the nursing profession. The nurse's ability to care for patients is contingent upon relationships. Nurses generally enter the profession out of a desire to help others. We "care" and very often form bonds with the patients and family members that we encounter in traditional health care settings. Caring, or the perceptions of whether the nurse "cared," has been attributed toward positive patient outcomes. In the correctional environment, nurses may have difficulty establishing relationships with a population of individuals who are historically unlikable in the eyes of society. For this reason, the nurse may have difficulty establishing a natural caring framework for this patient population.

In an ethically based caring framework, the caregiver is able to provide care based on doing what is right for the patient for the right reasons rather than the traditional natural caring framework (Maeve and Vaughn 2001). The health care staff must be able to balance the clinical and cultural needs of the patient with the security needs of the environment and facility (Maeve and Vaughn 2001). The ability of the health care staff to maintain an open nonjudgmental attitude and an ethically caring manner contributes to maintaining a therapeutic environment. The health care providers' ability to recognize clinical and cultural needs contribute toward their ability to develop an ethically based caring framework.

The ability of correctional health care staff to be able to formulate some type of caring perspective toward the incarcerated patient population is essential for avoiding a penal-harm environment. Correctional health care staff must consistently exemplify a nonjudgmental attitude toward the incarcerated patient population. Failure to separate the roles of the detention and medical staff can compromise the intent and mission of the medical caregiver (Maeve and Vaughn 2001).

Strategies to Avoid Penal-Harm Nursing

The ability to formulate a caring perspective, whether natural or ethical, is essential. Correctional health care staff must consistently exemplify a nonjudgmental attitude toward the incarcerated patient population, not only from an ethical, racial, or religious perspective but also toward the inmate patient's criminal charges. Role separation and recognition of the differing missions between detention and health care are essential. The creation of a therapeutic work environment assists in reinforcing the mission of health care. This can be achieved by equipping infirmaries with hospital beds and appropriate clinical equipment. Eliminate the double standard that exists where equipment and supplies are concerned because this is jail. Honor patient privacy and confidentiality and do not engage in behaviors that compromise the nurse-patient relationship. The collection of evidence by the health care provider is discouraged, and whenever possible, do not place the health care worker in this position of conflict. The inmate patient must trust that we as health care workers will do what is right.

Overcoming Obstacles

It is important to strike a balance between custody and caring. Care delivery systems should be designed to overcome the correctional jail setting. Staff education is essential. Detention staff may not always have an understanding of what is involved specific to patient care. This lack of understanding could compromise the quality of care; therefore, it is important for the medical staff to communicate with and educate the detention staff.

Studies have shown that one of the major obstacles encountered by correctional nurses is the perceived non-caring attitudes of coworkers. This was reported as a major obstacle for correctional nurses and as a major source of stress and negativity in the job. The literature has shown that displaying non-judgmental attitudes, showing compassion and respect, exhibiting concern, and treating the patients as human beings with dignity and respect are major ways for overcoming obstacles.

View the inmate population in a therapeutic light. Detention staff will frequently argue with health care staff over the use of the term "patient" versus "inmate." To the detention staff, the incarcerated individuals are inmates; however, to the medical staff, they are patients. The nursing staff must maintain a therapeutic nurse-patient relationship with the incarcerated individual. Consistently calling the patient an "inmate" detracts from the nurse's ability to view the patient in a therapeutic light. Nurses who stop referring to their patients as patients are at risk for engaging in penal-harm nursing by virtue of shifting their focus from a therapeutic nurse-patient relationship to a custodian-detainee perspective.

Avoid labels. Occasionally, detention staff and medical staff have preconceived ideas and opinions regarding inmate behaviors and medical complaints. Corrections and medical staff can label patients as malingerers. Malingering behavior is prevalent in jails and prisons. The inmate population can be viewed as manipulative individuals who malinger for secondary gain. This secondary gain can be a variety of things such as a change in housing unit, a medical excuse from a scheduled work detail, or an excuse to leave their cell to attend sick call.

Occasionally, the detention staff will advise the nurse that a patient, in the detention staff's opinion, is faking. Health care staff need to understand an individual's motivation for engaging in this type of behavior. The practice of viewing patients as malingering could have a negative impact on the patient's physical well-being because this label tends to follow the patient throughout the duration of his or her incarceration. Patients who malinger do get sick and preconceived ideas and opinions regarding the validity of the patient's clinical complaint can prohibit the medical provider from making an accurate assessment of the patient's problem. Nurses that accept the detention staff's opinion of malingering without performing a complete and thorough assessment of the patient's clinical situation are potentially engaging in penal harm nursing.

Conclusion

People do not enter medicine to do harm. As medical professionals, we have an ethical obligation to do the right thing. That includes taking care of the patients we serve, regardless of the care setting. We must take all steps necessary to avoid an environment that advocates patient harm. It is all right to touch a patient for the purposes of patient care. We must train our future staff that it is all right to develop working relationships with co-workers but not lose sight of the mission. We must not only talk the talk, but also walk the walk. This includes not remaining silent when an injustice is observed. We must not lose sight of our humanity in a sea of cynicism.

References

Allen, W. and K. Bell.1998. Death, neglect and the bottom line. Push to cut costs poses risks. *St. Louis Post Dispatch*. September 27. Retrieved from http://www.corpwatch.org/article.php?id=858

Bay County Boot Camp – Florida. 2006. March. Retrieved from http://www.teenhelpindustry.info/march06.asp

Beam, T. n.d. Military medical ethics. Section IV: Medical Ethics in the Military. Retrieved from http://www.bordeninstitute.army.mil/ethicsbook_files/Ethics2/Ethics-ch-13.pdf

Bright, S. 1999. Neither equal or just: The rationing and denial of legal services to the poor when life and liberty are at stake. The Justice Project. Retrieved from http://www.thejusticeproject.org/press/reports/neither-equal-nor-just-the-of.html

Estelle v. Gamble, 429 U.S. 97 (1976) Retrieved from http://biotech.law.lsu.edu/cases/prisons/Estelle_v_Gamble.htm

Lectlaw. (n.d.). Deliberate indifference.'Lectric Law Library. Retrieved from http://www.lectlaw.com/def/d037.htm

Maeve, M. K. and M. Vaughn. 2001. Nursing with prisoners: The practice of caring, forensic nursing, or penal harm nursing? *Advances in Nursing Science* 24(2): 47-64.

Miller, C. 2004. Jailed teen's death leads to charges; Two nurses are charged in the death of Omar Paisley, 17, who was pleading for medical attention at the Dade juvenile lockup. *Miami Herald*. January 28. Retrieved from http://www.nospank. net/n-l49r.htm

Riccardi, N. 2001. County called negligent in inmate's death; probe/Report says sheriff's department allowed mentally ill man to die in custody in 1999, unnecessary restraints and delayed CPR are cited. *Los Angeles Times*. October 14.

Time. 1968. Hell in Arkansas. Retrieved from http://www.time.com/time/magazine/article/0,9171,844402-1,00.html

Vaughn, M. and L. Smith. 1999. Practicing penal harm medicine in the United States: Prisoners' voices from jail. *Justice Quarterly* 16, 1. Mar.

Weiskopf, C. S. 2005. Issues and innovations in nursing practice: Nurses' experience of caring for inmate patients. *Journal of Advanced Nursing Practice* 49(4): 336-43.

About the Author

Victoria M. Scotti, M.S. N., R.N., CCHP, is the Program Administrator for Inmate Health Care at the Pinellas County Sheriff's Office in Clearwater Florida.

Cost-Effective Methods for Managing Contagious Diseases in the Jail Setting

By Rick Frey

The Centers for Disease Control and Prevention has determined that jails currently house what it refers to as its "target population." According to Centers for Disease Control studies, the jail inmate population includes a disproportionate percentage of people with hepatitis, sexually transmitted diseases (such as syphilis and HIV), and a variety of other contagious diseases.

Local jail systems have a transient population, and the same inmates the Centers for Disease Control has identified as its target population are returned to U.S. communities every day. Consider the following questions: How many inmates does a typical jail book and release every day? Do these released inmates pose a health risk to the community? Has everything been done to identify and treat them before they return to their neighborhoods?

Some jails have a policy mandating that unless inmates are symptomatic, the testing, treatment, and vaccination of the inmate population are the responsibility of the local health department. After all, with all of the demands placed on jails, why should the sheriff or jail administrator go to the expense of dealing with an issue that is someone else's responsibility?

The fact that local jails house the Centers for Disease Control's target population may be perceived two ways by corrections: as an additional burden or as an opportunity to better serve the community. For a jail considering a policy to take a proactive approach to addressing this population, the questions are how much does it cost and how can the jail pay for it? The answer is that testing, treatment, and vaccination programs can be much less expensive than expected and can be successfully administered inside any jail system in a cost-effective manner. The key to successfully developing and administering a cost-effective approach to addressing contagious diseases is in developing partnerships among the jail's health care provider and the local and state health departments responsible for the jail's jurisdiction.

How Broward County Did It

In 2003, Broward County, Florida, Sheriff Ken Jenne directed his jail administration to develop and implement a comprehensive approach to managing contagious diseases in the jail system. The jail has an average daily population of 5,600 inmates and books more than 70,000 people each year. Recognizing the potential to positively impact the community's health, the sheriff's office entered into a partnership with the Broward County Health Department and the State of

Florida Health Department—and thus began to take advantage of the opportunity the target population presented.

The process began with a meeting in Atlanta with Centers for Disease Control officials to discuss the vaccination and treatment of inmates with hepatitis. In January 2003, the Centers for Disease Control issued a *Morbidity and Mortality Weekly Report* titled "Prevention and Control of Infections with Hepatitis Viruses in Correctional Settings." The report indicated that between 12 and 39 percent of all Americans with hepatitis B or hepatitis C had been released from custody the previous year. Although focused primarily on prisons, the report made the following recommendations for all correctional institutions, including jails:

- All adults entering the jail should be medically evaluated, and, if they are determined to be high risk, they should be vaccinated for both hepatitis A and hepatitis B. The estimated cost for a combination A and B vaccine is approximately $78 for a series of three vaccinations over a six-month period.
- Inmates identified as high risk during entry medical evaluation should be tested for hepatitis C. If positive, further testing should be done. Treatment would be at the discretion of the health care provider.
- The jail should develop and maintain a database to track all vaccination-related data.

In reviewing the full report, Broward County jail officials clearly saw that the recommendations would not be easily implemented in any local jail environment. Broward County's average length of stay, as in most jails, was no more than twenty-eight days, not nearly enough time to complete the three vaccinations recommended during a six-month period. Because of that, the development of a database for the county's transient population would be useless if maintained in the jail.

To address these concerns, the jail's health-care provider along with administrators of the Broward County Health Department and the jail director met to discuss the potential of the jail partnering with the health agencies to both create the database and administer vaccinations. The discussion generated ideas on how to develop a comprehensive approach to not only hepatitis but also a variety of contagious diseases.

They exchanged ideas on testing, vaccination, and treatment of the inmate population. Their plans included not only the average daily population of 5,600 inmates, but all 70,000 inmates who were booked each year.

The jail director offered health officials full access to the inmate population. Further, the health department was offered office space in each of the five jail facilities to allow its staff daily interaction with the target population. As the discussions progressed, it was apparent that the health department representatives were surprised by the open access they were offered in each of the jails.

After discussion about funding and staff to administer the program, the health department, for most of the initiatives, offered to cover vaccination and lab costs if the health care provider agreed to draw blood for testing and administer the vaccine. The health care provider agreed to provide medication to treat identified diseases only as part of its contract for services. Gaps between the two health agencies were addressed by the jail administration, and, as different programs for treatment were discussed, it became clear that the cost was not as significant as first anticipated by the director. Money from the inmate welfare fund was offered as a short-term solution while sources of grant funding were explored.

To solve the problem of completing three shots during a six-month period, the health department offered to provide vouchers to the inmates who were released to encourage them to continue the program, thereby developing a post-release link between the inmate and the health department.

To further expand the impact on the overall target population, a plan was developed to include an education component for the inmates and their visitors and families. It was agreed that if the inmate were infected, there was a high probability the visitors and family were infected as well. The health department offered educational materials, and the jail purchased and installed television monitors and DVD players in all visitor-waiting areas. In addition to the availability of educational brochures, informational videos are continuously played in all lobby areas, providing information on all contagious diseases.

Recognizing that this program was voluntary, the jail system developed, as an inmate incentive, informational brochures that outline the overall program and emphasize that testing, treatment, and vaccinations were at no cost to inmates. Those brochures are distributed to each inmate passing through the system. The inmate handbook was revised, and the information was incorporated into the inmate-orientation video. To reinforce the initiative, jail administrators use every opportunity to educate inmates and promote the program.

Program Specifics

The original meeting was the beginning of a successful partnership that has seen the Broward Sheriff's Office fulfill its goal to develop and implement a comprehensive approach to managing contagious diseases in the Broward jail system.

Following are brief summaries of the various parts of the program along with the estimated costs for each. The key to the program's success has been the sharing of resources among its partners in providing testing, vaccination, and treatment.

HIV RAPID Testing

The Reducing AIDS Prevalence in Detention (RAPID) HIV Program offers testing for HIV infection to all inmates on a voluntary basis. In a collaborative effort, the Broward County Health Department has worked closely with the Broward Sheriff's Office to successfully implement this initiative. Information about the RAPID HIV Program is posted at intake and throughout the jail. Most testing is offered during the initial health assessment (within fourteen days of incarceration), and results are provided while the inmate is waiting. Pre- and post-counseling is provided for all individuals tested. A counselor is available at each jail site to conduct both the counseling and testing. All positive results are referred to the medical provider for further evaluation and treatment.

The RAPID HIV Program performs approximately 600 tests each month, with a monthly average of four new positive cases. Those newly identified with HIV are seen by the physician and have additional lab tests performed. After completing the evaluation and reviewing laboratory results, the physician and the patient formulate a treatment plan, including a potential medication program.

The program is currently funded by the Broward County Health Department, with costs of approximately $160 for each test and treatment at approximately $1,200 per month for each inmate treated.

Sexually Transmitted Disease Testing and Treatment

Most women infected with gonorrhea are unaware of their infection. The majority of men develop symptoms, but they might be unaware of their infection because symptoms may not be present during the first month of infection. Chlamydia infections are more common than gonorrhea and can be present in women and men without symptoms. Early detection and treatment of gonorrhea and Chlamydia reduce transmission and the risk of complications, which can include pelvic inflammatory disease, obstetric complications, infertility, and systemic illness.

Screening for women can be accomplished by performing a special DNA assay on a urine specimen. Results are available in a few days. Each lab test costs approximately $10, which is paid through a grant from the Broward County Health Department.

Screening for males is easier and can be accomplished with a urine dipstick that can detect the presence of white blood cells in the urine within a minute. Test strips cost approximately $0.40 each and are provided by Armor Correctional Health Services, the jail's health care provider. Treatment costs approximately $5 for each positive case, which is also paid by Armor.

Broward County has one of the highest rates of syphilis in the United States. A blood test remains the primary screening mechanism for determining syphilis infection. Many of the signs and symptoms of this disease are similar to those of other diseases, so diagnosing syphilis from signs and symptoms alone is difficult.

Pregnant women with syphilis can pass it to the babies they are carrying. Untreated syphilis may lead to serious health problems for the baby; it can cause death in the womb or death shortly after birth. Many people infected with syphilis have no symptoms for years yet remain at risk for late complications if they are not treated.

The Broward County Health Department processes the specimens at the state laboratory at a cost of approximately $5 each. Armor Correctional Health Services provides treatment for positive tests at a cost of approximately $50 each.

Hepatitis A and B Vaccinations

Most hepatitis A cases occur through person-to-person transmission (by the fecal-oral route) during communitywide outbreaks. Persons at greatest risk for hepatitis A include illicit drug users, men who have sex with men, and individuals with chronic liver disease.

The hepatitis B virus is carried by blood and transmitted when skin or mucous membranes are exposed to infected blood or body fluids such as semen. Although prevalence varies geographically, between 15 and 30 percent of inmates have been infected with hepatitis B. Injection drug use has been reported among 10 to 19 percent of patients infected with hepatitis B. Most hepatitis B infections among inmates are acquired prior to incarceration; however, the rate of new infection among inmates is approximately 1 percent per year.

Hepatitis A and B vaccination is recommended for all incarcerated adults, including those who lack proof of previous vaccination or previous hepatitis B infection, regardless of the length of incarceration. Because some individuals may be incarcerated only long enough to receive partial series doses, a tracking system should be in place to communicate with the outside public health system and ensure completion of the vaccination series. Even a partial series of vaccine confers significant protection. Vaccinating inmates in prisons and jails is feasible and cost-effective for the community. Among inmates offered a hepatitis vaccine, approximately 60 percent to 80 percent accept vaccination.

The complete series of vaccinations costs approximately $78. The vaccine is currently provided by the Broward County Health Department and administered by Armor Correctional Health Services staff.

MRSA Screening and Treatment

Methicillin-Resistant Staphylococcus Aureas is an emerging problem in many jail and prison environments throughout the country. Long ago, MRSA was often written off as "spider bites." Today, it is well known how contagious and serious a problem this can become if not identified and treated immediately. In March 2004, the Broward Sheriff's Office developed an aggressive approach to identifying and treating each inmate infection to prevent an epidemic. Not only does the medical staff conduct examinations, but an informational flier with color photos of wounds and sores consistent with the MRSA bacteria was posted in each housing unit to educate the inmates on what to look for. Although the initial focus was on the inmate population, the sheriff's office soon realized that the deputies and staff members appreciated the efforts of the sheriff's office. When the first case of MRSA was identified in May 2004, the staff expressed concern as rumors began about the seriousness of the infection. Fortunately, the education process had been under way for two months before this occurred. And when the first case was positively identified, all employees were fully briefed at roll calls (*see* Figure 1). Statistical data regarding any additional cases is provided to all commands on a weekly basis to keep all staff members informed.

Cultures of any suspected MRSA cases are taken by Armor Correctional, Health Services and positive cultures are treated by a course of antibiotics. The costs are approximately $28 for the culture and $5 for ten days of antibiotics.

Tuberculosis Testing

TB testing is mandatory for all inmates. Cost for the test is $0.68. All TB testing is conducted and paid for by Armor Correctional Health Services.

Flu and pneumonia vaccinations. Flu and pneumonia vaccinations are offered to inmates who may be at risk, consistent with the guidelines for those offered to the community at large (the elderly, and so forth). The costs are $10.40 for the flu vaccine and $25.60 for the pneumonia vaccine.

Health Education

Health education is a critical component to any program that addresses the management of communicable disease. It is important not only for the targeted inmate population but for their visitors as well. And health education for inmates and their visitors is expected to impact the community at large.The next page provides an example of just a few of the educational opportunities the Broward Sheriff's Office offers.

The POWERR (Providing Our Women Education for Risk Reduction) program is conducted by the Broward County Health Department. A health educator speaks to inmates and their visitors about prevention of HIV infection.

The health department provides periodic health education seminars to inmates in the Military Training Unit through the RAPID testing program. These are generally youthful first-time offenders who will be returning to the community.

Also through the RAPID testing program, the health department provides periodic health seminars in all programming units. All inmates are provided educational brochures and materials.

Because the sheriff's office knows it can positively impact community health, it continues to stress the importance of managing contagious diseases in the jail population. Managing contagious diseases in the jail environment can be done in both an efficient and cost-effective manner. The first step is deciding whether the target population presents an opportunity or a burden.

Figure 1. Excerpt from Roll Call Training Bulletin: MRSA Infection Control, March 5, 2004

Methicillin Resistant Staphylococcus Aureas (MRSA) in non-medical terminology is a staph infection that is resistant to penicillin. Because of such wide use of antibiotics over the years, some strains of infection have become resistant to antibiotics and that is when it becomes MRSA.

MRSA usually develops in hospitalized patients who are elderly or very sick or who have an open wound (such as a bedsore) or a tube going into the body such an IV catheter or a urinary catheter. In the community however, cases of MRSA have been associated with recent antibiotic use, sharing contaminated items, having active skin diseases, and living in crowded settings. Clusters of skin infections caused by MRSA have been described among injecting drug-users, incarcerated persons, players of close-contact sports, and other populations.

Staph infections can be treated with different antibiotics or by draining the sore. It is very important to complete the full course of antibiotic therapy for complete healing.

Staph bacteria and MRSA can spread among people having close contact with infected people: MRSA is almost always spread by direct contact, and not through the air. Spread may also occur through indirect contact by touching objects (such as towels, sheets, wound dressings, clothes, workout areas, sports equipment) contaminated by the infected skin of the person with MRSA or staph bacteria.

To prevent staph infection or MRSA:

1. Keep your hands clean by washing thoroughly with soap and water.
2. Keep cuts and abrasions clean and covered with a proper dressing until healed.
3. Avoid contact with other people's wounds or material contaminated from wounds.

About the Author

Lt. Col. Rick Frey is director of the Department of Detention at Broward Sheriff's Office in Fort Lauderdale, Florida.

The Use of Doulas for Inmates in Labor: Continuous Supportive Care with Positive Outcomes

By Marilyn C. Moses and Roberto Hugh Potter

"Doula" is a word of Greek origin that refers to a woman who cares for another woman. Today, this word is used to describe a trained lay birth attendant who advocates for and provides uninterrupted—prebirth to postbirth—nonmedical support; hands-on care; information; and encouragement to laboring women. Doula support for incarcerated women giving birth is an exemplary practice supported by a large body of scientific evidence.

Doulas are not nurses, midwives, physician assistants, or doctors. Although they do receive training, doulas do not have clinical responsibilities nor do they replace the roles played by the father and other family members during labor and delivery. A doula is a female companion who befriends the laboring mother, providing competent uninterrupted physical and emotional care and support. The doula provides low-tech care in a high-tech environment. The care is hands-on and may include nonsexual stroking and massage, assisting with relaxation techniques, providing continuous encouragement, anticipating and answering questions that mothers are likely to present, providing additional instruction on labor techniques, advocating for the mother when she is feeling overwhelmed by hospital authority figures—such as doctors, nurses, physician assistants, lab techs, and so forth—and providing other needed anxiety-reducing support.

More than twenty randomized trials of low-tech, minimal-cost doula support have yielded positive obstetric outcomes. Doula programs have been principally implemented in the general population but also have been tested with juvenile and other high-risk populations. Both prisons and jails have implemented doula programs and an evaluation of one such program (described later) has demonstrated positive results.

Birth is a joyful but stressful time for any woman. Although society has changed, with family members geographically dispersed and women having children later in life, the typical woman is still likely to have the father or some member of the family providing the crucial support needed during delivery. Incarcerated pregnant women, however, are not typical women; they often have high-risk pregnancies and are likely to deliver alone in adverse conditions and without support from anyone. While a doula is intended to augment the support that the woman is receiving, it is easy to understand why incarcerated laboring women, economically disadvantaged women, and other high-risk women laboring alone with no support might benefit the most from a doula's service.[1]

Pregnant Women in Jails and Prisons

On any given day in 2005, there were approximately 98,577 women housed in jails and 111,403 in prisons across the country, Bureau of Justice Statistics data indicated. Obtaining an accurate count of pregnant women in U.S. correctional settings is not easily accomplished. Estimates ranging from 6 percent to 10 percent are found in the academic and advocacy literature.[2] Bureau of Justice Statistics estimated that 5.2 percent of women in U.S. jails were pregnant during 2002. This is likely an underestimate, as it is based on self-reports from women detained long enough to respond to the nationally administered survey. For state and federal prisoner, there are few nationally representative data on the prevalence of pregnant women on any given day. Bureau of Justice Statistics reported that, in 1991, about 6 percent of the approximately 30,000 women entering state prisons were pregnant. Out of 3.2 million arrests of women at midyear 1998, Bureau of Justice Statistics reported that 5 percent of female offenders in state prisons were pregnant on entry, compared with an estimated 6 percent of those entering jail.

While the existing literature allows for rough estimates of the number and percentage of women who enter jails and prisons pregnant, knowledge in this area remains rudimentary. There is no information on the stage of pregnancy at which women enter, their histories of prenatal care prior to and following entry into the criminal justice system, or specific information on birth outcomes of incarcerated women. Therefore, correctional administrators and health care providers must rely on a small number of studies of this population and draw inferences from other studies of women in the general population who share the same socioeconomic background and behavioral risk factors—which often adds up to high-risk pregnancies with higher than average negative outcomes. Therefore, almost any practice that would mitigate negative outcomes would be worthwhile and welcome.

The Evidence Supporting this Practice

Rarely is there such a long history and sound body of positive evidence supporting a practice than there is for using continuous labor support. Studies assessing the value of continuous supportive care during labor began in 1980.[3] To date there have been more than twenty published randomized controlled trials comparing continuous support during labor with routine care. A published analysis of the first five studies resulted in positive support for the practice; women with doula support experienced significantly shorter labor, double the rate of spontaneous vaginal births, and a 50 percent reduction in the rate of Cesarean and forceps deliveries.[4]

In 2005, a second review of an additional fifteen randomized controlled trials of this practice was published. These studies were conducted between 1986 and 2002 and involved more than 12,000 women. Again, positive general findings were replicated: reduced rates in Cesarean delivery, operative vaginal births, and receipt of any anesthesia/analgesia.[5] Other reported beneficial outcomes include significantly shorter hospitalized labor time and higher Apgar scores[6] of health assessment for the baby at one and five minutes.

The common denominator of these and related studies is the continuous labor support provided to the mother. What varies across studies is who provided the uninterrupted support to the mother and how much training the doula or companion received to perform this role. The range of training levels across studies included student midwives, hospital employees, doulas, or other laywomen with minimal or extensive preparatory training.[7]

Why Doulas Produce Positive Outcomes

The clinical trials cited in this article provide sound evidence that continuous supportive care during labor produces a number of positive obstetric outcomes, and biomedical researchers have an educated guess as to why it works.[8] Recent psychological research suggests that males and females do not respond to stressful circumstances in the same way. The classic human response to a stressful circumstance is "fight or flight." Researchers now suggest, based on earlier animal and human studies, that fight or flight may be more appropriately categorized as a male response to stressful situations and that females respond differently—they "tend and befriend." That is, females tend to their children to ensure their safety and befriend other females in an effort to manage stressful situations. The female production of oxytocin[9] and naturally produced opiods[10] during the tend-and-befriend response are likely to be responsible for the gender-specific response to stressors.

It is widely accepted that women naturally produce catecholamines (epinephrine, norepinephrine, and dopamine) when experiencing pain, anxiety, or fear during the stress of labor. Increased catecholamine levels during labor results in reduced blood flow to the uterus and placenta and are associated with decreased uterine contractions, slower dilation rates, and longer labors.[11] It is believed that the uninterrupted and befriend nature of the mother-doula relationship results in the mother's production of oxytocin and naturally produced opiods, which counteract and reduce the catecholamine levels in her bloodstream. This, in turn, facilitates the positive obstetric outcomes observed in laboring women with doula companions.

Doulas in Correctional Settings

In response to the unique circumstance and stress experienced by pregnant women in detention who deliver babies, Seattle's King County Jail experimented with a doula birth support program. The jail-based program was a collaborative effort among local doulas, jail health care providers, correctional staff, and local hospital delivery personnel.

Prospective doulas were selected and received two hours of correctional orientation training provided by the facility and sixteen hours of doula-specific training by the Pacific Association for Labor Support. The doula training involved instruction on the hospital's delivery routines, an overview of the foster care system, and information on addiction and pregnancy, labor, past sexual abuse, and other related issues.

Pregnant women who would deliver while in detention were recruited for the program. Each woman was assigned a primary and back-up doula whom they met prior to delivery. Doulas were notified when the women arrived at the hospital in labor. Once there, they offered continuous support to the mother throughout labor, birth, and up to three days post-birth.

Eighteen women, attending nurses and physicians, and correctional officers, were surveyed post-birth. All expressed a high level of satisfaction with the perception of the offender response, doula services, and with the program overall.[12] Comments from the female offenders included:

- "I would have been absolutely petrified if I had been by myself."
- "It helped me have a positive experience even though I was in custody. There was a guard standing at the door, she let me forget he was there."
- "Nurses were very supportive in their medical way . . . monitoring, seeing I'm breathing, stimulating the baby's heart beat when it dropped . . . where the doula was holding my hand, telling me it was going to be OK."
- "The doula gives steady support and values you. Makes you feel good all over."
- "A lot of times I had no clue what [hospital staff] were talking about. . . . The doula was explaining to me about the epidural; it helped me focus."
- "I would do anything to help support this program. You need somebody to support you, not just an officer staring at you."
- "I felt like there was somebody on my side."

The use of doulas has a very strong evidence base among women in the general population as well as high-risk women. Doulas have been effectively used in correctional settings, and a case could be made that incarcerated women delivering alone may need this service most. For a relatively small investment of $50 for pre- and post-birth doula visits and a flat free of $175 for doula support at birth, regardless of the length of labor, this practice has demonstrated improved birth outcomes, as evidenced by study findings. These outcomes could reduce correctional facilities' health care expenses through the reduction of Cesareans, requests for epidurals, pain medication, forceps delivery, and shorter labor times; as well as invest in future healthy child development. While it is not known how widespread the use of doulas is in correctional settings, the correctional departments of the states of Oregon and Washington have long-standing programs.

Endnotes

[1] Kennell, J., M. Klaus, S. McGrath, S. Robertson, and C. Hinkley. 1991. Medical intervention—The effect of social support during labor in a U.S. hospital: A randomized controlled trial. *Journal of the American Medical Association* 265(17): 2197-2201.

Klaus, M., J. Kennell, S. Robertson, and R. Sosa. 1986. Effects of social support during parturition on maternal and infant morbidity. *British Medical Journal* 293(6547): 585-87.

Sosa, R., J. H. Kennell, M. Klaus, S. Robertson, and J. Urrutia. 1980. The effect of a support companion on perinatal problems, length of labor and mother-infant interaction. *The New England Journal of Medicine* 303(11): 597-600.

Wolman, W., B. Chalmers, G. Hofmeyr, and V. Nikodem. 1993. Postpartum depression and companionship in the clinical birth environment: A randomized, controlled study. *American Journal of Obstetrics and Gynecology* 168(5): 1388-93.

[2] Centers for Disease Control and Prevention. 2001. *Women, injection drug use, and the criminal justice system.* Atlanta: U.S. Department of Health and Human Services.

[3] Campbell, D. A., M. F. Lake, M. Falk, and J. R. Backstrand. 2006. A randomized control trial of continuous support in labor by a lay doula. *Journal of Obstetric, Gynecologic, and Neonatal Nursing* 35(4): 456-64.

[4] Zhang, J., J. W. Bernasko, E. Leybovich, M. Fahs, and M. C. Hatch. 1996. Continuous labor support from labor attendant for primiparous women: A meta-analysis. *Obstetrics and Gynecology* 88(4): 739-44.

[5] Hodnett, E. D., S. Gates, G. J. Hofmeyr, and C. Sakala. 2003. Continuous support for women during childbirth. *Cochrane Database of Systematic Reviews*, issue 3.

[6]The Apgar score is a simple and repeatable method of assessing the health of a newborn immediately after birth. It is determined by evaluating the newborn on five simple criteria on a scale from zero to two and obtaining the sum of the five values obtained.

[7]Campbell, et al. 2006.

[8]Ibid.

[9]Oxytocin is a hormone that acts as a neurotransmitter to the brain. In women it is released in large amounts after the distension of the cervix and vagina. In the brain, it is thought to be involved with social recognition, bonding, the formation of trust between individuals and generosity. *See* M. Kosfeld, M. Heinrichs, P. J. Zak, U. Fischbacher, and E. Fehr. 2005. Oxytocin increases trust in humans. *Nature* 435(7042): 673-676; P. J. Zak, A. A. Stanton, and A. Ahmadi. 2007. Oxytocin increases generosity in humans. PLoS ONE, 2(11): e1128; Stanton, A. A. 2007. Neural substrates of decision-making in economic games. *Scientific Journals International* 1(1): 1-64.

[10]An opiod is a chemical substance that causes a morphine-like reaction in the body; it acts as a pain killer.

[11]Campbell, et al. 2006.

Barton, M. D., A. P. Killam, and G. Meschia. 1974. Response of ovine uterine blood flow to epinephrine and norepinephrine. *Proceeding of the Society of Experimental Biology and Medicine* 145(3): 996-1003.

Lederman, R. P., E. Lederman, B. A. Work, and D. S. McCann. 1985. Anxiety and epinephrine in multiparous women in labor: Relationship to duration of labor and fetal heart rate pattern. *American Journal of Obstetrics and Gynecology* 153(8): 870-77.

Lieberman, A. B. 1992. *Easing Labor Pain: The Complete Guide to a More Comfortable and Rewarding Birth.* Boston: Harvard Common Press.

Myers, R. E. 1975. Maternal psychological stress and fetal asphyxia: A study in the monkey. *American Journal of Obstetrics and Gynecology* 122(1): 47-59.

Simpkin, P. and R. Ancheta. 2000. *The Labor Progress Handbook.* Malden, Massachusetts: Blackwell Sciences.

Wuitchik, M., D. Bakal, and J. Lipshitz. 1989. The clinical significance of pain and cognitive activity in latent labor. *Obstetrics and Gynecology* 73(1): 35-42.

Zuspan, F. P., L. A. Cibilis, and S. V. Pose. 1962. Myometrial and cardiovascular responses to alterations in plasma epinephrine and norepinephrine. *American Journal of Obstetrics and Gynecology* 84(7): 841-51.

[12]Schroeder, C. and J. Bell. 2005. Doula birth support for incarcerated pregnant women. *Public Health Nursing* 22(1): 53-58.

Schroeder, C. and J. Bell. 2005. Labor support for incarcerated women: The doula project. *The Prison Journal*, 85(3): 311-28.

About the Authors

Marilyn C. Moses is a social science analyst for the National Institute of Justice, chair of ACA's Children's Initiative, and member of both ACA's Exemplary Practices Committee and Research Council. Roberto Hugh Potter is a goal team leader for healthy institutions at the Centers for Disease Control and Prevention. After August 2008, Potter became a professor in the Department of Criminal Justice and Legal Studies at the University of Central Florida. Thank you to James Fort, for the National Criminal Justice Reference Service, for his assistance in preparing this article.

Flu Vaccination among General Population Inmates in a Large Urban Jail System— Los Angeles, 2007-2008*

By Shweta Namjoshi, M.P.H.; Armidia Miranda, B.S.N.; Ann Carter, B.S.N.; Frances Kamara, B.S.N., M.P.H.; Haroution Arslanian, B.S.N.; Michael Tadrous; and Mark A. Malek, M.D., M.P.H.

Outbreaks of influenza within correctional settings have been described; however, there has been no report of an influenza vaccination program in the jail setting. The researchers describe the first such reported vaccination campaign in a county jail system in the United States. Using free vaccine and pre-existing medical services infrastructure within the system, the Los Angeles Sheriff's Department's medical services staff vaccinated underserved individuals, particularly those at risk for severe complications from influenza. The Infection Control Unit collected demographic information and estimated the vaccination rate for the administered vaccine. A total of 5,076 inmates were vaccinated in the Los Angeles County jail system from December 2007 through March 2008, accounting for approximately 4 percent of all flu vaccines administered by the Los Angeles County Department of Public Health during the 2007-2008 flu season.

Introduction

Influenza is an orthomyxo virus best characterized by its epidemic behavior and its ability to swiftly and effectively cause pneumonia (Treanor, Mandell, and Dolin 2005). Outbreaks generally occur during the coldest part of the year, and vary somewhat with geography (Centers for Disease Control and Prevention 2008, County of Los Angeles Public Health 2008). In the United States, approximately 36,000 annual deaths are attributed to influenza (Centers for Disease Control and Prevention 2008), and in 2005, pneumonia and influenza were reported as the eighth leading cause of death overall for Americans (Kung, Hoyert, Xu, and Murphy 2008).

In correctional environments, the threat of communicable disease, including influenza, may be especially severe because infection control measures are often limited or inefficient (Bick 2007). Unique factors that facilitate transmission of infectious diseases in jails and prisons include crowding and suboptimal personal hygiene, inadequate sanitation and environmental cleaning, and high mobility and turnover of inmates (Bick 2007). Jails, in particular, defined as local

The findings and conclusions in this report are those of the authors and do not necessarily represent the views of the Los Angeles Sheriff's Department.

institutions accommodating inmates with short sentences and individuals awaiting trial (Perkins, Stephan, Beck, and Bureau of Justice Statistics statisticians 1995), house a highly transient population.

With approximately 13,000 to 17,000 bookings per month and an average daily inmate population of 20,000 inmates (range: 19,500 to 20,500), the Los Angeles Sheriff's Department operates the largest jail system in the United States. With such high turnover, jail health administrators face numerous challenges to prevent the spread of communicable diseases using standard precautions alone. The high mobility of inmates between and within facilities in the Los Angeles system, compounded by crowding, further precludes strict adherence to standard precautions and creates an ideal environment for transmission of communicable pathogens (Bick 2007). This mobility also limits continuity of care and complicates disease surveillance because jail patients have no consistent medical home.

In addition, incarcerated individuals have a higher incidence of pre-existing medical and mental health conditions compared with the general population, including HIV, hepatitis (A, B, and C), tuberculosis, and methicillin-resistant Staphylococcus aureus (MRSA) (Bick 2007). MRSA, in particular, is known to cause severe necrotizing bacterial pneumonia following infection with the influenza virus. Recent evidence indicates that many of the 40 million deaths that occurred worldwide during the 1918 influenza pandemic were attributable to secondary bacterial pneumonia, and men ages twenty-five-to-forty (an age range that largely characterizes the inmate population) were disproportionately affected (Awofeso 2004, Brundage and Shanks 2008, Morens and Fauci 2007).

Given the high rate of transmission in jails, compounded by the poor health inherent to the incarcerated population, vaccination is the prevention strategy against influenza for jails and prisons (Awofeso, et al. 2001, Bick 2007), particularly because of the link between necrotizing pneumonia due to MRSA following infection with the influenza virus (Chickering and Park 1919, David, Mennella, Mansour, Boyle-Vavra, and Daum 2008, Etienne 2005, Moran and Talan 2008, Pan, et al. 2003). For these reasons, the Advisory Committee on Immunization Practices recognizes that nonpharmacologic interventions, such as hand washing and respiratory hygiene, and community-level mitigation efforts, such as avoiding mass gatherings, are not as effective for control of influenza as mass vaccination efforts (Centers for Disease Control and Prevention 2008).

The first reported influenza vaccination program among general population inmates was in a U.S. jail system. Between December 2007 and March 2008, the Los Angeles Sheriff's Department's Infection Control and Epidemiology Unit initiated a pilot vaccination campaign using the services of pre-existing, jail-based medical staff to administer free vaccines obtained from the Los Angeles County Immunization Program. The foremost purpose of the campaign was to maximize influenza control and prevention within the jail facilities and in the Los Angeles community. In addition, the researchers aimed to establish an infrastructure within the jail system for future vaccination campaigns. To enable other jails to develop their own influenza vaccination campaigns, the demographics of Los Angeles Sheriff's Department's inmate-patient population, the implementation of the Infection Control Unit's influenza program, and unique barriers to influenza prevention and control within correctional settings are described.

Method

Clinical services and facilities. Between December 5, 2007, and March 25, 2008, Los Angeles Sheriff's Department offered flu vaccines to all individuals incarcerated in the county jail system, which is comprised of nine facilities at three sites across Los Angeles County. Los Angeles Sheriff's Department's medical staff includes more than 500 medical staff nurses, who provide clinical services and routine "pill call" (the procedure by which nearly one-third of all inmates receive daily medication) for inmates. The system also employs five public health nurses and forty-five physicians. In downtown Los Angeles, there is also a 196-bed state-licensed Clinical Treatment Center and two medical services wards that house inmates with chronic medical conditions in the Men's Central Jail.

Each facility has its own nursing director, who oversees provision of clinical care in his or her facility. All male inmates (approximately 400 to 600 new bookings every twenty-four hours) are asked sixteen medical and mental health screening questions when processed and booked at the Inmate Reception Center, which is located in downtown Los Angeles, adjacent to the Twin Towers Correctional Facilities and the Men's Central Jail. Tower I houses primarily mentally ill inmates (n = 2,500); Tower II houses violent offenders (n = 2,500); Men's Central Jail houses a variety of different detainees (n = 4,000 to 5,000). Approximately thirty miles north of downtown Los Angeles is the Pitchess Detention Center; many of these inmates (n = 7,000 to 8,000) have already been sentenced to state prison. This detention center consists of five facilities distributed over a large ranch-like area. The Century Regional Detention Facility houses women (n = 2,000 to 2,500) approximately fifteen miles south of downtown Los Angeles. This facility operates its own independent reception center and booking process, which also includes sixteen medical and mental health screening questions.

The Vaccine

The 2007-2008 vaccine contained an A/Solomon Islands/3/2006 (H1N1)-like virus, an A/Wisconsin/67/2005 (H3N2)-like virus, and a B/Malaysia/2506/2004-like virus, which were strains recommended both by the Food and Drug Administration and the World Health Organization (U.S. Food and Drug Administration 2007). Fluarix (Glaxo Smith Kline), Fluvirin (Novartis), and Fluzone (Sanofi) were administered using a 23-gauge needle. All three vaccines are approved to prevent infection with influenza A and B in adults older than eighteen.

The Los Angeles County Immunization Program provided the vaccine to the Los Angeles Sheriff's Department free of charge. The Infection Control Unit, which functions as a small-scale public health department for the jail system, received the vaccine weekly. Cold chain (an uninterrupted series of storage and distribution activities) was preserved between 35 degrees and 45 degrees in accordance with World Health Organization standards (Matthias, Robertson, Garrison, Newland, and Nelson 2007), and the vaccine was stored in a refrigerator supplied by a power source connected to an emergency power generator. The Infection Control Unit maintained daily temperature logs and reported them to the Los Angeles County Immunization Program monthly.

Vaccine Campaign

Vaccine was available to all inmates upon request from general medical services staff. Informed consent for vaccination was obtained from all inmates prior to vaccination, and the Influenza Vaccine Information Sheet was distributed prior to or at the time of vaccination. Both consent forms and an information sheet were provided the night before vaccination in the Pitchess Detention Center; the Influenza Vaccine Information Sheet was given on the day of vaccination in all other housing locations. Fact sheets were distributed routinely in English and Spanish, and in other languages, upon request.

Although the vaccine was available to all inmates, mass vaccination efforts focused on certain high-risk inmates due to limited nursing staff availability. These inmates were defined as high-risk for the purposes of the program because they had pre-existing medical conditions that increased the likelihood of severe infection with influenza (Treanor, et al. 2005) or because they made frequent contact with other inmates and staff increasing the risk of transmission of influenza throughout the jail system. For example, in the Century Regional Detention Facility, Tower I, Tower II, and the Men's Central Jail, these inmates included pregnant women, men in medical wards, and men in three separate men who-have-sex-with-men dormitories. Inmate workers in all facilities were also vaccinated.

Vaccination was tailored according to security concerns in each facility. Vaccination in Tower II, for example, was more difficult because access to inmates awaiting trial for violent crimes was limited. In the Inmate Reception Center, however, two nurses were specifically devoted to vaccine administration during all three eight-hour shifts. Because all inmates entering the Inmate Reception Center are screened for medical or mental health issues using sixteen standardized questions, vaccination was offered at that time. Furthermore, vaccination was added to the existing medical screening protocol for inmates fifty-five or older (electrocardiogram and laboratory tests).

For inmates already housed, there were two main methods of vaccination, administered by two groups of skilled nurses. First, five public health nurses in the Infection Control Unit vaccinated inmate workers and men who have sex with men and transgendered inmates in the Men's Central Jail and the Twin Towers Correctional Facilities. Of note, one of the public health nurses or the physician director of the Infection Control Unit, along with a senior deputy, provided these high-risk inmates with an educational and highly motivational message prior to vaccination. Second, the medical services nurses made a brief announcement without any educational component, offering the vaccine to all other inmates during regularly scheduled pill-call rounds. Many of these nurses were recruited to fill overtime assignments designated for flu vaccine administration, though some nursing staff administered flu shots in addition to their usual responsibilities.

Data collection and analysis. Infection control staff captured age, sex, and ethnicity data using the consent form. Nursing staff collected the consent forms and best effort was made to impute missing or illegible data based on housing location. Data were analyzed using Microsoft Excel. The researchers were only able to estimate vaccination rates for a number of housing areas (all inmate workers and men-who-have-sex-with-men dorms, as well as a sample of less than ten general-population-housing units) due to the limited availability of complete census data. In the few cases, where census data were complete, the vaccination rate was calculated as the estimated number of vaccinations divided by the estimated number of inmates housed in that particular unit.

Table 1. Demographics of Inmates Receiving Flu Vaccine, 2007-2008 Flu Season

	Vaccinated *(N = 5,076)*	
Age	*n*	%
18-49	3,837	75.6
50-64	995	19.6
65-84	75	1.5
85 and older	3	
Unknown	166	3.3
Gender	4,780	94.2
Male	294	5.8
Female	2	
Unknown		
Race		
Hispanic	2,479	48.8
Black	1,309	25.8
White	727	14.3
Asian	55	1.1
Other	227	4.5
Unknown	279	5.5

Table 2. Number of Inmates Vaccinated by Housing Facility

	Number vaccinated	Percentage	Days offered
Inmate Reception Center	2,359	46.5	67
Pitchess Detention Center	1,708	33.7	9
Men's Central Jail	413	8.1	5
Century Regional Detention Facility	294	5.8	24
Twin Tower I	166	3.3	5
Twin Tower II	91	1.8	4
Clinical Treatment Center	43	0.8	7
Unknown	2		
Total	5,076		67

Results

Vaccination Campaign

A total of 5,076 inmates were vaccinated in the Los Angeles County Jail from December 2007 through March 2008, which accounts for approximately 4 percent of all flu vaccines administered by the Los Angeles Department of Public Health during the 2007-2008 flu season (County of Los Angeles Public Health 2008). The researchers were able to target a small portion of high-risk inmates (that cannot be quantified due to insufficient census data) because they were clustered in specific housing areas, such as the men-who-have-sex-with-men dorms or medical wards, as well as inmates fifty-five or older using existing medical services protocols, such as those used in the Inmate Reception Center.

Demographics.

Of the 5,076 inmates vaccinated, 1,073 inmates (21 percent) were fifty-years-of age-or-older. Most (75.6 percent) inmates who received the flu vaccine were eighteen to forty-nine years of age, male (94.2 percent), and Hispanic (48.8 percent) or black (25.8 percent; *see* Table 1). Among those immunized, only black inmates were underrepresented (25.8 percent) compared with the jail's general population (35 percent). Percentages of inmates vaccinated within all other racial/ethnic and age groups mirrored the overall composition of the general population of the jail system.

Number of Inmates Vaccinated by Facility

In the Inmate Reception Center, 2,359 inmates (46.5 percent of inmates vaccinated) received the flu vaccine, where vaccination was offered during intake screening using the sixteen medical and mental health screening questions (*see* Table 2). The second highest number of vaccines was given at the Pitchess Detention Center, which is the only area where sign-up sheets and fact sheets were provided to inmates on the evening prior to vaccination. The vaccination rate in the inmate-worker dorms and the men-who-have-sex-with-men dorms ranged from 30 to 60 percent. The highest vaccination rates correlated with occasions when the physicians' director and a senior deputy delivered a strong educational and motivational speech prior to offering the vaccine. Finally, in the Clinical Treatment Center, where a physician's order was necessary for an inmate to receive vaccination, forty-three doses of flu vaccine were given between December 2007 and March 2008, which is less than 10 percent of the eligible patient population in that dormitory.

Discussion

The researchers describe the first reported influenza vaccination program among general population inmates in a U.S. jail and hope that their experience will serve as a guide to other jails and prisons that do not have vaccination programs. The Los Angeles County Immunization Program provided Los Angeles Sheriff's Department with free vaccine, and the Infection Control Unit took advantage of the existing medical services infrastructure to administer more than 5,000 vaccines, though medical services nurses did not begin vaccination until January. The researchers vaccinated underserved individuals, particularly nonwhite males between the ages of eighteen and forty-nine, who largely characterize the incarcerated population, as well as individuals at higher risk for severe complications from influenza infection, including men who have sex with men, individuals fifty-five and older, and pregnant women. They were also able to establish interpersonal relationships and a methodology within the jail system to improve the implementation of future vaccination programs. The infrastructure of this program will be enhanced for the current flu-season vaccination effort and has already been expanded to other programs to include hepatitis education and vaccination and pandemic flu preparedness.

The researchers identified four components that were critical to the success of the vaccination program. First, free or low-cost vaccines can increase the feasibility of vaccination and buy-in among administrative staff. Both international and domestic studies indicate that influenza vaccinations (including those administered in mass-vaccination clinics) are cost-effective for people fifty-to-sixty-four years of age, regardless of risk stratification, and availability of a free or low-cost vaccine makes the program even more attractive (Aballea, et al. 2007, Maciosek, et al. 2006, Prosser, et al. 2008).

Furthermore, the influenza vaccine requires only a single dose, making it an ideal candidate to introduce a vaccination program. Second, vaccination campaigns that use existing infrastructure and jail-based medical staff are most successful because jail health care workers are familiar with the correctional environment and have legitimacy among inmates, with whom they have daily contact. The researchers earned buy-in from senior Los Angeles Sheriff's Department leadership and administered the vaccine to deputies and inmates in plain sight of each other. This presumably helped to dispel irrational fears expressed by the inmates and created a sense of perceived benefit among deputies, who, in turn, sought vaccination for themselves. Third, the delivery of strong educational and motivational messages increased the inmates' sense of self-efficacy as well as vaccination rates. Finally, distribution of consent forms and linguistically and culturally tailored fact sheets the night before vaccination seemed to facilitate vaccine administration, particularly in large dorms. Distribution of these materials during the evening prior to vaccination also increased vaccination, apparently because inmates were more informed about vaccine availability and benefits.

Though there is no report of any other flu vaccination program among general population inmates in the United States, current literature supports illness prevention by means of influenza vaccination as the best method to limit the spread of disease in jails and in the general community (Bick 2007). As of January 2003, three influenza outbreaks were recorded in Australian prisons, and the strain represented in the summer prison outbreak in the most recent case became the predominant strain in the winter epidemic of that same year, replacing more common strains in the general population (Young, et al. 2007). In addition, inner city children with a household contact recently incarcerated in the Cook County Jail were found to have a higher incidence of MRSA infections (David, et al. 2008). As evidenced by the linkage between MRSA in the jail and the inner city, compounded by the potential for severe necrotizing pneumonia in otherwise healthy adults, there is a pressing need for preventive care in the jail setting. Immunization of inmates returning to these communities may benefit inmates, but may also help prevent transmission of influenza and severe infection to a largely unvaccinated population (David, et al. 2008, Francis, et al. 2008).

Inmates are in close contact with people from minority populations during incarceration and upon release, particularly children under the age of five and the elderly, who are at high risk for severe disease and death resulting from infection with the influenza virus. Some of these populations have already been identified by a branch of the U.S. Department of Health and Human Services, called *Healthy People* 2010 (http://www.healthypeople.gov) as severely lagging behind vaccination rate goals. Currently, only 24 percent of black patients and 25 percent of Hispanic patients between the ages of eighteen and sixty-four are vaccinated annually, and only 32 percent of people aged fifty or older are vaccinated, though the American Academy of Family Physicians recommends vaccination for all adults in these age groups (Aballea, et al. 2007, California Department of Public Health 2008). Vaccinating inmates may thus help address disparities in vaccination among underserved age and race groups.

There were several limitations to the pilot program. First, the researchers relied heavily on risk-based stratification, which is less cost-effective than age-based stratification, simply because the jail infrastructure permitted a risk-based stratification process (Aballea, et al. 2007). Yet, with the exception of inmates housed in men-who-have-sex-with-men dorms, inmates on medical wards, inmates older than fifty-five, and pregnant women, many high-risk individuals, such as those with chronic lung disease, remained unidentified in the general jail population.

Moreover, health care staff did not make maximum use of social marketing strategies to promote vaccination among inmates. Newer programs, including a hepatitis vaccine program, have made use of video programming and other communication methods, but the researchers were unable to employ such methods during the pilot program. Finally, rate-calculation methods based on jail census and surveillance data were limited. Limited vaccination rate estimates were calculated based on the gross number of individuals vaccinated in some housing areas, but influenza-like illness, comorbidities related to influenza, and laboratory diagnoses in the months following vaccination were not recorded.

In closing, successful duplication of this program will make use of free or low-cost vaccine, existing jail infrastructure, and tailored health education for a high-risk audience. Vaccination programs such as these present opportunities for collaboration between local public health departments and jail medical staff to engender a dynamic of prevention in jails and prisons. In the United States today, close to one of thirty-three Americans is incarcerated at some time in his or her life, and the high rate of recidivism and the transient nature of this population proves that correctional health is a community issue (Bick 2007).

For inmates, medical care is an entitlement, but for inner city children, pregnant women, and the elderly who make contact with former inmates, jail-based vaccination campaigns present a tremendous opportunity to eliminate health disparities, which would otherwise remain unaddressed. Jail-based vaccination programs also present an opportunity to train jail staff for pandemic flu emergency preparedness. A network analysis of incarcerated individuals and cases of influenza in the community may illustrate more concrete transmission patterns between jails and the community, though there can be little doubt that jail-based vaccination campaigns present a tremendous opportunity to reduce health disparities characteristic of underserved populations and play an important role in the domestic influenza prevention program.

References

Aballea, S., J. Chancellor, M. Martin, P. Wutzler, F. Carrat, R. Gaspanini, et al. 2007. The cost effectiveness of influenza vaccination for people aged 50-64 years: An international model. *Value in Health* 10(2): 98-116.

Awofeso, N. 2004. Prisons show prophylaxis for close contacts may indeed help in next flu pandemic. *BMJ* 329(7458): 173.

Awofeso, N., M. Fennell, Z. Waliuzzaman, C. O'Connor, D. Pittman, L. Boonwaat, et al. 2001. Influenza outbreak in a correctional facility. *Australian and New Zealand Journal of Public Health* 25(5): 443-46.

Bick, J. A. 2007. Infection control in jails and prisons. *Clinical Infectious Disease* 45(8): 1047-55.

Brundage, J. F. and G. D. Shanks. 2008. Deaths from bacterial pneumonia during 1918–19 influenza pandemic. *Emerging Infectious Disease* 14(8): 1193-99.

California Department of Public Health. 2008. *Healthy California 2010 progress report* (2008 Update). Retrieved October 3, 2008, from http://www.cdph.ca.gov/ data/indicators/goals/Pages/HC2010Progress.aspx.

Centers for Disease Control and Prevention. 2008. Recommendations of the Advisory Committee on Immunization Practices. *ACIP* 57(RR07), 1-60.

Chickering, P. T. and J. H. Park. 1919. Staphylococcus aureus pneumonia. *Journal of the American Medical Association* 72(9): 617-26.

County of Los Angeles Public Health. 2008. Influenza summary 2007-2008. Retrieved March 5, 2009, from http://www.lapublichealth.org/acd/docs/Flu/ Influenza%20Summary_07-22-08.pdf.

David, M. Z., C. Mennella, M. Mansour, et al. 2008. Predominance of methicillin-resistant Staphylococcus aureus among pathogens causing skin and soft tissue damage in a large urban jail: Risk factors and recurrence rates. *Journal of Clinical Microbiology* 46(10): 3222-27.

Estelle v. Gamble, 420 U.S. 97, 1976.

Etienne, J. 420 U.S. 97, 1976. 2005. Editorial commentary: Panton-Valentine Leukocidin: A Marker for staphylococcus infection? *Clinical Infectious Disease* 41(5): 591-93.

Francis, J. S., M. C. Doherty, U. Lopatin, et al. 2005. Severe community-onset pneumonia in healthy adults caused by methicillin-resistant Staphylococcus aureus carrying the Panton-Valentine Leukocidin genes. *Clinical Infectious Disease* 40: 100-07.

Kung, H. C., D. L. Hoyert, J. Q. Xu, et al. 2008. Deaths: Final data for 2005. *National Vital Statistics Report* 56.10. Hyattsville, MD: National Center for Health Statistics.

Maciosek, M. V., L. I. Solberg, A. B Coffield, N. M. Edwards, H. S. Khanchandani, and M. J. Goodman. 2006. Influenza vaccination: Health impact and cost effectiveness among adults aged 50-64 and 65 and older. *American Journal of Preventive Medicine* 31(1): 72-79.

Matthias, D. M., J. Robertson, M. M. Garrison, et al. 2007. Freezing temperatures in the vaccine cold chain: A systematic literature review. *Vaccine* 25(20): 3980-86.

Moran, G. J. and T. A. Talan. 2008. MRSA-acquired pneumonia: Should we be worried? *Annals of Emergency Medicine* 53(3): 366-68.

Morens, D. M. and A. S. Fauci. 2007. The 1918 flu pandemic: Lessons for the 21st century. *Journal of Infectious Diseases* 195(7): 1018-28.

Pan, E. S., B. A. Dies, H. A. Carleton, et al. 2003. Increasing prevalence of methicillin-resitant Staphylococcus aureus infection in California jails. *Clinical Infectious Disease* 37(10): 1384-88.

Perkins, C. A., J. J. Stephan, A. J. Beck, and Bureau of Justice statisticians. 1995. Jails and Jail Inmates 1993-1994: Census of Jails and Jail Surveys. Washington, DC: U.S. Department of Justice, Office of Justice Programs. April.

Prosser, L. A., M. A. O'Brien, N. M. Molinari, et al. 2008. Non-traditional settings for influenza vaccination of adults: Costs and cost effectiveness. *Pharmaco Economics* 26(2): 163-78.

Treanor, J. J. 2005. *Mandell, Douglass, and Bennet's Principles and Practice of Infectious Disease*, 6th ed. Philadelphia: Churchill Livingstone.

U.S. Food and Drug Administration. 2007. Influenza virus vaccine 2007-2008 season. Retrieved October 3, 2008, from http://www.fda.gov/CbER/flu/flu2007.htm.

Young, L. C., D. E. Dwyer, M. Harris, et al. 2005. Summer outbreak of respiratory disease in an Australian prison due to an influenza A/Fujian/ 2002 H3N2 like virus. *Epidemiology and Infection* 133: 107-12.

About the Authors

Haroution Arslanian, B.S.N; Ann Carter, B.S.N.; Frances Kamara, B.S.N., M.P.H.; and Armidia Miranda, B.S.N., are public health nurses in the Infection Control and Epidemiology Unit, Medical Services Bureau for the Los Angeles County Sheriff's Department. Mark A. Malek, M.D., M.P.H., is director of the Infection Control and Epidemiology Unit, Medical Services Bureau for the Los Angeles County Sheriff's Department. Shweta Namjoshi, M.P.H., is a student with the Infection Control and Epidemiology Unit, Medical Services Bureau for the Los Angeles County Sheriff's Department. Michael Tadrous is a deputy in the Custody Support Services Division of the Los Angeles County Sheriff's Department.

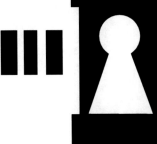

Section 7

Jail Mental Health Care

Identifying and Treating Mental Illness: One Jail System's Story

By Jeff Blum

S omeday, modern medicine may allow the exact diagnosis and treatment of brain disorders with the same level of certainty that exists for physical maladies such as diabetes or cancer. Currently, however, there is a great deal of subjectivity inherent in the process of diagnosing and treating what is commonly referred to as mental illness. For correctional facilities, this process can be particularly daunting because the lines between what is recognized as severe and persistent mental illness, personality disorders, trauma, addiction, and just plain meanness is often blurred.

Female Offenders and Mental Health

Diagnosis and treatment of mental illness in the female offender population has presented a challenge for the Davidson County Sheriff's Office in Nashville, Tennessee. As in most correctional facilities, the female population has doubled in the past fifteen years. All female pretrial detainees, convicted misdemeanants, and convicted felons at the sheriff's office with up to a six-year sentence were under the care of a private prison provider between 1994 and 2004. The private provider had total responsibility for the detention and incarceration of the offenders in addition to the diagnosis and treatment of mental illness.

In 2004, the sheriff's office constructed a stand-alone women's facility and began the process of transitioning the 400-plus female inmates from the private provider to the Correctional Development Center—Female. The sheriff's office decided to keep all medicated inmates on the same medication for a period of six weeks after the transition. At the time of the transition, almost 70 percent of the women were diagnosed as having a mental illness and were receiving psychotropic medication.

As the offenders acclimated to the new facility and the sheriff's office mental health care provider had an opportunity to review files, there was a concern that many of the offenders were being unnecessarily medicated. When the period of transition was complete, some medications were changed and others discontinued entirely if the mental health provider determined that the diagnosis of mental illness was inaccurate. As new female inmates cycled through the system and a more careful medication policy was instituted, the percentage of women on psychotropic medications was reduced by about 25 percent to an average of 45 percent.

A Change in Mental Health Care

In October 2005, the sheriff's office awarded the contract for medical services to Correct Care Solutions, which had subcontracted with the Mental Health Cooperative as the provider of mental health services. Mental Health Cooperative came into the contract with extensive knowledge of the sheriff's office's client base and the criminal justice system.

As the largest provider of case-management services and the only provider of crisis services in Davidson County, Mental Health Cooperative had been a primary player in the development of an extensive network of community and institutional mental health services focused on the criminal justice system. Mental Health Cooperative also brought to the process a database containing information on more than 60,000 individuals encountered during its ten years of case-management and crisis services. The information in this extensive database was critical to the changes in mental health care that would come later to the county's female offender population.

A History of Collaboration

Collaborative efforts between the Mental Health Cooperative and other mental health care providers in the criminal justice system started in 1994. The Criminal Justice and Mental Health Task Force was established through a modest grant from the Tennessee Bar Association, and—for the first time in Tennessee—the mental health community and criminal justice professionals sat at the same table and discussed common issues and clients.

It quickly became obvious that a core group of individuals with mental health and (in many instances) substance-abuse issues were cycling through mental hospitals, community agencies, and the jail. Despite a heavy investment of time and resources in these individuals by each agency, there was no sharing of information, or even the knowledge that these clients were receiving additional community services. Each agency was "reinventing the wheel" regarding these individuals without the benefit of critical information from the other care providers. The rapid but confidential sharing of information became the primary goal of the task force.

The current collaborative effort depends on the sheriff's office admissions list, which is distributed daily by e-mail to all the community mental health centers in Davidson County. Since arrests are public information, the distribution of this list in no way breaches confidentiality. To permit the reciprocation of confidential information from community providers, mental health consumers who come under the care of any Davidson County community mental health centers sign releases that allow for contact with the sheriff's office regarding diagnosis, medication, and mental health history if the client is arrested. Each morning, the providers compare the e-mailed admissions list with their client roster and contact the sheriff's office with critical information, making it possible to expedite diagnosis and medication.

The information provided by the community mental health centers is also entered into the "case notes" module of the sheriff's office jail management system, where offenders' names are flagged with a special-needs symbol that allows for quick identification, statistical analysis, and the development of comprehensive reports.

The sheriff's jail docket report, containing vital information, such as diagnosis and community mental health provider, is printed daily and used by a sheriff's office mental health case manager, who serves as a liaison to the courts on issues of mental health. The mental health case manager has been instrumental in diverting a significant number of defendants with mental illness out of the criminal justice system and back to the community.

A comprehensive jail management system report, providing individual biographical, diagnostic, release, and treatment information, is used in weekly case-review meetings attended by the sheriff's office mental health staff, clinicians from community mental health centers, and sheriff's office representatives from classification, security, administration, case management, discharge planning, and medical care. The information contained in the report, plus information from the broad spectrum of professionals attending the meeting allows for careful monitoring of offenders during incarceration and interdisciplinary collaboration at the time of discharge.

A New Protocol

During the weekly case-review meetings, information from the comprehensive report brought into question the sheriff's office's longstanding policy of uncritically accepting diagnoses from past incarcerations and community providers. Over a period of six months of these weekly reviews (where the arrest, incarceration, and release of chronic offenders were charted), a pattern was recognized.

Many of the female offenders were initially diagnosed either by a private medical care provider or during a previous incarceration at the private facility when 70 percent of the population was being medicated. Although medicated while in custody and provided with a discharge plan that referred them to a community mental health center upon release, a majority of these offenders did not pursue treatment or medication in the community, returning to prostitution or other drug-related activities. Upon rearrest, offenders would request their previously prescribed medication even though they were not taking the medication in the community. And, because of the aggressive medication policy of the sheriff's office, the medication was being provided based on the offenders' past history.

Clinicians from the community mental health centers began questioning many of the diagnoses and the prescribed medications. The sheriff's office policy of providing medication based on previous history, and this particular population's use of crack while in the community, resulted in their being under chemical influence for years at a time. Therefore, a protocol was instituted that allowed for a thirty-day period of detoxification for any offender entering the system whose profile included a questionable diagnosis, substance abuse, and a pattern of medication compliance only while incarcerated. During this thirty-day period, offenders were closely monitored for any negative effects from the detoxification process and medicated if they developed clear symptoms of a psychotic disorder.

More than Statistics

The results were startling. The percentage of women on psychotropic medication was cut by more than one-third, from 48 percent to 30 percent in six months—and the percentage has remained stable at 25 to 28 percent for the past five months. More importantly, however, many of the women learned through the detoxification protocol and substance abuse treatment that they can cope well without legal or illegal drugs.

In a sense, while trying to be part of the cure, the previous medication policy of the sheriff's office had been encouraging the very dependence upon chemicals that its treatment programs were trying to eliminate. Proper diagnosis allowed these offenders to confront and deal with the issues that had locked them into a cycle of chemical dependence and criminality.

The Opposition

As the new policy was implemented, and the amount of medication being distributed among the inmate population decreased, opposition arose from two distinct groups: inmates and correctional officers.

For many inmates, a mental health diagnosis had become an excuse for their criminal behavior—and the medication a substitute for the chemicals they abused on the street. Taking away the diagnosis and the medication forced them to come to grips with the true circumstances of their behavior and experience thought and emotion unaffected by chemicals.

For correctional officers, medication had become a chemical restraint. Under previous mental health care providers, powerful medications were administered for "sleep disorders," and many inmates literally slept through their period of incarceration. With the discontinuation of these medications, officers complained that the inmates were "too active" and "weren't sleeping all day," which made their jobs more difficult.

A Healthy Debate

Some mental health professionals may take issue with the sheriff's office medication policies. They may credit the drop in the percentage of inmates on psychotropic medication as a function of under-diagnosis rather than careful screening, observation, and medication management.

Recent headlines generated by the Bureau of Justice Statistics' Special Report, "Mental Health Problems of Prison and Jail Inmates," indicate that more than 55 percent of male inmates and 73 percent of female inmates are mentally ill. It is only by delving deeper into the substance of the report that one learns that "The surveys did not assess the severity or duration of the symptoms, and no exclusions were made for symptoms due to medical illness, bereavement or substance use." In other words, if in the past year an individual experienced psychosis while high on cocaine, according to the Bureau of Justice Statistics study, he or she had a "mental problem" rather than a substance-abuse problem. If while incarcerated an offender learns of the death of his or her mother and that offender felt sad, it was counted as a "mental health problem" rather than a normal and healthy expression of grief.

By using the subjective label "mental problem," based on symptoms that may not be the result of the more clinical and objective finding of a severe and persistent mental illness, the Bureau of Justice Statistics may have furthered the negative public perception that inmates are "crazy" and, therefore, unpredictable and dangerous. Painting with such a broad brush inexorably links mental illness with criminality. It also exacerbates the existing stigma for individuals with a true, severe, and persistent mental illness, who never encounter the criminal justice system, as well as for those discharged with mental illness,who have been stabilized during incarceration and present no imminent danger to the community.

Toward a More Humane Treatment Philosophy

Recent changes in treatment and medication policies in the Davidson County Sheriff's Office can be seen as an admission of a past error in judgment; it equated a liberal diagnosis and medication policy with humane treatment of the offender population. As an institution, the sheriff's office had bought into the hype that pervades American culture and is prevalent in the offender population—that every problem can be solved with a label and a pill.

With guidance from professionals at the Mental Health Cooperative, the administrators in the sheriff's office have come to the realization that the most humane treatment is the least-intrusive intervention, free from stigmatizing labels, false promises, and excuses for behavior. This is not an institutional excuse for minimizing services; rather, it is a mandate to expend the necessary resources to ensure accurate diagnosis and appropriate treatment. With this focus on proper diagnosis, the Davidson County Sheriff's Office reaps the benefits of a reduction in unnecessary and possibly harmful medication, while addressing the real issues that lock many inmates into an almost endless cycle of addiction, crime, and incarceration.

About the Author

Jeff Blum is the mental health coordinator for the Davidson County Sheriff's Office in Nashville, Tennessee.

Judge Steven Leifman Advocates for the Mentally Ill*

By Susan L. Clayton

"When I became a judge, I had no idea that I was becoming a gate-keeper to the largest psychiatric facility in the state of Florida— the Miami-Dade Jail," said Miami-Dade Judge Steven Leifman, keynote speaker at the Healthcare Professional Interest Section's Special Session and Luncheon at ACA's 2009 Winter Conference in Kissimmee, Florida. Since April 2007, Leifman has served as special advisor on criminal justice and mental health for the Florida Supreme Court.

Leifman began his address by sharing *The Forgotten Floor*, a video filmed by local Miami-Dade media in 2006. It highlighted some of the challenges faced by the Miami-Dade Jail in dealing with mentally ill offenders and the unfavorable conditions that these offenders lived in at the time of their convictions. Although the video was disturbing in spots, Leifman noted that "If we don't look at what is really going on out there, we will never be able to fix it." He said the video was an example of the difficult and complex problems facing the justice system.

Leifman stressed the need to decrease inappropriate and costly involvement of people with mental illnesses in the criminal justice system by increasing access to comprehensive and cost-effective community-based services that target specialized treatment needs.

Leifman, who also serves as chair of the 11th Judicial Circuit of Florida's Mental Health Committee, created the 11th Judicial District Criminal Mental Health Project. This initiative, which includes both pre-arrest and post-arrest diversion programs, brings together the justice system, law enforcement, and community resources to divert low-level offenders with mental illnesses away from incarceration. Miami-Dade County has seen reductions in arrests and recidivism rates among people with mental illnesses; the burden of providing psychiatric services through the jail has decreased; and the county is saving money.

Leifman became involved with mentally ill offenders about eight years ago when he promised a couple that he would help obtain treatment for their son who was mentally ill and had been convicted of a low-level crime. As a county court judge at the time, he could not involuntarily hospitalize someone. Leifman realized there was nothing he could do, and he would not be able to keep his promise to the offender's parents.

From this experience, Leifman said, he learned three important things. The first is that Miami-Dade has the largest percentage of people with mental illness of any urban area in the United States. In fact, 9.1 percent (more than 210,000 people) of the general population in Miami-Dade County have a serious mental

*ACA thanks MHM Correctional Services, Inc. for its very generous sponsorship of this event.

illness. Because the state is only treating 13 percent of them, many others end up in jail, Leifman said. "On any given day we have approximately 1,200 people on psychotropic medication, making us the largest psychiatric warehouse in the state of Florida—occupying nine floors of our main jail. Because conditions are not conducive for treatment, people with mental illness in jails are staying eight times longer than those without mental illness."

Second, Leifman learned that this is not a local problem; instead, it is a local, state, and national problem. Finally, he learned that Florida's mental health system and crisis care system, as in most states, was developed more than forty years ago when most people with serious mental illnesses were still in state hospitals. "And they [state hospitals] were never developed and designed to handle the most acute population among people with mental illnesses. We have the most fragmented, inadequate, antiquated systems of care for people with mental illness that is in need of great reform."

According to Leifman, there are fewer than 40,000 hospital beds for the mentally ill in the United States. Ninety percent of the country's mental health hospital beds have been closed, and the nation has experienced a 400 percent increase in the mentally ill offenders entering the criminal justice system. Last year, 1.1 million people with severe mental illnesses were arrested, Leifman said. He added that on any given day, there are about 500,000 people with mental illnesses in the nation's jails and prisons, and about another 500,000 on probation. Leifman noted that in the late 1970s, the Supreme Court came out with an order for the deinstitutionalization of state mental hospitals. But because there was no community mental health system at the time, the country never deinstitutionalized, Leifman said.

"Instead we transferred people from hospitals to jails giving them criminal records and making it much more difficult for them to go into recovery." Having a criminal record makes it harder to obtain housing and employment. Leifman noted that jails are now the primary place to house people with severe mental illnesses. "This is one area of civil rights we have gone backwards on, and it certainly speaks more about us as a society than it does about people with mental illnesses." The consequences of this failed policy, Leifman said, include an increase of homelessness, police injuries, police shootings of people with mental illnesses, and wasted tax dollars. "We have made mental illness a crime in this country," he said.

Last year, Florida initiated more involuntary hospitalizations than the number of arrests for robbery, burglary, and grand-theft auto combined, Leifman said. He noted that the fastest growing public mental health dollars are going to a forensic hospital, where people go after they have committed a felony. Funding for this has increased 72 percent. Florida's forensic hospital houses about 3,000 people a year (1,700 beds) and costs the state more than $200 billion a year, meaning one-third of its mental health budget, is dedicated to 1,700 beds. It is projected that in the next eight years the number of beds and the cost to the state will double, Leifman said. He also pointed out that in the last ten years there has been a 145 percent increase in the number of people with mental illnesses entering the prison system. "One hundred eighty percent of people with moderate or severe mental illness—8,000–17,000 people—will grow to about 35,000 in the next eight-to-ten years . . . Florida needs ten new prisons over the next five to six years just to house people with mental illnesses. The cost to the taxpayers will be $3.6 billion, which is more than our existing budget today."

Leifman told attendees that there was a crisis in Florida that led to the state chief justice appointing him to his current advisory position. Florida law states that once one is found competent to stand trial, he or she must be moved to a forensic hospital within fifteen days of the finding. Because this issue had been ignored for so many years, the hospital ran out of beds. So, according to Leifman, as the numbers continued to grow, people with mental illnesses got stuck in jails. Lawsuits resulted and the public defenders and sheriffs came together and sued the state of Florida and the secretary of the Department of Children and Families. A judge found the secretary in criminal contempt of court, fined her $80,000 and was on the verge of putting her in jail. The state took an appeal and lost.

In an effort to rid the backlog, the legislature and the governor allocated $48 million to rent 300 beds. "They did nothing to resolve the underlying problem that caused this in the first place," Leifman said. "We could have provided mental health care for more than 260,000 children or 60,000 adults. Instead, we rented 300 beds, which will be full by this summer." Leifman said Florida is now on the course for another constitutional crisis. In an effort to avoid this, the chief judge ordered a bipartisan multibranch task force to try to come up with a plan to resolve this problem. Leifman thinks they have.

The task force began by examining as much data and research as possible. Its members found that most people with mental illness in Florida have never come into contact with the system, but a small group of people keep recycling again and again. Leifman noted that the people with the highest need and the least access to services end up in the criminal justice system.

Leifman said that the problem should be looked at not as a criminal justice issue but as a medical one. With physical illness, Leifman said, "when we catch people early, they go into treatment, then go into recovery and most do fairly well." When people with a physical illness get sicker they see a doctor; however, when people with mental illness get sicker, they go to the one institution that cannot say no— jails and prisons.

Leifman said the task force found a huge gap between how science dictates how mental illness is treated and how it is actually delivered to communities. He pointed out that 50 percent of people with bipolar disorder are not only on the wrong medication, but the medication they take actually exacerbates their mental illness. He also noted that almost 100 percent of women in jails and prisons with mental illness were sexually abused as children and now suffer from severe post-traumatic stress. Yet, most communities do not offer trauma-related services to mentally ill people coming out of jail. According to Leifman, almost 75 percent of men in jails and prisons with severe mental illnesses suffer trauma. "As we continued to look at the system we realized that the case management services at the community level were inadequate. There was a lack of day activities, a lack of affordable housing, and a lack of employment opportunities, and very little coordination between the criminal justice system and the local community."

In response, the task force created a document that serves as a guideline and blueprint for Florida and other states that focuses in on the problem and creates an appropriate level of services in the community for this population. This is also tied into a reentry plan. "We will intercede and try to provide an entire level of services so you do not continue to recycle," Leifman said. "If you do not have housing on the day you leave jail and you have a severe mental disorder, it is almost impossible that you will succeed."

Leifman said that Florida has created a program based on one in Tennessee called "Crisis Intervention Policing," which trains local law enforcement on how to identify people who are in crisis situations, how to deescalate the situation, and where to take them as opposed to arresting them. In Miami-Dade County alone, there are more than 1,800 police officers trained. Correctional officers are also trained. This along with diversion programs help to keep people with mental illnesses out of the criminal justice system whenever possible. "The guiding light for us is if you are in jail because of your mental illness, we want to get you out. If you are in jail in spite of your mental illness, you need to serve," Leifman said.

According to Leifman, the task force's work and recommendations have been turned into legislation. "We got very close last session with approval in the Florida House of Representatives and it barely failed in the Senate. We are very hopeful that we will make some adjustments and we will be able to get it passed," he said. The legislation will help someone with mental illnesses as he or she goes through pre-arrest diversion, is found incompetent to stand trial, or is released from jail or prison.

"We take you and wrap our arms around you and we build the system that provides six essential elements: good diagnosis and medication, intensive case management services, day activities, trauma-related services, support for housing, and support for employment," Leifman said. "If you offer that, you can save the states billions of dollars in unnecessary spending to keep people out of the system or take care of them when they come out."

For example, Leifman said, 50 percent of the people with mental illnesses who go back to prison go back not for committing a new offense but for some kind of technical violation. According to Leifman, Florida has to build a prison a year just to house people who are violating the terms of their probation. "We have a long way to go, but we do think we have figured it out. I am very hopeful that at the end of the day this legislation passes and we will finally succeed in what the Supreme Court was trying to do in the 1970s when it ordered the deinstitutionalization."

About the Author

Susan L. Clayton is the managing editor of *Corrections Today*.

Managing the Mental Health Population at the Broward Sheriff's Office

By Winifred McPherson

S tudies estimate that as many as 700,000 adults entering jails each year have active symptoms of serious mental illnesses,[1] with the majority (60 percent) of symptoms related to major depression, mania, or psychotic disorders.[2] One study shows that the U.S. prison population will grow by 192,000 inmates (13 percent) from 2007 to 2011, and Florida is one of four states and the federal system that will account for 45 percent of this increase.[3] Unfortunately, these figures do not even take into account jail growth. The Broward Sheriff's Office has developed some innovative ways to manage inmates with mental health issues. To meet the needs of this population, a certified mental health team of correctional staff, mental health practitioners, and medical staff who are trained in managing the needs of mentally ill offenders has been selected.

Background

Brief History of Broward Sheriff's Office

Broward County has a population close to 2 million and only one jail system. Broward Sheriff's Office Department of Detention operates the twelfth largest local jail system in the United States with 5,722 beds and five jail facilities housing male and female misdemeanants, felons, and juvenile inmates for all the municipalities in the county. The facilities operate under the Florida Model Jail Standards and are fully accredited by the American Correctional Association, the National Commission on Correctional Heath Care, and the Florida Correctional Accreditation Commission (FCAC).

The jail's five housing facilities are the following: Main Jail, which is a podular jail that houses maximum/medium-custody inmates; North Broward Bureau, which is podular and houses the medium security general population, the infirmary, and the Mental Health Unit; and the Sheriff's North Jail; the Conte Facility; and the Stockade, which are direct supervision jails that house medium/misdemeanor-custody inmates. The five jails average approximately 5,300 inmates, of which about 850 (16 percent) are on prescribed psychotropic medication to treat serious mental illnesses.

The North Broward Bureau operates a 375-bed Mental Health Unit for male and female inmates experiencing severe symptoms of mental illness and those requiring specialized housing and treatment services. In 2007, the average length of stay for the mental health population was 76.28 days, compared with 29.02 for the entire inmate population. The units are divided into classification categories based on an inmate's level of psychiatric functioning and demonstrated institutional behavior. The "open" mental health units house the general mental health population, whereas the "closed" units house inmates requiring some level of segregation for safety and security reasons. There are also specialty units for intake, suicide watch, psychological evaluation, and transitional programs.

Certified Correctional Staff

Inmates with mental health issues are supervised and managed primarily by the certified correctional staff who oversee their housing, recreation programs, meals, and all other activities. The certified staff are administratively selected for these positions based on their work ethic and input from supervisors. They are then given specialized training to help them manage the mental health population.

Beyond the standardized training for correctional staff mandated by the state, Mental Health Unit staff are given a block of basic mental health training in the academy and during their annual in-service training. In addition, the mental health staff must attend forty hours of specialized, advanced mental health training. This specialized training, implemented in 2004, was used in 2006 as a model by the Florida Department of Law Enforcement's Criminal Justice Standards and Training Commission to develop a certified forty-hour advanced training class, "Managing and Communicating with Inmates and Offenders"[4] for law enforcement, correctional staff, and correctional probation officers.

Through this training, participants gain an increased level of safety and management skills; learn about social, emotional, and organizational intelligence to enhance human interaction skills; and practice communication skills to help them interact with individuals who have mental illness, substance abuse problems and co-occurring disorders. While initially costly, this investment in training has paid enormous dividends in terms of enhancing staff performance and morale and in reducing negative incidents. After implementation of this training, the Department of Detention saw a tremendous decrease in violence and behavior issues in several categories in the Mental Health Unit of the jail. The trend has continued as shown in Table 1 and Figure 1.

Table 1. Number of Negative Incidents in the Mental Health Unit by Category, 2003 – 2007

Year	Founded Grievances	Restraint Chair	OC Pepper Foam	Inmate-on-Inmate Battery	Inmate-on-Staff Violence
2003	44	81	107	262	70
2004 (First year of training)	53	57	64	218	38
2005	51	27	45	210	40
2006	22	37	54	174	52
2007	19	4	39	151	35

Figure 1. Percent of Decrease in Negative Incidents in the Mental Health Unit, 2003 – 2007

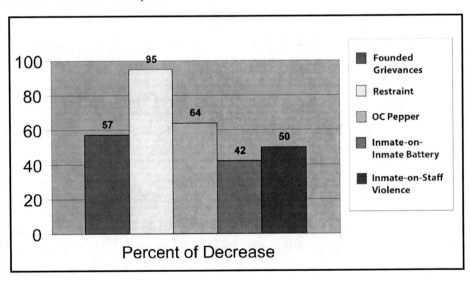

As a result of the training, there is a tremendous difference in officers' ability to recognize problems, communicate with inmates, observe behaviors, and interact with the medical practitioners on the needs of the mental health population. These performance changes are noted by the unit sergeants, who supervise correctional staff and inmates in the mental health unit. The sergeants prefer to have trained individuals working in their units because they understand the process.

Broward Sheriff's Office Mental Health Services Division Staff

The Mental Health Services Division consists of a licensed psychologist, a treatment supervisor, two doctoral interns, four mental health specialists, and two discharge planners. This team is dedicated to meeting the needs of the mental health population by developing initiatives, providing programs and other services, and tracking and interacting with the court system for proper placement of mentally ill offenders in the criminal justice system. The team also provides a variety of services for treatment that incorporate individual therapy, psycho-social group programs, psycho-education, psychological assessments, release/discharge planning, and deputy training.

In 2007, the division conducted more than 1,200 individual and 3,000 group therapy sessions for nearly 18,000 treatment contacts on the Mental Health Unit. Inmates receiving these services have consistently rated them very highly on quarterly program satisfaction surveys. Team members have advanced degrees in behavioral health care and are appropriately trained, credentialed, and/or supervised to provide mental health program services.

Contracted Medical Provider's Mental Health Staff

Broward Sheriff's Office has contracted with a medical vendor who provides mental health services to inmates who are incarcerated within the Broward County Jail system. These services consist of screening for mental health problems at intake, initial psychiatric evaluations, medication evaluations/renewals, crisis intervention, individual psychotherapy, and discharge planning. These practitioners include two licensed psychiatrists, a licensed psychologist, a licensed social worker, a licensed mental health counselor, a mental health sick call nurse, four advanced registered nurse practitioners, a discharge planner, and an administrative assistant.

The medical provider holds treatment team meetings to discuss cases that are of particular concern and to develop strategies for effective intervention as a crisis-prevention strategy. When not on duty, a psychiatrist is on call and protocols are in place to address medication issues and involuntary hospital admission. Agreements have been established with local hospital receiving facilities and the Crisis Stabilization Unit to accept inmates in need of involuntary hospitalization.

Special Needs Management Team Meeting

A special needs meeting is chaired by the facility administrator to address the most high-risk or volatile inmates. The meeting, held once a week, rotates between the day and evening shifts to include input from staff on each shift. The meeting is attended at a minimum by the North Broward Bureau's major, captain, executive officer, shift lieutenants, unit sergeants, and a deputy from each housing area, department mental health administrator/staff, contracted medical/mental health provider's administrator/staff (which includes psychiatrists), and the classification supervisor.

Not only do these meetings aim to promote teamwork, but they also provide opportunities for communication among the various service providers for identifying and resolving inmate problems and planning for any upcoming concerns. *Corrections Today* magazine, the *Correctional Law Reporter*, and the *Correctional Mental Health Report* are a few sources of literature reviewed for best practices and training for staff. Minutes from these meetings are available by e-mail and on unit bulletin boards to all medical, certified, and civilian staff working in the Mental Health Unit.

The multidisciplinary team approach employed by the Special Needs Management Team has proved successful in the management of mentally ill inmates. There are a number of key components to this approach:

- Teamwork is critical. It is more than a philosophy; it is a well-organized structure, which is the result of careful planning with specific mental health staff, North Broward certified administrators, and mental-health-trained correctional officers.
- The team provides consistent interactions, which enhance inmates' stability and result in good treatment, management, and security.
- The team operates under policies and procedures that reflect the needs of individual inmates. Understanding that each inmate is different and that his or her level of functioning changes, the team uses individual and group plans in the treatment and management of inmates.
- Team members understand that inmates are held accountable for their behavior and that discipline combines safety issues with psychiatric need and individual levels of functioning.

Mental Health Program

According to Martin Drapkin's 2003 book, *Management and Supervision of Jail Inmates with Mental Disorders*, there are basic elements regarding the management of the mentally ill inmates that should be present in every jail mental health service program.[5] The Broward Sheriff's Office Department of Detention has met and surpassed the basic elements of Drapkin's model by mandating mental health training for staff and implementing programs that rehabilitate mentally ill inmates and challenge them to prepare for transition back into society.

Discharge Planning

Discharge planning is a coordinated effort among the Broward Sheriff's Office Mental Health Division and security personnel, the jail's contracted medical provider, the courts, and the community mental health and substance abuse service providers. Considerable effort has been made to strengthen the partnerships among these entities with a focus on system integration processes to facilitate inmate transition planning. Broward Sheriff's Office and the contracted medial provider participate on the community's Forensic Task Force, which focuses on diversion of the mentally ill involved in the criminal justice system.

In addition, Broward Sheriff's Office convened its own task force, which includes local government agencies, and their contracted community mental health providers, to focus on jail discharge planning issues and link inmates to community-based providers upon release from jail. A seven-day supply of psychotropic medication is given upon release, plus bus passes for transportation, when needed. Community providers and case management teams from community mental health centers are notified when a patient they have been providing services to is arrested or when an incarcerated patient is about to be released. The Department of Community Control provides a *Reentry Guide* on local and other resources to link inmates to community-based services upon release.

Crisis Intervention

Broward Sheriff's Office uses Crisis Intervention Teams to assist with pre-booking diversion of offenders with mental illnesses. This program brings law enforcement officers trained in crisis intervention together with community personnel and mental health professionals to provide services to mentally ill individuals and their families. In the case of incarceration, certified staff work with the mental health professionals to bring the necessary services to the inmates. As a post-booking diversion, in addition to other programs mentioned, Broward County has a Mental Health Court, which was the first of its kind in the nation, to transition the mentally ill out of the corrections system.[6]

Mental Health Unit Housing and Programs

The Mental Health Unit is podular in design with twelve "open" dormitory-style housing units of twenty-one beds each and twenty-three "closed" segregation units, which have between three and seven beds each. Mental health beds are also allocated in the jail's infirmary. A number of different mental health programs are offered to inmates on the Mental Health Unit that are designed to meet the needs of inmates at different levels of psychiatric functioning. A more detailed description of the housing units and the mental health programming follows:

Open Unit Housing—These units house inmates with psychiatric diagnoses or moderate adjustment and/or impulse control problems that require scheduled periodic-to-frequent clinical monitoring. Inmates are able to manage their psychiatric symptoms for the most part and interact with fellow inmates and staff with minimal problems. Interventions focus on continuing or maintaining improvements in psychiatric functioning and the provision of various programming options. The open, dormitory-style units allow for increased freedom of mobility and access to programming and recreation areas. After a period of demonstrated stability of symptoms and behaviors, inmates may move to the general population.

Open Unit Programs—Psycho-social group programs are held on a daily basis in one of the open units. A monthly schedule is developed informing clients on each of the open housing units when group programs will be offered to their specific unit and the topic of focus for each week. Each of the open housing units is offered group programming at least once per week, and they are exposed to a broad range of psycho-educational topics. These include: understanding mental illness, mood management/emotional awareness, self-esteem, feelings, anger management, stress management, substance abuse, harm reduction/coping skills, thinking errors, communication skills, medication management, life skills, relapse prevention, discharge planning, and video therapy.

Intensive Program Unit—The Intensive Program Unit aids individuals in the development of behavioral options and the socialization and coping skills they need for transition to the general inmate population and the community. Individuals can be referred to or volunteer for these services and are screened for inclusion into the program. The program meets five times a week and offers a morning community meeting and an afternoon group program. This program unit, located in one of the male and female open units, uses a therapeutic community modality.

Closed Unit Housing—Inmates housed in this unit are in acute psychiatric crisis, present as a danger to themselves or others, or are grossly impaired in their ability for self-care, and as a result may pose a safety or security concern. This area houses inmates who may need to be segregated from others for safety and security purposes, and it constitutes the highest level of service need outside of the infirmary. Although inmates are housed in single, segregated cells, these units are not disciplinary segregation. As such, officers are expected to allow each inmate as much out-of-cell time as possible and may even let inmates out together to interact, if deemed appropriate.

Closed Unit Programming—Currently, mental health staff provide programs in these units to decrease the harmful effects of isolation such as increases in psychiatric symptoms and paranoia. This programming entails individual counseling, psycho-social groups, and therapeutic recreation and leisure activities. The overall goal of these activities is to engage inmates in the treatment process, reduce isolation, increase pro-social behaviors, stabilize psychiatric symptoms, and eventually move inmates to a less-restrictive-housing environment.

Transitional Program Unit—Inmates are referred to the Transitional Program Unit from closed units by mental health staff and officers when the inmate is identified as interested in, and in need of, the support and skills offered in an open unit. These units house inmates who require closed unit housing but are willing—and deemed appropriate by both clinical and security staff—to participate in a more intensive programming component that will assist with adjustment to incarceration and movement to less-restrictive housing. More intensive treatment services are provided and inmates are generally afforded dayroom access with the goal of teaching social and coping skills that will make relocation to an open unit successful. Individuals who voluntarily participate in this program receive individual and group counseling focused on effective coping skill areas such as socialization, communication, conflict resolution, anger management, and stress management, as well as any mental health or substance abuse issues they may have. Improvement in functioning is accompanied by increased privileges, time out of cell, and ultimately movement to an open unit.

Outcome Study

An outcome study was conducted to examine the efficacy of the Transitional Program Unit in meeting three primary program goals: 1) increased inmate socialization and engagement; 2) reduction in psychological symptomology; and 3) movement to a less-restrictive environment. Significant findings suggest that inmates who received fewer negative incident reports, complied with medication, and attended group counseling were more likely to transfer to less-restrictive housing upon program completion. Furthermore, inmates in the study demonstrated a significant reduction in the intensity of the symptoms over time. The findings suggest that for at least some of the inmates participating in the program, the Transitional Program Unit is meeting its stated goals and has effectively assisted them in attaining the level of functioning required for movement from segregation to a less-restrictive-housing environment.

Individual Therapy

Referrals for individual therapy are received by the Mental Health Division staff from the inmates, through inmate request forms, or from the contracted medical provider or detention staff. Upon request, inmates are assessed to determine the nature of their mental health issues. They then give written consent to participate and are assigned to a therapist, accordingly. Individual therapy is conducted weekly, or as often as deemed necessary.

Video Programming

The Mental Health Division staff conduct video programming with special needs inmates in all housing areas of the Mental Health Unit. These individuals are offered daily educational video programming several times per week, focusing on the mental-health-treatment-curriculum topics addressed throughout the week. The overall goal of these activities is to engage the individuals in the treatment process and provide them with additional educational materials addressing mental health and/or co-occurring concerns.

Summary

Every effort is made to identify the inmates who need mental health assistance and provide them with stabilization and rehabilitation services when they arrive at the Broward County Jail system. Correctional staff are afforded advanced mental health training to manage and communicate with the inmate population. The internal and contracted mental health providers, along with certified staff, collaborate in a Special Needs Management Team meeting to make collective decisions on the best care for inmates while they are incarcerated. This team effort is significant to the successes of the management of the inmate population.

The Broward Sheriff's Office has put a great deal of time, effort, and resources into designing a program that meets the needs of the mentally ill inmate population. It will continue to strive to ensure creative measures are used to deliver the best service possible to assist in inmate rehabilitation. From a jail administrator's perspective, these efforts have resulted in tremendously positive outcomes in terms of operations, security, staff morale, and inmate management.

Endnotes

[1] Osher, F., H. J. Steadman, H. Barr. 2002. A best practice approach to community re-entry from jails for inmates with co-occurring disorders: The APIC model. Delmar, N.Y.: National GAINS Center.

[2] James, D. and L. Glaze. 2006. *Mental health problems of prison and jail inmates.* Washington, D.C.: U.S. Department of Justice, Office of Justice Programs, Bureau of Justice Statistics. Retrieved from www.ojp.usdoj.gov.

[3] Deitch, M. 2007. Public safety, public spending: Forecasting America's prison population 2007 – 2011. *Correctional Law Reporter* 18(6): 81-96.

[4] For more information, visit the Florida Department of Law Enforcement, Criminal Justice Standards and Training Commission website at www.fdle.state.fl.us/cjst/Commission/.

[5] Drapkin, M. 2003. *Management and Supervision of Jail Inmates with Mental Disorders*. Kingston, N.J.: Civic Research Institute.

[6] Lerner-Wren, G. 2000. *Broward's mental heath court: An innovative approach to the mentally disabled in the criminal justice system*. Williamsburg, Va.: National Center for State Courts.

About the Author

Winifred McPherson is a major in the North Broward Bureau of the Broward County Sherriff's Office. Special thanks to Timothy Ludwig, Ph.D., Broward Sheriff's Office inmate mental health manager; Denise Vasquez, Psy.D., director of behavioral health for Armor Correctional Health Services; and Louis Diamond, classification supervisor at the Broward Sheriff's Office, for their input in this chapter.

Chapter 8

Aging in Jail

Aday Addresses the Needs of the Aging Correctional Population

By Susan L. Clayton

At the 2008 Health Care Professional Interest Section's Luncheon, Ronald H. Aday, Ph.D., professor of sociology at Middle Tennessee State University and author of several books on corrections' aging population, urged attendees to respond to the growing needs of older offenders in the criminal justice system. Aday began by pointing out similarities between the students with whom he works and the offenders with whom the audience works. These similarities include trying to prepare them for life in the real world, dealing with security issues, incorporating the use of distance learning in education, and attempting to control the use of cell phones. Acknowledging that he has never actually been employed in a correctional facility, Aday expressed his respect for corrections professionals. "I certainly appreciate the work that you do."

Aday noted various observations about aging inmates in jails and prisons, such as:

- The aging prison population represents one of the most dramatic changes in the jail and U.S. prison system
- The increase in aging prisoners is having far-reaching effects on all components of the criminal justice system
- The graying of the American prison system is a reflection of society
- The aging jail and prison population is also an international issue with other countries engaging in research and policy discussions.

"It is unfortunate that we are here today talking about geriatric inmates and that we have a society where we are keeping people incarcerated until the end of their lives," Aday said. Given that mandate however, Aday said the key is figuring out how corrections professionals can provide quality care to this population and how to prepare aging inmates to possibly transition back into the community.

Because older offenders often lack preventive care, engage in risky behaviors, have a greater risk of chronic and infectious disease, experience longer and more frequent hospitalizations, and incur higher health care expenditures, Aday has categorized inmates fifty-years-old and older as elderly or geriatric. He noted however, that the exact age is not what matters, rather it is the challenges the older population presents.

The number of geriatric offenders in jails and prisons continues to grow. Aday pointed out that in 1991, there were 33,499 inmates age fifty and older in prison. This number increased to 113,358 in 2001. Today, there are more than

190,000 inmates fifty and older in state and federal institutions. The same holds true in jails. He said that a 2002 national study of jail inmates found that 2.2 percent were elderly and that another national study of jails in 2005 reported that one in four jails has experienced an increase in elderly (sixty and older) admissions.

"It is necessary to manage diverse health care needs of elderly offenders in jails and prisons," Aday said. Corrections professionals must deal with elderly offenders first incarcerated after age fifty, chronic or career criminals, and offenders who are serving long sentences. Aday also noted that it is important to look at race and gender when developing a health-care delivery strategy.

Many aging inmates are mentally and physically frail. Aday cited several mental health concerns including:

- Forty percent of state prisoners, 36 percent of federal prisoners, and 52 percent of jail inmates report at least one mental health problem
- Forty-nine percent have received treatment with one-third after admission (25 percent—major depression and 27 percent received prescribed medications)
- Mentally ill/repeat offenders are serving longer sentences
- Three-quarters of female inmates have mental health issues and 50 to 70 percent of these report physical or sexual abuse
- Dementia is becoming more common among older offenders (memory/cognitive disorders)
- Some elderly inmates are transitioning into the correctional system for the first time
- Older inmates suffer from anxiety disorders, emotional problems, alcohol/drug abuse, posttraumatic stress disorder (PTSD)
- They may exhibit grief reaction to losses (life without parole, physical health, death of family members)
- Some have mood disorders, impulse control problems, and sexual disorders
- Many have high rates of depression and personality disorders
- Many experience stress related to fear of dying in prison or an unsafe living environment

Concerns of victimization must also be addressed, Aday said. He noted that inmate-on-inmate victimization is frequent, and said that there is a direct link between victimization and health. Aday interviewed 327 inmates in five states and found that "older female inmates abused as children or adults are less adjusted and more likely to report significantly higher levels of depression, somatization, anxiety, interpersonal sensitivity, and chronic health problems."

Aday said that older inmates exhibit a variety of chronic health problems such as hypertension, diabetes, arthritis, cancer, emphysema, kidney problems, heart problems, sensory losses and related disorders, hepatitis and infections, and vascular diseases. He also pointed out that some older offenders require special needs units and twenty-four-hour care, are frail and/or terminally ill, and experience incontinence. Correctional professionals must address these needs.

End-of-life care is expensive, Aday said. "Medical costs for older inmates require expenditures two-to-three times that of younger, healthier inmates." As an example, he pointed out that it costs $1,500 per week to care for an eighty-year-old inmate with lung cancer. Aday also noted that according to a 2006 study by physician B. A. Williams, et al., older inmates often cannot perform corrections-specific functions such as dropping to the floor for alarms, standing for head count, climbing on and off the top bunk, getting to the dining hall for meals, and hearing directions/orders from staff.

Aday outlined the following strategies for effective health care delivery:
- Trends toward managed care
- Geriatric facilities/prison nursing homes or assisted living
- End-of-life services (hospice, dementia)
- Assistance with activities for daily living levels of care
- Health promotion (nutrition, education, activities) and self-care

Additionally, he mentioned several best practice models around the country including the Northern Nevada Correctional Center's True Grit program that incorporates physical fitness, diversion therapy, and music programs. Aday noted that programs like this can be run inexpensively. "Success is a matter of using the resources that are available." Aday stressed that it is important to give older offenders things to do to keep their minds and bodies active, such as counseling, reentry programming, outings, health and wellness education, and job assignments. Individual and group work therapy (counseling, recreation groups, life history groups, grief groups, sexual abuse groups, and so on) are also helpful. "We don't engage enough in group work, which reduces depression and enhances one's outlook on life."

According to Aday, successfully transitioning back to the community for this population involves effective case management planning and public health partnerships. Case management includes looking at discharge planning and community placement orientation; Medicaid, disability and Medicare; veterans or Social Security benefits; volunteer companion services; family connections; occupational therapy skills; health records; medications; and treatment plans. Public health partnerships with nursing homes, public housing, home and community-based care, hospice/palliative care, and public and mental health agencies facilitate the reentry process.

Reentry challenges remain, Aday said. Many older offenders suffer from institutional dependency and feel secure in prison settings. Many have outlived family members or have disengaged themselves. In some jurisdictions there is a lack of compassionate release/discharge. Mental illness and crime histories are also barriers. Also, there can be a lack of organized structures available for inmates to succeed.

Aday noted that challenges for health care delivery still remain including:

- Crowding and financial constraints
- Rising cost of medical care
- Staff attitudes/knowledge of aging
- Physical barriers in most secure prisons
- Lack of community support
- Lack of correctional policies, programs, and facilities
- Diversity of aging inmate population
- Politics favoring "get tough" legislation

"Where do we go from here?" Aday asked. "Moving toward a geriatric justice system where we look at mental health issues of people who commit crimes later in life," is a step in the right direction. Sentencing alternatives for older offenders with mental illness also should be explored. Aday said the expansion of geriatric facilities and policies will be a must in the future. He also suggested that consideration be given to house arrest or safe community alternatives, as well as a second chance for lifers and compassionate release. "In other words, we are going to have to look at a lot of different options."

About the Author

Susan L. Clayton is the managing editor of *Corrections Today*.

Section 9

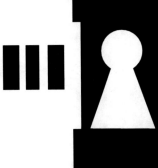

Reentry

SOAR: Access to Benefits Enables Successful Reentry

By Deborah Dennis and Dan Abreu

Reentry for state prisons and jails has become a national priority. Ninety-five percent of state prisoners will eventually return to their communities; an estimated 600,000 people return to their communities from state prison each year.[1] In addition, there are more than 12 million bookings into jail each year, with the majority of people detained less than one month.[2]

Reentry and Mental Illness

The Bureau of Justice Statistics reports that 16 percent of people in jail have a mental illness, and a similar proportion is estimated for people in prisons.[3] Advocacy groups and federal agencies alike have addressed diversion and reentry for people with mental illness, with comprehensive reviews of barriers and thoughtful recommendations for legislation, policy change, and program design.[4]

Transition or reentry services for people with mental illnesses and co-occurring substance use disorders include service linkage processes used in diversion and jail or prison reentry programs. Transition services reflect the shift of care from one system to another. They acknowledge the shared responsibilities of multiple systems to ensure continuity of care and service engagement as people move between the community and the criminal justice system.[5]

Providing transition services from jails or prisons is complex due to many factors: quick turnover of jail cases; the distance between prisons and home communities; the array of services needed to comprehensively address multiple needs; perceptions by the provider community that justice-involved people with mental illness are not responsive to services; and post-transition gaps in benefits that limit access to treatment and essential medications.

Despite the difficulty, there are compelling reasons to address transition. First, transition services are important from a public health standpoint. *The New England Journal of Medicine* reported that within the first two years of release, the death rate for those released from prison is 3.5 times higher than that of the general population.[6]

Second, poor reentry planning is costly. A study of releases from New York State prisons to shelters showed increased re-arrest rates.[7] In a recent study, providing people with transition and supportive services demonstrated a 53 percent reduction in jail days and an annual cost reduction of almost $3,000 per person.[8]

Lastly, there may be an emerging liability for jails and prisons that neglect reentry planning. The *Brad H.* case in New York City found that inmates with mental illness were released from the Rikers Island Jail with a MetroCard and a bag of medication.[9]

The court ruled that the New York City Department of Corrections had to develop specific release plans for inmates with mental illness and ensure community linkages, which included applying for Medicaid benefits for high-need inmates.

Importance of Benefits

Key to successful transition is obtaining access to Medicaid and Social Security disability benefits. Although benefit programs provide essential funding for mental health services and medications, few states or communities have developed legislation or policy to ensure their availability for people with mental illness upon release.[10] Consequently, hundreds of thousands of people with mental illness are released each year without the ability to pay for needed health and behavioral health treatment and medications. Without medication and comprehensive services to address housing and mental health and substance abuse treatment needs, people with mental illness have a greater risk of violation and rearrest.[11]

States and communities struggle to develop timely and efficient procedures that result in access to public benefits upon release from jail or prison. Many initiatives have focused almost exclusively on access to Medicaid. While helpful, focusing on Medicaid alone has some serious limitations. First, legislation enacted in some states, including Oregon, Illinois, New York, and Florida, allows for Medicaid to be suspended rather than terminated upon incarceration. Few states have fully implemented this, however, and the full impact of this legislation has not yet been demonstrated.[12] Second, most people with mental illness are not receiving benefits upon incarceration,[13] so Medicaid suspension does not help them. Few communities have developed procedures to process new Medicaid applications prior to release.[14] Finally, Medicaid provides only medical benefits and does not address the need for basic subsistence or housing.

In contrast, the Social Security Administration (SSA)'s Supplemental Security Income (SSI) program is automatically accompanied by federal Medicaid benefits in most states.[15] SSI provides a monthly payment that can be used to provide for basic needs and to access many subsidized housing programs. Housing is critical for justice-involved people with mental illness. The Bureau of Justice Statistics reports that inmates with mental illness are more than twice as likely to be homeless in the twelve months prior to arrest than inmates without mental illness.[16] Shelter use, both before and after prison, is associated with increased risk of return to prison.[17] Thus, housing is key to successful reentry, and for people with mental illness leaving jail or prison, SSI is key to accessing housing.

SSI focuses limited local and state resources on people with the highest needs and on people who use a disproportionate amount of unreimbursed services in the community. For example, a study in Rhode Island found that forty-eight "high utilizers" used almost $32,000 per year of services. Once provided with supportive housing and case management, costs for services were reduced by $8,800 per person per year.[18] Without SSI in place upon release, many prison and jail detainees with mental illness are destined to be homeless for extended periods and to face delays in treatment because of inability to pay.

The process of applying for SSI, however, can be difficult. This is particularly true for people with mental illness or co-occurring substance use disorders. Recently, best practices have emerged to address the complexity and challenges inherent in the SSI application process, and specific programs have begun to show consistent success in access to SSI upon release.[19]

The SOAR Initiative

The SSI/Social Security Disability Insurance (SSDI) Outreach, Access and Recovery (SOAR) initiative evolved to address the difficulties associated with applying for SSI for people who are homeless. Funded by the federal Substance Abuse and Mental Health Services Administration, SOAR provides technical assistance to help states and communities increase access to SSI/SSDI for adults with disabilities who are homeless. The initiative is based on an SSA demonstration project for people experiencing homelessness in Baltimore, through which 96 percent of individuals identified as eligible received approval upon initial application. SOAR, currently implemented in thirty-four states, combines strategic planning among key players; training of case managers and others to complete SSI applications using a specific approach; and follow-up technical assistance to address challenges along the way.

In 2009, thirty-two states in the SOAR program reported that 71 percent of 4,386 initial applications were approved in an average of eighty-nine days.[20] These results stand in stark contrast to the estimated approval rate of 10 to 15 percent for people who are homeless and the approval rate of 37 percent for all people who apply for SSI. There are limited, but positive, indications that SSI approval leads to quicker placement in housing. In Atlanta, all people approved for SSI through SOAR were placed in housing after being homeless for an average of three years. SSI applicants assisted in Nashville, Tennessee, homeless for an average of seven years, found housing within forty days after receiving benefits.

Application of SOAR to criminal justice settings. Some states and communities have developed prerelease agreements with SSA that allow submission of SSI applications prior to release from prison, and there is early evidence that the SOAR approach can be generalized to jail and prison settings with results equal to those seen in community settings. Implementing SOAR in jail and prison settings requires partnerships with community providers, including SSA and community mental health providers; training for jail/prison staff on sharing of information and improving procedures for acquiring pre-prison medical evidence; and translating prison functioning as it relates to ability to work in the community.

SSI outreach in prison. In New York, the Center for Urban and Community Services (CUCS) was funded to coordinate the entitlement process for people with serious mental illness exiting Sing Sing Prison. Beginning in 2005, CUCS piloted the SOAR approach and currently has an approval rate of 88 percent on initial applications in fifty-nine days on average.[21] In Oklahoma, the departments of correction and mental health collaborated to initiate SSI applications using SOAR-trained staff. According to Randy May of the Oklahoma Department of Mental Health, approval rates approached 90 percent. In both New York and Oklahoma, adaptations to the SOAR approach and curriculum[22] were required to successfully implement prison-based SOAR initiatives.

SSI outreach in jail. The SOAR approach has also been used in jails. The Miami-Dade County jail diversion program is using SOAR-trained staff to assist inmates to apply for SSI. Most individuals entering the program were homeless at the time of arrest, and more than 70 percent have co-occurring substance use disorders. Roughly 85 percent of program participants are diagnosed with schizophrenia or another psychotic disorder. With 146 SSI decisions received thus far, the Miami-Dade County SOAR initiative has an application approval rate of 84 percent in sixty-one days on average. The SOAR program is credited with relieving crowding in the county jail, as well as providing immediate access to safe housing with the necessary treatment and wraparound services. According to Cindy Schwartz of the Miami-Dade jail diversion program, early results show recidivism decreasing from 70 to 22 percent.

Using SOAR to make the outcomes of SSI applications more predictable, the Miami-Dade jail diversion program leveraged pending SSI and Medicaid benefits to advance county dollars for housing and medications. The expectation is that upon approval of SSI and receipt of Medicaid (both of which are retroactive to the date of filing or the date of release from incarceration), the funds could be reimbursed for use with other program participants. The individual consumer has the benefit of immediate access to housing upon admission to the jail diversion program and release from jail. In Miami, this strategy is an effective and cost-efficient way to improve the transition of individuals from the criminal justice system to the community.

In Atlanta, judges frequently require housing and treatment options to be in place before people with mental illness are released from the Fulton County Jail. Thus, many people arrested primarily on misdemeanors spend unnecessarily long periods of time in jail waiting for mental health assessments and post-release housing and treatment linkages. Working with the public defender's office, the chief jailer, and the local Social Security office, the Georgia state SOAR team leader helped to establish a prerelease procedure that includes SOAR assistance with SSI applications. Members of the SOAR team were given security clearance and access badges for the Fulton County Jail to conduct assessments and work on SSI applications on the units. Though a fairly new pilot, the SOAR Fulton County Jail project, according to former Georgia state SOAR team leader Kristin Lupfer, has already secured benefits for people almost immediately upon release.

Case Study[23]

A.D. is a twenty-two-year-old single male who was diagnosed with paranoid schizophrenia at age eighteen. He was raised in a low-income neighborhood with limited resources amidst family turmoil. His mental health began to deteriorate but went largely untreated and undiagnosed until he was involuntarily committed in 2005 with an acute exacerbation of symptoms, including delusions and psychosis. A.D. dropped out of school in the ninth grade and for the next three years was in and out of crisis units. His family lacked the economic resources and health care benefits to access treatment and services. They could not afford medications and did not know where to go or whom to ask for help.

In 2008, A.D. was arrested for aggravated assault after becoming irate, throwing a large rock at his mother and yelling, "Next time I will kill you." He spent the next twenty days in jail where the chief psychiatrist contacted the Miami-Dade jail diversion program. Program staff interviewed A.D. in jail several times until he agreed to a voluntary psychiatric hospitalization. The jail diversion team immediately began requesting records from previous hospitalizations and compiled a complete application for SSA disability benefits utilizing the SOAR model. His SSI application was approved in four days. Upon discharge from the hospital, A.D.'s housing and medication were paid for by county "gap" funds until he got his Medicaid card and started receiving SI checks.

Today, A.D. has a positive outlook on life that he attributes to the people who helped him get his benefits and housing when he got out of prison. He lives in what he describes as a "shockingly beautiful" home in a middle-class neighborhood where he has his own private room. A.D. has not been hospitalized and has not been arrested since reentry. He has achieved a level of recovery that enables him to help others as a volunteer at a nearby outpatient clinic where he also receives treatment and support services.

Conclusion

People with mental illness face extraordinary barriers to successful reentry. Without access to benefits, they lack the funds to pay for essential mental health and related services, such as medication, and they frequently face long waiting lists before being able to access care. They cannot access supportive housing and, without family, frequently become homeless upon release.

Acquiring benefits is essential to the success of any reentry plan. The SOAR approach has been implemented in more than thirty-four states, and there is programmatic evidence that the approach is transferable to correctional settings.

The SOAR Technical Assistance Center is positioned to assist new states and communities wherever there is the commitment to implement the SOAR approach. Acquiring Social Security and Medicaid benefits provides the foundation for the reentry plans to succeed. For more information about implementing SOAR in your jurisdiction, contact the SOAR Center at soar@prainc.com.

Endnotes

[1] Hughes, T. and D. J. Wilson, 2003. *Reentry Trends in the United States*. Washington, D.C.: U.S. Department of Justice, Office of Justice Programs, Bureau of Justice Statistics.

[2] Sabol, William J. and H. Couture, 2007. *Prison and Jail Inmates at Midyear 2006*. Washington, D.C.: U.S. Department of Justice, Bureau of Justice Statistics.

[3] Ditton, P. M. 1999. *Mental Health and Treatment of Inmates and Probationers*. Washington, D.C.: U.S. Department of Justice, Office of Justice Programs.

[4] New Freedom Commission on Mental Health. 2004. *Subcommittee on criminal justice: Background paper*. Rockville, Md.: Department of Health and Human Services. Pub. No. SMA-04-3880; Council of State Governments. 2002. *Criminal justice/mental health consensus project*. New York: Council of State Governments; Bazelon Center for Mental Health Law. 2009. Lifelines: Linking to federal benefits for people exiting corrections. Available at www.bazelon.org/issues/criminalization/publications/Lifelines/Lifelines.htm; Osher, F., H. J. Steadman, and H. Barr. 2002. *A Best Practice Approach to Community Re-entry from Jails for Inmates with Co-occurring Disorders: The APIC Model*. Delmar, N.Y.: The National GAINS Center.

[5] Osher, F., H. J. Steadman, and H. Barr, 2002.

[6] Binswanger, I. A., M. F. Stern, R. A. Deyo, et al. 2007. Release from prison—A high risk of death for former inmates. *The New England Journal of Medicine* 356 (2): 157-65.

[7] Metraux, S., D. Culhane, and T. Hadley, 2001. *The New York/New York agreement cost study: The impact of supportive housing on services use for homeless people with mental illness in New York City*. Philadelphia, Pa.: Center for Mental Health Policy and Services Research, University of Pennsylvania.

[8] Corporation for Supportive Housing. 2009. *Getting out with nowhere to go: The case for supportive reentry housing*. New York: Corporation for Supportive Housing. Available at www.csh.org.

[9] *Brad H. et al. v. The City of New York et al.* 2003. Stipulation of Settlement of the Supreme Court of the State of New York. Jan. 8.

[10] Council of State Governments. 2005. *Report of the Re-Entry Policy Council: Charting the Safe and Successful Return of Prisoners to the Community.* New York: CSG Reentry Policy Council.

[11] Porporino, F. 1995. The prison careers of mentally disordered offenders. *International Journal of Law and Psychiatry* 18(1): 29-44.

[12] Bazelon Center for Mental Health Law. 2009.

[13] Ditton, P. M. 1999.

[14] Council of State Governments. 2002.

[15] In eleven states, known as 209(b) states, the state uses at least one criterion that is more restrictive than the SSI program's criteria for determining eligibility for Medicaid. The eleven states are the following: Connecticut, Hawaii, Illinois, Indiana, Minnesota, Missouri, New Hampshire, North Dakota, Ohio, Oklahoma, and Virginia.

[16] Ditton, P. M. 1999.

[17] S. Metraux, D. Culhane, and T. Hadley. 2001.

[18] Hirsch, E. and I. Glasser. 2007. *Housing First Program: First Year Evaluation.* Providence, R.I.: State of Rhode Island and the United Way of Rhode Island.

[19] Dennis, D., Y. Perret, A. Seaman, and S. Wells. 2007 *Expediting access to SSA disability benefits: Promising practices for people who are homeless.* Delmar, N.Y.: Policy Research Associates, Inc. Available at www.prainc.com/soar/soar101/PromisingPractices.pdf.

[20] SOAR Outcomes. 2009. Available at www.prainc.com/soar101/pdfs/SOAR Outcomes2009.pdf.

[21] SOAR Outcomes. 2009.

[22] Perret, Y. and D. Dennis. 2006. *Stepping stones to recovery: A training curriculum for case managers assisting adults who are homeless with SSA disability and supplemental security income applications, participant guide.* Rockville, MD: SAMHSA.

[23] Personal communication. October 27, 2009. Cindy Schwartz, Miami-Dade jail diversion program.

About the Authors

Deborah Dennis is vice president of Policy Research Associates Inc. Daniel J. Abreu is associate director of the National GAINS Center.

Enhancing Continuity of Care through Medical Discharge Planning at a Large Urban Jail

By John P. May, M.D. and Nazim Hamid, Ph.D. *

Release from jail into the community can be challenging for inmates, particularly for those with health conditions that require ongoing care. This chapter describes a medical discharge planning program at the Hillsborough County Jails (Tampa, Florida) that connects patients to health and community services. During a two-year period, 1,872 inmates received discharge planning services. For those who needed health care coverage, 94.5 percent applied and were approved for the county's health care plan. Of these, 70.8 percent attended the community health center to which they were referred upon release. Program feedback from inmates was positive. Medical discharge planning fills an unmet need for inmates to continue care and for practitioners to transition care.

Introduction

Continuity of care is considered to be a defining characteristic of primary care medicine and a standard of correctional health care. The Institute of Medicine defines continuity of care as a core attribute of primary care medicine (Committee on the Future of Primary Care 1996). The American Correctional Association requires that continuity of care be established from admission to transfer or discharge from the facility, including referrals to community-based providers, when indicated (ACA 2002). Discharge planning for inmates with serious health needs should include formal linkages between the facility and community-based organizations; lists of community providers; discussions with the inmate that emphasize the importance of appropriate follow-up and aftercare; and specific appointments and medications arranged for the patient at time of release (NCCHC 2003).

This chapter describes a program of medical discharge planning at the Hillsborough County Jail, a large urban jail system in Tampa, Florida. The jails are comprised of two main facilities with a 2008 mid-year average daily population of 3,985 (Minton and Sabol 2009). Admissions to the jails in 2008 totaled 72,211, with 71,744 released. The program to provide formal continuity of care for inmates being released with serious health care needs began in 2006, under the direction of a private health care vendor, which contracted to begin medical and mental health services at the jails in late 2005. The cost of the program is primarily the staffing of a single, full-time employee, and discharge medications comprising less than 1 percent of the total health care budget.

* The authors would like to acknowledge the involvement and support of Sara Seltzer, Lisa Coyle, Dr. Bethany Weaver, Dr. Scott Hopes, Tampa Family Health Centers, and the Hillsborough County Sheriff's Office.

The Needs of Incarcerated Persons

For some, incarceration can be redemptive, a time for coming to terms and reform from harmful behaviors, addictions, dangerous environments, and illicit activity. But for many, incarceration can be destructive, especially for those removed from their fragile social support and network. Due to incarceration, many lose jobs, housing, property, employability, reputation, and/or family and friend support. For these individuals, the release from jail or prison where the basic needs of food, shelter, safety, and health are met, into communities without structure, support, or resources can be overwhelming. Discharge planning can improve the likelihood that this transition is successful.

For nonincarcerated persons with complex health care needs, care is frequently transferred and required in multiple settings. Incarcerated persons with these needs are particularly vulnerable and experience interruptions in quality of care and care fragmentation (Coleman 2003). Recognizing the risks associated with these transitions, and delivering patient-centered care, helps to mitigate the problem and bring better outcomes.

Every human being needs to meet the basic physiological needs of food, shelter, safety, and health. These were described in the classic analysis of human behavior by psychologist Abraham Maslow (Maslow 1942). Maslow's Hierarchy of Needs is often depicted as a pyramid consisting of five levels referred to as motivational needs (*see* Figure 1). The lower the needs in the hierarchy, the more fundamental they are and the more a person will tend to abandon the higher needs to pay attention to meeting the lower needs. In this context, the priorities and behaviors of inmates being released from jail or prison can be understood.

Figure 1. Maslow's Hierarchy of Needs

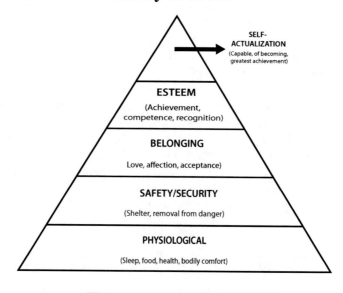

Before a former inmate can be successful within his or her community, he or she must seek to meet basic needs. An example of this pathway is represented in Figure 2.

Figure 2. Motivational Needs

The model of discharge planning at the Hillsborough County Jail identifies an inmate's level of need and serves to set the inmate on a path to meet those needs. Since health is one of the basic needs, it must be satisfied before higher functioning can be achieved.

The Medical Discharge Planning Program

The primary intent of the Medical Discharge Planning Program in Hillsborough County is to connect inmates in the jails who have ongoing health needs to community health centers upon release. The program also assists inmates in meeting other post-release needs such as housing and employment through a network of social service agencies. Inmates receiving medical discharge planning services are those with chronic health problems, including mental illnesses or substance addiction. Most are indigent, and many are homeless or transient dwellers.

In the development of the program, partners were solicited and developed by the medical vendor and sheriff's office and included the Hillsborough County Department of Health and Social Services, the Florida Department of Public Health, local federally qualified health centers, and various community medical and mental health providers. The discharge planner and sheriff's office social worker served as the liaisons with all partners. As the program grew, a part-time social worker from the Department of Health and Social Services was assigned to the jail through a federal grant to work closely with the medical discharge planner. Multiple social service agencies, including those providing employment assistance, job training, housing, drug addiction treatment, and other services, joined to participate in the effort. Meetings with primary partners occur once monthly, and all organizations meet at least twice yearly to identify ways to respond to the needs of those being released from the jails.

The Process of Discharge Planning

The coordination of meeting health care needs upon release begins when the inmate is first identified with a chronic health condition, typically during the health screening at the booking process. The inmate—now a patient—is referred to the jail's health care providers for evaluation and care. A treatment plan is developed that might include a referral to the discharge planner if the patient does not have an identified medical home in the community. The discharge planner then schedules an encounter with the patient, now client, to conduct a needs assessment. Clients are also referred to the discharge planner via self-referral, public defenders, or custody staff.

Based on the needs assessment, the client is prepared for release and reentry into the community. If the client cannot identify a preexisting medical home in the community, or does not have private health insurance, Veteran's benefits, Medicare, Medicaid, or other coverage, an application is completed to the Hillsborough County Health Care Plan, Hillsborough Healthcare. This plan was established in 1991 through an act by the county commissioners and funded through a one-half cent per dollar sales tax. It is a comprehensive managed health care plan for indigent residents with incomes up to 100 percent of the federal poverty level who do not qualify for other coverage. Recipients must live in the county for at least one year, be a citizen or legal resident of the United States, and not have more than $5,000 in assets among other criteria. Services are provided by a network of primary and specialty care providers, hospitals, mental health providers, and dental clinics through contracts with public and private providers. The plan is administered by the Hillsborough County Department of Health and Social Services with oversight by a community advisory board. A provision added in 2005 excludes persons with three or more felony convictions from qualifying for the plan.

Prior to 2006, there had been little formal effort to enroll or connect inmates in the county's jails to the county health plan. The medical discharge planning program changed that. The application is usually completed within fifteen minutes during a single session with the client, and requires demographic, employment, schooling, and financial information. The jail's booking "mug shot" is used for the application's photograph requirement. The completed application is then delivered by courier or facsimile to the county agency responsible for processing applications. Review and approval, including preparation of a laminated identification card, are typically completed within a few days. Priority approvals can be obtained within a few hours and a machine has been installed at the jail to print and produce the cards on-site.

The discharge planner identifies the participating community health center located closest to the client's primary residence. If the client is homeless, a shelter is selected with a nearby health center. Clients also receive detailed information about the clinic including location, hours, and scope of services. For some, appointments are made if the release date is known. If the client was receiving Medicaid or Medicare prior to incarceration, an application to the county health care plan is not completed, but instead the discharge planner provides information on how to reapply for benefits after release.

An individualized packet of materials is reviewed with and prepared for each client. The health care provider completes a medical summary and copies pertinent laboratory or diagnostic test results and information on how to contact the provider if more information is required. In complex cases, the provider will call ahead to the clinic. If medications are being taken, a nurse discusses their indications, dosing instructions, and side-effects. The packet is placed at the property desk for the client to retrieve upon release from the jail. Contents vary, but can include:

- A three-day supply of general medication or a seven-day supply of psychotropic medication, depending on the individual's need
- A prescription for a thirty-day supply of medication that can be filled at designated pharmacies or health centers in the county
- A completed summary of the individual's clinical history
- A Hillsborough County Health Care Plan identification card
- A transition package with information on short- and long-term housing, employment, food and clothing assistance, social service assistance including food stamps, disability benefits, and Social Security, as necessary
- A Community Resource Guide
- A public bus transit pass
- A contact telephone number for the jail's discharge planner

Results

Three preliminary indicators were selected to reflect the value and effectiveness of the Hillsborough County Jail Medical Discharge Planning program during the first two years of the program: a) approvals for health coverage following applications to the county health care plan, b) attendance at the designated community health centers following release from jail, and c) statements from clients receiving discharge planning. These indicators were measured from

March 2006 through February 2008, during which time comprehensive medical discharge planning services were provided to 1,872 clients, an average of 78 each month, or four new clients each weekday.

Approvals for Health Coverage

Of the 1,872 clients with chronic health conditions seen by the jails' discharge planner during two years, 1,521 (81.3 percent) did not have preexisting health coverage and completed applications to the county health care plan. The remainder (18.7 percent) had private insurance, veteran's benefits, Medicare, Medicaid, or other coverage. Of the 1,521 different applications submitted to Hillsborough Health Care, 1,437 (94.5 percent) were approved.

Community Health Center Attendance

Those qualifying for the county health care plan, 1,437 of 1,872 (76.8 percent), were referred to community health centers within the plan's network including several federally qualified health centers. These community health centers were later queried to determine if the clients used their health care services within the first month following release from jail. Of these, 1,017 (70.8 percent) attended and received a health care visit at a participating health center within the first month of release from jail.

Of the others, 351 (18.8 percent) did not require referrals to health centers because they already had a primary care provider, private insurance, received care at the Veterans Affairs hospitals, or previously qualified for Medicaid or Medicare benefits. The remaining 84 (4.4 percent) needed health coverage, but did not qualify for the county health care plan for various reasons. They were provided instructions on how to access public health clinics outside of the plan's network. It was not possible to track the health care utilization of those not needing or qualifying for the plan because they may have sought care at a wide variety of institutions.

Statements from Clients

Formal evaluations or surveys from clients receiving discharge planning services had not been done. Several clients during the two years, however, provided feedback on their own initiative to relate their experience with the Discharge Planning Program. A sample of unsolicited letters or statements follows:

- "I think this is going to help me by taking better care of my health and this is a chance for me to get myself together. I think this is a good thing for people like me. Thank you."

- "My life has been in shambles these past few years and now I have hope and help to change my life. I now have the county health insurance so that I can have free medical and a place to stay. No more homelessness."

- "I am just amazed that this program exists and I am thrilled about the great help I am being offered. This is an excellent opportunity for me to get 're-started' in life. I intend to use this chance to better my life. I hope this program would continue for those following me. Thank you."

- "It is most pleasant to meet and talk with the discharge planner to get help. When you feel optimistic, there is hope. I believe that this program is very useful and will help many as I intend to do. The discharge planner needs to be on a TV show for giving people hope in the future."

Discussion

Practitioners and investigators have long recognized that persons entering jails are unlikely to have preexisting private or public health care coverage (Conklin, Lincoln, and Tuthill 2000, Lee, Vlahov, and Freudenberg 2006, Wang, et al. 2008). For those who do, these benefits are often suspended or terminated during the incarceration, and reinstatement following release can be complicated and contain barriers (Gibbons and Katzenbach 2006).

Yet, even in a county that has offered health coverage for the indigent for more than fifteen years, we found a large number of persons (81.3 percent) identified with chronic illnesses at the jail who did not have health coverage or a medical home. The Hillsborough County Health Care Plan provides a unique vehicle for jail-based medical discharge planning as most states or counties do not provide universal health coverage, or something similar. Even so, other local and federal programs, such as the more than 1,000 federally qualified health centers throughout the United States, which accounted for more than 63 million patient encounters in 2007 (Henry J. Kaiser Foundation 2009), bear promise to jails for continuity of care when transitioning into the community.

At the Hillsborough County Jail program, nearly all (94.5 percent) who needed health coverage qualified and were approved for the health plan, and most (70.8 percent) followed up at their medical clinic within one month after release from jail. Although the long-term follow-up of clients receiving medical discharge planning services was not measured in this review, the short-term results are encouraging. The need was there, and the majority sought to fill it.

The results are similar to other jail-based medical discharge planning programs such as the Hampden County Correctional Center (Springfield, MA) where 65 percent kept their first medical appointment and 70 percent their first mental health care appointment within 30 days (Lincoln, et al. 2006). Research into continuity of care remains limited by differing definitions and measurement techniques. Visit patterns showing longitudinal continuity are a means to an end; they are not the ends in themselves (Saultz 2003). Patient satisfaction is another, and many patients expressed satisfaction. In the final analysis, jail medical programs should be most concerned with involving the patient in the process—from integrating patient-centered care at the initial booking function, through periodic chronic care clinic visits, and into the transition to strong, enduring medical homes in the community.

Limitations to the assessment of this program include the difficulties replicating linkages in a county that does not have a comprehensive health care plan for indigent residents. Also, outcomes related to the seriousness, complexity, or overlap of various physical, mental, and additional health conditions were not distinguished.

It is a muddle of medicine. Persons whose conditions require complex, continuous care frequently require services from different practitioners in multiple settings, but practitioners in each setting often operate independently, without knowledge of the problems addressed, services provided, information obtained, medications prescribed, or preferences expressed in previous settings (Institute of Medicine 2001). These patterns are even more blatant in correctional medicine. Recognizing the hazards inherent in failed health care transition planning, the American Geriatrics Society (Coleman and Boult 2003) issued positions that are also lessons to correctional medicine:

- Clinical professionals must prepare patients and their caregivers to receive care in the next setting and actively involve them in decisions related to the formulation and execution of the transitional care plan.
- Bidirectional communication between clinical professionals is essential to ensuring high-quality transitional care.
- Policies should be developed that promote high quality transitional care.
- Education in transitional care should be provided to all health care professionals involved in the transfer of patients across settings.
- Research should be conducted to improve the process of transitional care.

A jail-based medical discharge planning program can build transitions so that continuity of care happens. It must be patient-centered, providing care that is respectful of and responsive to individual patient needs. It should identify persons within the community who need, but lack, health care coverage and connect them to services and medical providers. The costs are minimal, and the payoffs can be substantial. Previously disconnected persons can receive health maintenance, preventive care, motivation for risk behavior modification, and access to social and support services to meet basic needs. Together, these resources can slow the progression and consequences of chronic disease, reduce acute events or deterioration requiring hospitalization or costly interventions, generate social service referrals and resources, and stabilize otherwise chaotic and fragile lives, thereby allowing individuals to reach for more and achieve higher level needs.

References

American Correctional Association. 2002. *Performance-Based Standards for Correctional Healthcare in Adult Correctional Institutions*, 1st ed., 1-HC-1A-04. Updated by *2010 Standards Supplement*. Alexandria, VA.

Coleman, E. A. 2003. Falling through the cracks: Challenges and opportunities for improving transitional care for persons with continuous complex care needs. *Journal of American Geriatrics Society* 51: 539-55.

Coleman E. A. and C. Boult. 2003. Improving the quality of transitional care for persons with complex care needs. Position statement of the American Geriatrics Society Health Care Systems Committee. *Journal of the American Geriatrics Society* 51: 556-57.

Committee on the Future of Primary Care. 1996. *Primary Care: America's Health in a New Era*, 1st ed. Washington, D.C.: Institute of Medicine, National Academy of Sciences.

Conklin, T. J., T. Lincoln, and R. Tuthill. 2000. Self-reported heath and prior health behaviors of newly admitted correctional inmates. *American Journal of Public Health* 90: 1939-41.

Gibbons, J. and N. Katzenbach. 2006. *Confronting Confinement: A Report of the Commission on Safety and Abuse in America's Prisons*. New York: Vera Institute of Justice.

Henry J. Kaiser Family Foundation, The. 2008. National Association of Community Health Centers, Inc., *Analysis of the 2007 Uniform Data System*, Bureau of Primary Health Care, Health Resources and Services Administration, Department of Health and Human Services.

Institute of Medicine. 2001. *Crossing the Quality Chasm: A New Health System of the 21st Century*. Washington, D.C.: National Academy Press, 1-22.

Lee, J., D. Vlahov, and N. Freudenberg. 2006. Primary care and health insurance among women released from New York City jails. *Journal of Health Care for the Poor and Underserved 17*: 200-17.

Lincoln, T., S. Kennedy, R. Tuthill, C. Roberts, et al. 2006. Facilitators and barriers to continuity healthcare after jail: A community-integrated program. *Journal of Ambulatory Care Management* 29(1): 2-16.

Maslow, A. H. 1942. A theory of human motivation. *Psychological Review* 50: 370-96.

Minton, T. D. and W. J. Sabol. 2009. *Jail inmates at mid-year 2008* (NCJ 225709).Washington, D.C.: Bureau of Justice Statistics.

National Commission on Correctional Health Care. 2003. *Standards for Health Services in Jails*, J-E-13. Chicago: NCCHC.

Saultz, J. W. 2003. Defining and measuring interpersonal continuity of care. *Annals of Family Medicine* 1: 134-43.

Wang, E. A., M. C. White, R. Jamison, et al. Discharge planning and continuity of health care: Findings from the San Francisco County Jail. *American Journal of Public Health* 98: 2182-84.

About the Authors

John P. May, M.D., is chief medical officer at Armor Correctional Health Services and clinical associate professor at NOVA Southeastern University College of Osteopathic Medicine in Miami, Florida. Nazim Hamid, Ph.D., is a discharge planner at Armor Correctional Health Services in Tampa, Florida.

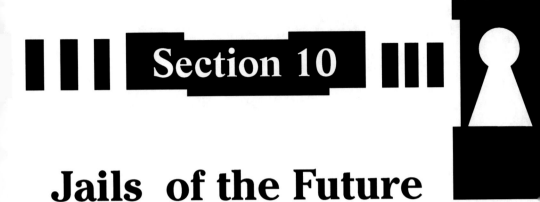

Section 10

Jails of the Future

Jails of the Future: Design, Operations, and Offenders

By William Sturgeon

Now that the first decade of the twenty-first century has past, the future of the criminal justice world is becoming clearer. It is obvious to this writer that the criminal justice world will have to make some significant changes to cope with the challenges that it is facing.

My personal experience with jails goes back thirty-five years when the majority of the offenders were in jail for petty misdemeanors. Many were addicted to alcohol. Back then, there was the occasional "really bad guy," the murderer, armed robber, and rapist. Yet, these "really" bad guys were in the minority of most jail populations. Today, the county jails have been transformed into first-rate penal institutions.

Over the past several years, a great many jails have been designed to be operationally efficient while also being pleasing to the eye. The current jails have become masterpieces of architecture. I am not sure that this is how the jails of the future will look. There are a great many areas in play when one tries to look into the future. Some of the areas that I have referenced prior to writing this chapter are the following:

- Worldwide terrorism
- Worldwide economics
- Greening of America
- Characteristics of future offenders
- Characteristics of future staff

These areas above will greatly influence the design, operations, and staffing of the jails of the future.

Worldwide Terrorism

With the advent of worldwide terrorism, external attacks on jails and/or other criminal justice facilities are becoming commonplace in other areas of the world. It is not too far a stretch to see these tactics used here in America. Jails/prisons have been attacked over the past several years by a variety of terrorist groups in an attempt to free their compatriots, kill their opponents, and/or embarrass the government. American jails have never been constructed to repel attacks from external forces and, therefore, are vulnerable to attack.

Worldwide Economics

At the writing of this chapter, the world, in general, and the United States, in particular, is experiencing a severe recession. California and other states are toying with declaring bankruptcy. As a cost-saving endeavor, California is considering releasing non-violent inmates early. How will worldwide economics affect the construction, operations, and staffing of the jails of the future?

The jails constructed over the past 100 years have a multiplicity of different types of design and construction materials. These jails were constructed during much different eras, when money was more available and the construction of jails and prisons appeared to be the answer to America's problems.

My belief is that the jails of the future will take on an entirely new look and will have completely new operational methodologies. Staffing levels will be drastically reduced. Society, I believe, has come to the realization that it can no longer afford to incarcerate the numbers of people that it currently has in its jails and prisons using the same methods they are currently using.

The Greening of America

The jails of the future will have to conform to all of the energy-efficient standards for construction and operations. Additionally, recycling will become an integral part of the day-to-operations. Years ago, some jails and a great many prisons started a recycling effort. After a time, many of them abandoned the effort due to an excess of contraband, as well as health and safety issues. Perhaps the future jails will not experience the same issues with recycling.

Characteristics of Future Offenders

Anecdotal evidence shows that future offenders will be younger and more violent. Street and prison gang members will constitute a significant percentage of the general populations.

Additionally, these future offenders will be poorly educated and will have few if any skills that could be used in jail (plumbers, electricians, carpenters, cooks, and so forth). A number of the future offenders will be high school dropouts.

In the future, county jails will continue to incarcerate an inordinate number of offenders with mental health issues. This unique segment of jail populations of the future will continue to cause considerable budget issues. The cost of psychotropic drugs, specialized staffing, and housing areas will add to already strapped budgets.

Characteristics of Future Staff

I believe that it is safe to predict that the jail of the future will have far fewer staff to operate them than they do currently. The reason for this is because of the cost of human resources (staff), their salaries and benefit packages. I believe that new jails will be designed differently than current facilities to insure that fewer staff will be needed.

Jails of the future will fully incorporate cutting-edge technology into their daily and emergency operations. This technology will help in reducing staff demands, and will assist in controlling offenders. The staff of the future will be better educated and trained so that they can operate the high tech equipment and be able to interact with the offenders, which may be through a monitor in the offenders' cells. This increase in educational requirements will require the staff to be better compensated than current staff.

Design

While the jails of the 1990s and early 2000s are pleasing to eye, they are, in my opinion, vulnerable to external attacks. With terrorists using car bombs, satchel charges, and other types of explosives, these beautiful buildings could become killing zones. Here is just one example: Many of these new jails have glass fronts that make them susceptible to explosions where the glass could become deadly shrapnel.

Perimeters have taken on new a role, that of being the first defense to intruders rather than their old correctional job of being the last barrier to escape. It is my belief that perimeter security will have to take these things into consideration:

1. Depending on the physical location of the jail, "blast walls" may have to be installed.
2. The exterior walls of the facility will be constructed of blast-resistant materials.
3. High-rise metro jails will become a thing of the past because of the difficulties of providing post 9/11 security.
4. Beautifully designed criminal justice centers will become things of the past. The attack of September 11, 2001, on the World Trade Center has made it clear that criminal justice agencies must separate their resources so that one event will not destroy and/or render them ineffective.
5. Strengthened/re-enforced perimeter security will be essential (Install more cameras; add additional razor ribbon, tangle foot [barbed wire], firing points, lighting, and early-warning intrusion devices.)
6. Extend the distance of the perimeter from the institution and establish "fields of fire" within the internal perimeter.

7. Increase the speed at which vehicle sallyport gates open and close. Most jails and other correctional facilities have older slow moving sallyport gates, which could be easily breached.

8. Reduce the number of times the vehicle sallyport is opened and closed. Monitor very closely why and when the sallyport is opened.

9. Increase the number of "high" quality color video cameras on the perimeter. Use video surveillance of the external areas of a facility as a "pro-active" technique to prevent an incident from taking place.

10. A staff person (who has been trained in intelligence gathering) will be assigned to review DVD recordings from external video cameras. This person(s) will be looking for individuals who might be casing the institution, leaving contraband, visitors exiting and leaving their vehicles, checking and running license plates, and keeping surveillance on external patrols.

11. All roads leading up to the facility should be constructed to prevent any vehicle gaining enough speed to break through the outer perimeter barrier and/ or sallyport gates.

12. Designated "fields of fire" for towers should be established around the external perimeter.

13. External street patrol units will be the first responders should a jail come under an attack. Ensure that the agency emergency plans determine which units respond to the jail and which units stay back at a predetermined second perimeter. If international, domestic terrorist and/or narco-paramilitary-gangs attack the facility, they will have conducted in-depth surveillance prior to the attack.

Internal Design

Most of the jails that have been built over the past twenty years have been designed to support the direct supervision model of offender management. I believe that, for the most part, this model will continue to be used for general populations, although staffing will be done through cameras and monitors.

I anticipate that some changes will be in the "Special Management" detainees/offenders area. "Special Management" areas, I believe, will have to be enlarged to meet the needs of the changing offender population (more violent, domestic/international terrorists, younger offenders, and/or narco-paramilitary-gang members.)

The special management cell should be totally self-contained, that is, the shower should be an integral part of the cell. Incorporating the shower in the cell will reduce moving the special management detainees/offenders to and from showers. Showering special management detainee/offenders is a staff-intensive activity, currently. Most jails currently require two officers to escort special management detainee/offenders during the showering process.

Each special management cell will have a 20-inch monitor microphone and speakers that will be used to communicate with the detainees/offenders.

The detainees/offenders will use the same system to communicate with staff members, such as security, for education, medical issues, visiting, and other activities. When these monitors are not being used for official purposes they can be used by the detainees/offenders to watch television. All monitors are controlled at the unit control center. All detainee/offender information will be in the language of the detainee/offender.

Each of these "Special Management" cells will have its own exercise yard that has been attached to the exterior wall of the cell. Additionally, in certain circumstances, some of these "Special Management" cells could house up to four detainees/offenders, but the majority will be made up of one-person cells.

Lighting, heating and cooling will be done incorporating the most up-to-date methods:

- ✓ Solar
- ✓ Geothermal
- ✓ Wind
- ✓ Fossil fuels

Operations and Staffing

Controlling detainees/offenders' movement in the jail of the future will be crucial because of the reduced staffing levels. Correctional staff will be replaced by design innovations and technology.

For the jails of the future to meet the public budgeting demands to be more cost effective, staffing levels will have to be reduced. Day-to-day operations will be "contained" in several small units. Detainees/offenders movement will be restricted to these several small units.

In the event of an emergency situation, the facility will have the ability to isolate each of the small units.

Program staff will be contracted on an as-needed basis. For example, if there are a number of younger offenders incarcerated at specific times and there is a need for a G.E.D. class, the jail will contract for that program, rather than maintain teachers on staff.

Medical and psychological programming will also be contracted with a baseline staffing level. In the event that additional medical or psychological staff is needed, they will be brought in on a temporary basis.

A word of caution before becoming too involved with any recycling initiatives. Some years ago I knew of several correctional facilities that became very involved with recycling. While the thought was good, the actual process became a nightmare. They were collecting cans, glass, paper, and plastic. What eventually happened was that the recyclable became a source for contraband. Additionally, as the recyclable supply chain broke down, and there were few recyclable vendors, the recyclables began to become health and safety issues because tons of paper products were not picked-up for months.

The most distinctive change in operations will be that a great many jails will be "operated" by private companies. The business practice of public/private partnerships will replace the current practice of the government agencies owning and operating jails. There will be several reasons for this transfer of operations from the public to the private sector:

- To reduce the number of employees on government payrolls, therefore, reducing salaries and benefit costs to the county
- Private companies can employ the economies of scale (depending on their size) to purchase products and materials used in the operation of the jails. These products will include, but not be limited to:
  - Heating fuel
  - Food products
  - Staff and detainees' uniforms
  - Furnishings and equipment for the jails, and so forth
- Private companies will have more options for promoting and transferring staff
- Private companies will not be encumbered by or obligated to adhere to existing contracts
- Private companies will have the ability to sub-contract with other private companies to provide services such as:
  - Food service
  - Medical services
  - Psychological services
  - Transportation services
  - Staff training
  - Educational services, and other services
- Economically, moving staff positions from the public sector to the private sector will become a necessity in the future. I believe that federal, state, county, and city governments will, in the very near future, come to the realization that there can be some real cost savings in privatizing their correctional facilities and other government services.
- Private jails will (by contract) be required to maintain insurance that guarantees operational issues and paybacks if they do not adhere to the terms of the contract.
- The challenges for the government agencies will be to develop Request for Proposals (RFP) that permit the responding vendors the freedom to be creative and innovative with their designs, management, technology, and staffing patterns.
- Another major challenge will be to write an operational contract that will delineate with a great deal of specificity what exactly the government agency requires along with the fines and penalties should the vendor fail to perform.

Summary

No one can perfectly predict the future, so what I have written is my best guess. I have been in the field of criminal justice for more than thirty-five years and I have seen the field enjoy years of unlimited growth. During the 1980s and 1990s, the country tried to build its way out of the correctional crowding problems. Agencies went on a hiring spree and most agencies grew substantially.

Now that we are entering the second decade of the 2000s, governmental entities realize that they can no longer afford to operate jails or prisons. The money pool has dried-up while the crime problem has not. I believe that within the next twenty years the small jails (under 500 detainees/offenders) will disappear—just because they are too expensive to operate and maintain.

As a nation, we have no choice but to find better, more efficient and effective ways to incarcerate detainees and offenders. I believe that the jails of the future will be technological masterpieces whose designs and operations will be decidedly different than those of today. The cost of operations will be the driving force.

About the Author

William "Bill" Sturgeon is president of the Institute for Adult Education and Training in Pittsfield, Massachusetts. He has more than thirty-five years of broad experience in jails and prisons. He is the author of two books for ACA.